Aldeburgh Studies in Music

Volume 1

Britten's *Gloriana*

ESSAYS AND SOURCES

Aldeburgh Studies in Music

ISSN 0969–3548

Britten's *Gloriana*

ESSAYS AND SOURCES

EDITED BY

Paul Banks

THE BOYDELL PRESS

THE BRITTEN–PEARS LIBRARY

First published 1993 by The Boydell Press, Woodbridge
in conjunction with
The Britten–Pears Library, Aldeburgh

The Boydell Press is an imprint of Boydell & Brewer Ltd
PO Box 9, Woodbridge, Suffolk IP12 3DF, UK
and of Boydell & Brewer Inc.
PO Box 41026, Rochester, NY 14604, USA

ISBN 0 85115 340 2

British Library Cataloguing-in-Publication Data
Britten's "Gloriana":Essays and Sources. –
(Aldeburgh Studies in Music; Vol.1)
I. Banks, Paul II. Series
782.1092
ISBN 0–85115–340–2

Library of Congress Cataloging-in-Publication Data applied for

The paper used in this publication meets the minimum requirements
of American National Standard for Information Sciences –
Permanence of Paper for Printed Library Materials, ANSI Z39.48–1984

Printed in Great Britain by
St Edmundsbury Press Ltd, Bury St Edmunds, Suffolk

Contents

Preface

The origin of this volume was an event associated with one anniversary – a study course devoted to *Gloriana* at the Britten–Pears School in 1991 which coincided with the 90th birthday of Joan Cross, who created the role of Elizabeth I in 1953 – and its appearance coincides with a second – the fortieth anniversary of the opera's ill-fated première. Happily the latter event is also marked by the first appearance of *Gloriana* on CD: perhaps the opera will now receive its well-merited reassessment. If so this collection of studies and bibliographical material may contribute to a more informed debate about the work – its intrinsic qualities, and its place in Britten's operatic canon – but the differences in emphasis and evaluations offered by the team of authors also suggest that the debate will raise fundamental critical issues and may not be characterized, wholly, by unanimity of view. Except, that is, the view that *Gloriana* deserves (and survives) a more penetrating examination than it received in 1953.

All the contributors to the volume took part in the 1991 study course, and of the first five chapters all except the third were given as papers during the weekend. The background to the list of sources is outlined in the preliminary notes to chapter six; the bibliography grew out of the research which formed the basis of chapter three. There is no conventional list of the sources cited in the text, but if they do not fall within the parameters of the bibliography, such sources are included under the author's or editor's name in the index.

The idea of publishing papers from a Britten–Pears School study course had been mooted in the past, but it is thanks to the interest and commitment of Richard Barber of Boydell & Brewer Ltd that such good intentions have been realized. Not only that: with this volume a series is launched which it is hoped will reflect in diverse ways the astonishing musical heritage, extensive archival resources and vibrant musical life of Aldeburgh and, more broadly, East Anglia. Much of that richness has its roots in the lives of three outstanding musicians – Benjamin Britten, Peter Pears and Imogen Holst – and it is inevitable that the pre-eminence of their contribution will be reflected in the series. But not exclusively. A new generation of composers and performers is now heard in Aldeburgh, new music education projects are promoted by the Aldeburgh Foundation and the libraries – the Britten–Pears Library in Aldeburgh, and the Holst Library at Snape – have collections which extend into unexpected repertoires. The series will try to encompass this diversity.

Paul Banks
March 1993

Acknowledgments

First and foremost I have to thank the contributors, not just for their papers, but the patience with which they have shown when little seemed to be happening, and the speed and helpfulness of their responses to often unreasonable requests as the inevitable deadlines approached.

This volume reflects, to varying degrees, the help and co-operation of five organizations. Kathy Wolfenden and her team at the Britten–Pears School ensured that the original course was enjoyed by all who attended, and thus created the harmonious background out of which this collaboration has emerged. Since then many of the mundane but essential chores entailed in producing a scholarly volume have fallen onto the shoulders of the staff of the Britten–Pears Library; in particular I would like to thank Pam Wheeler for innumerable insights from the archive, and Judith Henderson, without whose painstaking checking the text would have been far less accurate or complete than it is.

Even a cursory glance through the list of sources will reveal the extent of our debt to Boosey & Hawkes Music Publishers Ltd. Some publishers seem intimidated by requests for detailed information about their publications, but from the outset Boosey & Hawkes have offered their fullest co-operation and have devoted considerable time and energy to the project. In particular I would like to thank Tony Fell, Paula Rainsborough, Jo Daly, Malcolm Smith and Ian Julier for their tireless efforts. The result offers some small indication of the immense work undertaken on Britten's behalf by Boosey & Hawkes, and also a fascinating glimpse into the world of British music publishing in the mid-twentieth century.

In the last stages of course it has been Richard Barber and the staff at Boydell & Brewer who have borne the brunt of the project, which they have done with good humour and patience. Throughout the book has been enthusiastically supported by the Trustees of the Britten–Pears Foundation, and in particular by Hugh Cobbe, the Chairman of the Library Committee: to them my warmest thanks.

Finally it is a pleasure to record the gratitude of all the contributors to those individuals who have responded to our requests for information and help with great generosity: Martin Aylmore (Royal Artillery Band), Chris Banks (British Library, Music Library), Jonathan Burton (English National Opera, Music Library), Richard Chesser (British Library, Music Library), Timothy Day (British Library, National Sound Archive), John Dingle, Osian Ellis, Colin Graham, Lord Harewood, Sir Rupert Hart-Davis, David Stone, Tom Tillery

(Royal Opera House, Music Library). I have one personal appreciation: to my wife Chris, who has not only been a source of advice and encouragement throughout, but has also borne the burden of a husband distracted by the demands of editorship, with exceptional good humour.

Music examples 1–9 are © Copyright 1953 by Hawkes & Son (London) Ltd. Reprinted by kind permission of Boosey & Hawkes Music Publishers Ltd.

List of Abbreviations

bar.	baritone	no.	number
BBC	British Broadcasting Corporation	ob.	oboe
		p., pp.	page, pages
bsn	bassoon	perc.	percussion
cl.	clarinet	picc.	piccolo
cm.	centimetre(s)	pl.	plate
db.	double bass	*r*	*recto*
dbsn	double bassoon	rec.	recorder
desc.	descant	ri	rear outer wrapper/cover
ed.	edition; editor	ro	rear inner wrapper/cover
EOG	English Opera Group	rpm	revolutions per minute
Ex.	Example	sax.	saxophone
fi	front inner wrapper/cover	sc.	scene
fl.	flute	s.l.	sine loco
fn.	footnote	s.n.	sine nomine
fo	front outer wrapper/cover	sop.	soprano
fol.	folio(s)	ten.	tenor
hn	horn	tp	title page
hp	harp	tr.	translator, translated
ht	half-title	trb.	trombone
in.	inch(es)	treb.	treble
ips	inches per second	trpt	trumpet
mezzo	mezzo-soprano	*v*	*verso*
min.	minute(s)	vcl.	violoncello
LSO	London Symphony Orchestra	vla	viola
ML	Music & Letters	vln	violin
ms.,	manuscript	vol.	volume
mss	manuscripts	vols	volumes
MT	*Musical Times*	wm	watermark
n.d.	no date		

Library sigla

GB-ALb	Britten–Pears Library, Aldeburgh
GB-ALhf	Holst Foundation, Aldeburgh
GB-ALrs	Collection of Rosamund Strode, Aldeburgh
GB-Lbbc	BBC Sound Archive

GB-Lbh	Boosey and Hawkes Music Publishers Ltd., London
GB-Lbl	British Library, London
GB-Leno	English National Opera, London
GB-Lnsa	British Library, National Sound Archive, London

Conventions

Scenes are normally identified by the *New Grove Dictionary of Opera* convention. Thus Act two, scene three would be represented by 2.iii; individual numbers are identified in the form 2.iii.5. The only exceptions appear in the list of sources where such abbreviations are sometimes avoided because of the predominance of numerals in the surrounding description. Particular bars are identified using rehearsal numbers (which appear only in the fourth edition of the vocal score ((M)/V17) and the study score ((M)/F11)) with superscript numerals were necessary. Thus two bars before Fig. 167 would be represented as 'Fig. 167^{-2}', and four bars after, by 'Fig. 167^{+4}'.

Specific sources listed in the list are usually identified in the form (M)/F7, where the letter in parentheses indicates the work or variant concerned, and the characters after the oblique stroke the source listed under that work or variant.

1

'Happy were He': Benjamin Britten and the *Gloriana* Story[1]

ROBERT HEWISON

Of all of Benjamin Britten's major works, there is only one that has not subsequently become a commercial recording, on CD, tape or disc. That is his opera for the Coronation of Queen Elizabeth II, *Gloriana*. For almost forty years, the complete recording of *Gloriana* has been missing from the record catalogues, apart from a specialist video recording.[2] There may be technical reasons for this – a difficulty in getting the right singers, or orchestra or conductor – but the likeliest reason is that, in the words of one of those most closely connected with the project, Lord Harewood, the first night of *Gloriana* was 'one of the great disasters of operatic history'.[3] I am going to argue that the reasons for this disaster were not musical, but cultural. I hope to show that the failure was not Britten's but that of his audience, and that with the perspective of history, we can now see that *Gloriana* was a more prescient work than was realized on that terrible first night on the 8 June 1953. To do so requires some consideration of the circumstances in which Great Britain found itself at the beginning of our present Queen's reign, and of the political and social climate in which *Gloriana* was commissioned and composed. Artists are of course individuals, with their own creative imperatives, but the distinctly public nature of this 'Royal' opera placed special demands on Benjamin Britten's genius.

Ever since the success of *Peter Grimes* in 1945, Britten had enjoyed a growing reputation, to the point where he could almost be considered as an official artist. This position was confirmed when the Arts Council decided in 1949 that he should be commissioned to write an opera as part of the celebrations

---

[1] This essay is a revised version of a lecture given at the Aldeburgh Festival, 25 June 1992, and originally presented at the Study Course on *Gloriana* in September 1991. The author would like to express his thanks to Lord Harewood for his help in preparing this paper.

[2] A recording of the 1984 production by English National Opera was undertaken and it was planned that this would be issued in all sound and video formats (see Nicholas John, ed., *Peter Grimes, Gloriana*, Opera Guide 24 (London: John Calder, 1983), 127), but in the event only a video cassette and laser disc were ever published. Fortunately other important, but unpublished, recordings of the opera and related works, survive (see the List of Sources, pp. 95–170 below).

[3] Lord Harewood, *The Tongs and the Bones* (London: Weidenfeld and Nicolson, 1981), 138.

connected with the Festival of Britain in 1951. That opera was *Billy Budd*. As it happens, *Billy Budd* cannot be described as particularly festive, nor for that matter was it performed until after the Festival was officially over, but in terms of the context in which *Gloriana* must be seen, there is an important connection between the Festival of Britain in 1951 and the Coronation in 1953. The Festival and the Coronation were *state* events. Looked at together, they mark the passage from the immediate post-war austerity of the late 1940s to the growing affluence of the 1950s. At a deeper level, they were both concerned with questions of national identity, and how that identity could not only be asserted, but renewed in the difficult social and economic climate of the post-war period.

Yet, while I shall argue ultimately for a continuity between the Festival and the Coronation, there is a key local difference between the sponsors of the two events. The Festival of Britain was the last party given by the Labour government that had set out to create the Welfare State in 1945. The Coronation was one of the first thrown by the Conservative government that was to manage the political consensus of the 1950s. It is not unusual for governments to organize great expositions or other public spectacles as a way of demonstrating recovery after a period of national danger and stress. The French did it after the Revolution and the Terror that followed, and again after the debacle of the Franco-Prussian war in 1870. The Americans did so after the Civil War. Perhaps it is significant that both these countries are republics, and therefore had to invent the spectacles that a monarchy might more spontaneously have engendered.

The idea of marking the centenary of the Great Exhibition of 1851 had been first mooted in 1943. The message of national recovery was explicit in the terms of reference of the Ramsden Committee, set up in 1945 to consider a 'Universal International Exposition' in Hyde Park, that would demonstrate to the world the recovery of the United Kingdom from the effects of war in the moral, cultural, spiritual and material fields.[4] When the decision to go ahead was taken in 1947 the idea was whittled down to a national, rather than international exhibition, but it remained for Herbert Morrison, the Government minister responsible, 'a great symbol of national regeneration'.[5] Morrison described the Festival site as 'new Britain springing from the battered fabric of the old'.[6]

The Festival was planned by a special directorate, under the control of a Festival Council operating at what we would now call 'arm's length' from the Government. The Festival Council worked closely with the Council of Industrial Design, which helped select the exhibits, while the accompanying arts events were made the responsibility of the Arts Council, then a relatively fledgling body, set up in 1945 following the success of the wartime Council for the Encouragement of Music and the Arts (CEMA). While Morrison was not

---

[4] Mary Banham and Bevis Hillier, eds, *A Tonic to the Nation: The Festival of Britain 1951* (London: Thames and Hudson, 1976), 27

[5] Bernard Donoghue and G.W. Jones, *Herbert Morrison: Portrait of a Politician* (London: Weidenfeld and Nicolson, 1973), 492.

[6] *Loc. cit.*

unaware of the potential political benefits to Labour of the event, he was scrupulous in excluding direct party political propaganda. This did not stop the Conservative opposition making party political points against the alleged extravagance of the Festival at a time of extreme material shortages, but Churchill's criticisms were muted by the choice of his former Chief of Staff, Lord Ismay, as Chairman of the Festival Council. Opposition was further muted when the King and Queen became patrons of the Festival in 1950. The most consistent opposition came from Beaverbrook's *Evening Standard* and *Daily Express*.

With a budget of £11 million, the Festival consisted not only of the South Bank exhibition, but the Pleasure Gardens in Battersea, architecture in Poplar, science at South Kensington, industrial power in Glasgow, farming in Belfast, a travelling exhibition, and a Festival ship, the converted aircraft carrier *Campania*. There were also a great many local celebrations, encouraged, but not financially supported by the Festival Council. The Arts Council organized a special season of exhibitions, music and drama in London, and gave extra help to local arts festivals, some of which, like Aldeburgh, were already in existence, while others were specially mounted for 1951.

The lasting imagery of the South Bank exhibition, the Dome of discovery and the Skylon, the struts and wires, the abstract 'atomic' designs and the fabric patterns derived from crystals, suggest that the Festival of Britain was a little more forward-looking than it really was. The theme was 'the Land and the People',[7] comfortably democratic words that created a space within which to explore the way a nation had shaped its environment and been shaped by it. The emphasis was on 'the arts of peace',[8] imperial echoes sounding only in the celebration of British explorers in the Dome of Discovery.

The modernist, technological vision promoted by the South Bank was diluted by an indigenous neo-romanticism that had flourished during the war. The artists brought in to decorate the site, among them Graham Sutherland, Henry Moore and John Piper, tended to add a biomorphic or vegetable overlay which softened the designers' abstractions. The site was too cramped for any imposing architectural master plan; the English picturesque, barely under control in the Lion and Unicorn pavilion dedicated to the British character, ran riot in the Battersea Pleasure Gardens. There John Piper and Osbert Lancaster's Grand Vista, and Rowland Emmett's Far Tottering and Oyster Creek Railway, offered a comic alternative to the modernist styling favoured by the Council of Industrial Design.

The celebration of national identity – which was sufficiently self-conscious to suggest an uncertainty about the durability of that identity – was highlighted as the Festival's theme in the sermon given by Archbishop Fisher at the opening service of dedication. 'The chief and governing purpose of the Festival is to declare our belief in the British way of life ... It is good at a time like the present

---

[7] Introduction to the Official Guide to the South Bank Exhibition, reproduced in M. Banham and B. Hillier, eds, *op. cit.*, 74–5.

[8] *Loc. cit.*

so to strengthen, and in part to recover our hold on all that is best in our national life'.[9] The parenthetical 'and in part to recover' suggests that that hold was not as secure as people would wish. The 'dangers and anxieties'[10] besetting Britain which the Chairman of the Arts Council Sir Ernest Pooley hinted at in his introduction to the Council's report covering the Festival were real enough. There had been a long term economic crisis since 1947, compounded by the need for a massive rearmament programme following the outbreak of the Korean war in 1950. The conflict brought with it the very real threat of a third world war involving atomic weapons. The need to pay for rearmament had caused the Labour Government to abrogate the principle of a completely free National Health Service, provoking resignations which weakened it in the run up to the 1951 General Election. All in all, the Festival of Britain did not take place in the political and economic climate it had been planned for: for that matter, it also rained a great deal in the summer of 1951.

Yet the Festival was undoubtedly a popular success. Herbert Morrison had wanted 'to see the people happy. I want to hear them sing'[11] and by all accounts the break from austerity was welcomed. The Festival was mounted in a remarkably short time, in the face of considerable difficulties. It had had to be about that keyword of the post-war period, *planning*. The masterminds were young architects and designers; many people working on the Festival had seen war service, and the combination of military and design skills met in the complex art of logistics that on opening day had the painters and cleaners leaving by the exit just as the first visitors entered by the turnstiles. When you recall that the Festival's service of dedication ended with the hymn 'Jerusalem', it is tempting, in retrospect, to see the Festival as one little bit of the Welfare State that worked.

Yet if we are to consider the Festival of Britain as a particular manifestation of post-war culture, we must see that culture for what it was. In 1963 Michael Frayn published a brilliant essay on the Festival which argued that it was not the beginning of anything, rather the end of the period when a certain social group had held sway. These were 'the radical middle-classes – the do-gooders; the readers of the *News Chronicle*, the *Guardian*, and the *Observer*, the signers of petitions; the backbone of the BBC. In short, the Herbivores or gentle ruminants.'[12] The tone of the Festival, wrote Frayn, was 'philanthropic, kindly, whimsical, cosy, optimistic, middlebrow, deeply instinct with the Herbivorous philosophy so shortly doomed to eclipse'.[13] That eclipse was to be brought about by the Carnivores, 'the upper- and middle-classes who believe that if God had not wished them to prey on all smaller and weaker creatures without

[9] *Ibid.*, 35.
[10] Arts Council of Great Britain, *Annual Report 1950/51*.
[11] B. Donoghue and G.W. Jones, *op. cit.*, 323.
[12] Michael Frayn, 'Festival' in *Age of Austerity*, ed. Michael Sissons and Philip French (London: Hodder & Stoughton, 1963), 319.
[13] *Ibid.*, 320.

4

scruple, he would not have made them as they are'.[14] Frayn was writing of the 1950s; the Carnivores have ruled the earth with even greater ferocity since then.

Frayn's point is that although the Festival celebrated 'the Land and the People' the people, for the most part, and certainly the working-class, had little say in how they were celebrated. In so far as the Festival had any socialist colouring, it was socialism of a distinctly Fabian kind. Reyner Banham describes the Festival as being run by 'kindly ex-officers and gentlemen'[15] and the principal beneficiaries of the state's patronage were not so much the individual artists who received commissions, as the institutions through which Festival funds were channeled. This is especially true of the Arts Council, given direct responsibility for the cultural programme, and an extra £400,000 by the Treasury. This show of confidence in the Arts Council seems in turn to have given the Council confidence to go beyond its then fairly hesitant practice of giving small subsidies and guarantees against loss, and to commission work for the first time.

Given Benjamin Britten's growing reputation it is not surprising that he should have been one of the favoured artists. (Vaughan Williams declined the offer of a commission, George Lloyd was commissioned to write *John Socman* for the Carl Rosa Company, and there were four further opera scores commissioned following a competition.[16]) The English Opera Group had been receiving £3000 a year since 1947; the commission for *Billy Budd* was agreed in 1949. The question of suitability of an all-male opera and the change of proposed production house from Sadler's Wells to Covent Garden need not detain us here. The Arts Council's report noted dryly that 'it was perhaps unfortunate that circumstances made it impossible for this opera . . . to be played during the Festival season; but the production, when it came, was hailed as being an excellent one.'[17] Britten was further honoured with a special season at the Lyric Hammersmith by the English Opera Group, although financially this was not a great success.

In general the musical events arranged by the Arts Council were well-received, but the Festival drama was neither particularly distinguished nor, thanks to professional rivalries, well organized. But the Arts Council itself emerged with credit, and indeed a small financial surplus. It was also by now a far less radical body than its wartime predecessor CEMA had been. If there ever had been any question that 'the arts' were to be defined as those professional activities sanctioned and encouraged by the Arts Council, or that institutions like the Royal Opera House were the most appropriate recipients of funds, that question was closed in 1951. In that year the Council appointed a new Secretary-General, W.E. Williams, who concluded that, although the Council had a double duty to 'raise and spread' the standards and appreciation of the arts, the Council could not afford to broaden its activities. 'If an emphasis must

---

14 *Loc. cit.*
15 In M. Banham and B. Hillier, eds, *op. cit.*, 197.
16 None was performed as part of the Festival. See below, p. 51, fn. 14.
17 Arts Council of Great Britain, *Annual Report 1951/52*, 38.

be placed somewhere in that motto of 'Raise and Spread' it seems wiser and more realistic to concentrate on Raise.'[18]

In spite of the genuinely popular appeal of the Festival of Britain to a wide section of the population, its organizers, like their counterparts in the Arts Council, or for that matter in the BBC, who had launched the Third Programme in 1946, shared the assumptions of their time. They saw their cultural landscape in terms of a high ridge of artistic achievement towering above a middleground of average endeavour, which fell away to the lowlands of popular pursuits. These lower reaches of recreation were menaced by invaders from across the sea: the bearers of crass American entertainment. 'Culture' – with a capital 'C' – was what it had been even before Matthew Arnold's day, not just the alternative to Anarchy, but a defense against the corruptions of industrialization and the mass society that threatened to blot out all sweetness and light. Yet if culture was the pursuit of the enlightened minority, by the 1950s it was firmly in the realm of public policy. The need to organize societies for the massive efforts required of them in wartime – ironically, to defend cultural values – made culture the responsibility of governments dedicated to the management of industrialism for the benefit of mass society.

The recognition that these changes had made culture a matter for institutions – be they the Arts Council or UNESCO – was one of the motives for T.S. Eliot to publish his *Notes Towards the Definition of Culture* in 1948. It is a scrappy little book, made up of essays and broadcasts that go back to 1943, but it made an impression, partly because Eliot was then at the height of his reputation – he was awarded the Order of Merit and won the Nobel Prize that year – and partly because it was, as far as I know, the only book to raise the theoretical issues involved at that time. It may also have made an impression because it was so hostile to the way things appeared to be going.

Eliot is concerned that culture should have become a matter of state concern. While claiming to do no more than ask what the word 'culture' might mean – answering that it is 'the creation of the society as a whole'[19] – he raises objections (with a distinctly cold-war anti-Russian inflection) to the Welfare State notion that culture can be planned, and argues that contemporary plans, in terms of the creation of state institutions and educational policy, will be damaging to the organic, hierarchical culture which he discerns and defines as 'the creation of society as a whole'. If the landscape metaphor used earlier appears at all far-fetched, it is less so than Eliot's claim that the 'headlong rush to educate everybody' has been 'destroying our ancient edifices to make ready the ground upon which the barbarian nomads of the future will encamp in their mechanized caravans'.[20] (Do we see here Matthew Arnold's Dover Beach becoming a caravan site?) Eliot positively fears a classless society, arguing that it is good for the culture of society as a whole that the culture of the minority and the elite should remain qualitatively distinct, and that no conscious effort

---

[18] Arts Council of Great Britain, *Annual Report 1952/53: The Public and the Arts*, 12.

[19] T.S. Eliot, *Notes Towards the Definition of Culture* (London: Faber and Faber, 1948), 37.

[20] *Ibid.*, 108.

should be made to make it accessible to those outside the minority. It is a romantic, conservative defense of the traditional cultural pyramid, and true to the pessimism inherent in romantic conservatism, he goes so far as to warn of a coming period 'of which it is possible to say that it will have *no* culture'.[21]

To judge from the opinions of the other major cultural commentator of the period, F.R. Leavis, that condition had already been reached. Even Eliot's book did not come up to the standards set by Leavis's critical journal *Scrutiny*. Leavis made no direct comment but the general conclusion of a symposium of articles on the book was that it failed 'to arouse any interest in those who are actively engaged in the study of society'.[22] Yet Leavis shared Eliot's fears about the institutionalization of culture. An unsigned, but characteristically Leavisite comment on the composition of the panel selected to judge the Festival of Britain poetry prize expresses astonishment that the Arts Council 'should have been able without bracing itself for a storm of protest or ridicule to invest with supreme critical authority a Panel so composed. It seems to us that, given for fellow members any five of this Panel, no critic truly qualified would have consented to serve on it.'[23] Leavis not only believed in the preservation of minority culture over against mass civilization, but in the sustenance of a clerisy of critics whose duty was to puncture the pretension of the metropolitan elite. Rooted in pre-War Bloomsbury, this elite had flourished as a result of the institutionalization of culture and, it would appear, the political changes that had encouraged the process. In the final number of *Scrutiny* in 1953 Leavis wrote: 'the BBC, the British Council and the related institutions are manifestations of the same modern developments as those which issued in the Welfare State'.[24]

It was to be some years before the Labour government's cultural dispositions were to be criticized for being, not too radical, but not radical enough. Since 1945 the majority of British intellectuals had moved to the Right. Raymond Williams, who was to open a new agenda with his study *Culture and Society* in 1958,[25] published a small volume, *Reading and Criticism*, in 1950, which is notable for its fulsome acknowledgement to Leavis.[26] One of the reasons for the relative silence on the Left in the early 1950s was that this was the early phase of the Cold War. Those ex-Communists who did not explicitly break with their past found themselves in a difficult position. Williams, who was dishonourably discharged from the Army Reserve for refusing his recall to fight in Korea, has written of 'the pain and confusion of a younger generation for whom communism had not been a god but who were trying to reject Stalinism and to sustain, under heavy attack, an indigenous socialism'.[27] For the moment, the field of

---

21 *Ibid.*, 19.

22 D.F. Pocock, 'Symposium on Mr. Eliot's "Notes"', *Scrutiny, a Quarterly Review* xvii/3 (Autumn 1950), 275.

23 'The Logic of Christian Discrimination', *Scrutiny, a Quarterly Review* xvi/4 (Winter 1949), 343.

24 F.R. Leavis, *Scrutiny, a Quarterly Review* xix/4 (October 1953), 327.

25 Raymond Williams, *Culture and Society 1780–1950* (London: Chatto & Windus, 1958).

26 Raymond Williams, *Reading and Criticism* (London: Frederick Muller, 1950), ix.

27 Raymond Williams, '1956 and all that', *Guardian*, 2 April 1981.

theoretical debate about culture was dominated by Eliot, as Williams ruefully acknowledged in *Culture and Society*. 'The next step, in thinking of these matters, must be in a different direction, for Eliot has closed almost all existing roads.'[28]

The Festival of Britain officially ended when the South Bank exhibition closed on 30 September. The Labour administration folded soon afterwards, when Parliament was dissolved on 5 October. There is debate to this day as to what extent the victorious Conservative Administration acted deliberately vindictively towards the Festival. There had been discussion of the possibility of a second season in 1952, but the buildings were temporary structures, and part of the site was needed for further work on the Festival Hall. The new Minister of Works, David Eccles, quickly ordered the clearance of the site, with the exception of the Riverside Restaurant, the Telekinema (which became the National Film Theatre) and the walk along the new Embankment. The rest of the site remained empty until 1961, and part of it is still what most of it became – a car park. 'I am unwilling to become the caretaker of empty and deteriorating structures' Eccles declared in 1952, adding that he wanted the site cleared so as to be available for use as a garden in time for the Coronation.[29]

King George VI had died in February 1952, and preparations began for the Coronation of his successor, Queen Elizabeth II. It may be argued that a festival, deliberately conceived as a matter of public policy, is of a different order to a coronation, which must necessarily follow on the death of the previous monarch. But, as the wedding of the present Prince of Wales in 1981 reminds us, royal occasions are both authentic tribal rituals, and carefully stage-managed spectacles. The Festival of Britain was one attempt at national renewal, the arrival of a new sovereign on the throne provided an even better opportunity for another. Emblematically, Hugh Casson, architect of the Festival exhibition on the South Bank, also designed the Coronation decorations, and Britten, composer of a Festival opera, now provided one for the Coronation.

The significance of the Coronation was analyzed at the time by two sociologists, Edward Shils and Michael Young, who argued that the popularity of the event was more than simply the product of commercialism, hysteria or the desire for a national binge. These explanations, they argued, 'overlook the element of communion with the sacred'.[30] On the eve of Coronation day, they noted, there was 'an air of gravity accompanied by a profound release from anxiety' as the celebrations became an affirmation of family and community ties.[31] Shils and Young lost some of their academic distance as they too became swept up in the celebration of national myths of solidarity and resistance. 'Something like this kind of spirit had been manifested before – during the Blitz, the Fuel Crisis of 1947, the London smog of 1952, even during the

---

[28] Raymond Williams, *Culture and Society* (Harmondsworth: Penguin, 1961), 238.

[29] Quoted in M. Banham and B. Hillier, *op. cit.*, 38.

[30] Edward Shils and Michael Young, 'The Meaning of the Coronation', *Sociological Review* (New Series) 1 (December 1953).

[31] *Ibid.*, 67.

Watson–Bailey stand in the Lord's Test or Lock's final overs at the Oval.'[32] They also drew political significance from the event, which they said marked 'the assimilation of the working-class into the moral consensus of British society', adding that 'it appears the popularity of the Conservative Administration was at least temporarily increased by the Coronation, and at the time much newspaper speculation centred on the question whether Mr Churchill would use the advantage to win a large majority for his Party in a General Election.'[33]

There was one sense in which Shils and Young were right to describe the Coronation as a family occasion. It was not just that the Monarch was now presented as part of a 'Royal Family', but also that many people watched the ceremonial at home gathered around their newly-acquired television sets. As the Commonwealth contingents marched through the rain, the Coronation marked a fitting close to the era of Empire, just as the Festival of Britain had brought down the curtain on the aspirations of 1945.

Every nation lives partly in reality, and partly in myth. The war had created its own myths of community and grim endurance, but the reality of the post-war period was that the sacrifices of wartime had not left Britain with an enhanced position in the world. In order to reassert and modernize the British sense of identity following the disappointments and uncertainties that had been felt since 1945, what was needed was a new version of the national myth. If Britain was to feel young and expansive once more, fresh symbols of potentiality and aspiration had to be found. What the Festival had artificially tried to stimulate was almost spontaneously supplied by the youth and name of the Monarch herself. The *Daily Express*, for instance, which had been a scourge of the Festival, was quick to celebrate the arrival of the New Elizabethan age.

'New Elizabethanism' can be traced back to the cultural nationalism of the Second World War. The conservative critic A.L. Rowse was predicting a New Elizabethan age in the *Evening Standard* as early as June 1942. It was an obvious tag for a hoped-for period of revival that at the same time reassuringly circled back to the past.[34] This renewal also implied a break with the immediate past of the post-war years, just as the return of Winston Churchill as Prime Minister suggested a return to wartime solidarity. In 1953 the popular journalist Philip Gibbs published a survey of British youth, *The New Elizabethans*, which contained this revealing rhapsody:

Our poets loved the song of the cuckoo heralding the summer – and all the flowers of an English spring and the drowsy days of summer with the ripple of a streamlet nearby, and the song of the lark rising high, and the love song of the nightingale in the dusk of starlight nights and the peace and delight of English fields. They would grieve that so much of English beauty is being defaced and destroyed by the ugliness of sprawling cities, the blight of

[32] *Ibid.*, 72.
[33] *Ibid.*, 76.
[34] A tag which had not escaped the attention of the Royal Family itself: see below, p. 27.

factories, the utter wantonness of those who grab and invade our heritage of beauty when often they might spare it – these Borough councils and governmental tyrants who do not care a jot for any loveliness of our countryside.[35]

The state – meaning the Welfare State created since 1945 – is the bureaucratic and industrial enemy of the sweet pastoral of Deep England – Hardy's Wessex, Tennyson's Lincolnshire, Elgar's Worcestershire, John Piper's Derbyshire, Graham Sutherland's Pembrokeshire, even Benjamin Britten's East Anglia – to which British notions of heritage are so firmly attached. On Coronation Day the poet laureate, John Masefield, published in *The Times* 'A Prayer for a Beginning Reign' which covertly pleaded for release from governmental tyrants, hoping

> That she may re-establish standards shaken,
> Set the enfettered spirit free.[36]

The most modernizing aspect of the Coronation itself was the recognition of the importance of the mass media, especially television. Although the Coronation Commission set up under Prince Philip in April 1952 had initially resisted televising the ceremony, the Coronation had to be a dramatic national spectacle. The government minister responsible, David Eccles, said: 'My job is to set the stage and build a theatre inside Westminster Abbey.'[37] He was speaking literally, but *theatre* is a powerful metaphor, not only for the drama of the Coronation itself, but for the national celebrations that went with it. It is worth recalling, by the way, how different material conditions were in 1953. As though to give everyone a share in the official feasting, in Coronation week food rationing was relaxed, and everyone was allocated an extra pound of sugar and four ounces of margarine.

The total cost of the Coronation was over a million pounds. (The Festival had cost eleven.) Although on a much smaller scale than that of the Festival of Britain, the celebrations included a cultural programme. The Queen and Prince Philip attended the première of Tyrone Guthrie's production of Shakespeare's *Henry VIII* at the Old Vic, the first Royal appearance at a première since the reign of Edward VII. The Arts Council mounted exhibitions of Gainsborough, Graham Sutherland and John Piper, and spent £750 on music commissions, among them William Walton's march *Orb and Sceptre*. With Arts Council support the London County Council gave a series of Royal Philharmonic concerts at the Festival Hall featuring British composers. But the most significant event – both in terms of its context and the issues of patronage and identity that it raised – was Britten's opera *Gloriana*. The House of Windsor has not been known for its enthusiasm for the arts. It was unfortunate that this occasion should turn out so badly.

* * *

35 Philip Gibbs, *The New Elizabethans* (London: Hutchinson, 1953), 18.

36 *The Times*, 2 June 1953. I am grateful to Boris Ford for drawing my attention to Masefield's poem.

37 Quoted in Conrad Frost, *Coronation June 2 1953* (London: Arthur Barker, 1978), 26.

Shortly after the opera received its gala performance in the presence of the Queen six days after the Coronation, the composer Vaughan Williams wrote a letter to *The Times*, asserting that 'for the first time in history the Sovereign has commanded an opera by a composer from these islands for a great occasion'.[38] But although the opera has been seen as a rare case of not just state, but royal patronage, its origins are more complex, and its status less certain.

That a cousin of the Queen, Lord Harewood, should be not only a passionate admirer of the work of Benjamin Britten but also on the staff of the Royal Opera House, Covent Garden, is an accident of history. But Britten stood out among British composers, even more than his contemporary Michael Tippett. As Harewood records in his autobiography, *The Tongs and the Bones* (1981), the idea for a coronation opera was the result of a conversation about national musical identity between Harewood, Britten and Peter Pears, while Harewood and his wife were on a skiing holiday with Britten and Pears at Gargallen, early in 1952.

> What was 'national' expression in opera, we asked ourselves: what were the 'national' operas of different countries? . . . 'For the Italians undoubtedly Aida,' said Ben. 'It's the perfect expression of every kind of Italian nationalist feeling, national pride – but where's the English equivalent?' 'Well, you'd better write one.' The next three or four hours were spent discussing a period – the Merrie England of the Tudors or Elizabethans? and a subject – Henry VIII? too obvious and an unattractive hero. Queen Elizabeth? Highly appropriate! What about a national opera in time for next year's Coronation?[39]

The problem, of course, was that an opera would take time to write, and Britten had a number of other projects and commitments, including concerts with Pears that Pears for one was reluctant to drop. It was this, rather than a desire for prestige, that led Britten to suggest that 'his Coronation opera was made in some way official, not quite commanded but at least accepted as part of the celebrations'.[40] Britten did not seek a Royal commission, and there was no question of money changing hands. But if Britten was to clear his desk in order to be able to write the work in time, he needed a Royal reason for doing so. Pears was not pleased.

Lord Harewood, who suggested using Lytton Strachey's *Elizabeth and Essex* (1928) as a basis for the libretto, was well placed to arrange Royal approval for the project. The Queen was his cousin, and so was her private secretary, Sir Alan Lascelles, who gave Harewood an enthusiastic reception when he discussed the idea informally with him. Harewood then put his proposal in a letter which was shown to the Queen, and permission was given for the project to go ahead in May 1952. This was on the understanding that it would be in

---

[38] *The Times*, 18 June 1953.

[39] Lord Harewood, *op. cit.*, 134. For a detailed examination of the opera's early creative evolution, see chapter 2.

[40] *Ibid.*, 135.

association with the Coronation, rather than a direct commission. The dedication in the vocal score, published in a deluxe edition issued at the time of the première, reads: 'This work is dedicated by gracious permission to Her Majesty Queen Elizabeth II in honour of whose Coronation it was composed.'[41] The principal sign of Royal approval came on 1 June 1953, when Britten was made a Companion of Honour in the Coronation honours list.

In the light of what was said earlier about the Festival of Britain and the Coronation, we should not be surprised that Britten, Pears and the Harewoods should be discussing the question of national musical identity. But the issue was of importance to more than just them. The Royal Opera House, Covent Garden, had reopened in 1946 with David Webster as General Administrator, and with full Arts Council support for an all-year-round programme of opera and ballet. While the ballet company under Ninette de Valois, which had transferred from Sadler's Wells, prospered, opera productions at Covent Garden were much criticized in the early years. The policy was to perform in English, which limited the choice of singers severely, and it became a regular practice to have mixed language productions, with perhaps the tenor singing in German and the bass in English. The prospect of an opera in English, by a leading English composer, was therefore especially significant. Webster assured Britten that if the Treasury was not forthcoming, the money for the production would be found by the Opera House. In the event, there was an additional grant of £15,000 from the Arts Council for Covent Garden's Coronation season, which also featured a new production of Strauss's *Elektra* conducted by Erich Kleiber. *Gloriana* was to be given its première at a gala in the presence of the Queen and Prince Philip, produced by Basil Coleman, conducted by John Pritchard, and designed by John Piper, with Joan Cross as Elizabeth, and Peter Pears as Essex. The libretto was to be prepared by William Plomer, with whom Britten had been considering other musical projects, although this was to be his first exercise in full-length opera.

Britten's sponsors should have realized that he was too serious an artist to sacrifice his creative imperatives to courtly prudence. There had already been controversy about *Billy Budd*, an all-male opera whose discreet homosexual sub-text may have been one reason why it was not performed, as originally intended, at Sadler's Wells.[42] The homosexual theme is deeply hidden in what might be read as a cold-war allegory: the rules of war and the menace of revolution demand unbending conformity to public discipline, though at great personal cost. It should also be noted that at a period when homosexual acts were criminal offences, strict outward conformity was a requirement for public figures who had homosexual private lives. The conflict between private desires and public responsibility surfaces once more as the theme of *Gloriana*.

Britten was clear that some kind of cod-Elizabethan pastiche would not be appropriate to the New Elizabethanism the Coronation was intended to

---

[41] For a full description of this publication, see List of Sources, (A)/V7.1.

[42] See also Mervyn Cooke and Philip Reed, *Benjamin Britten: Billy Budd* (Cambridge: Cambridge University Press, 1993), 60–1.

12

encourage. He wrote to William Plomer that he wanted 'lovely pageantry'[43] but it is to his credit that he was intending to create more than that. He told Lord Harewood, 'It's got to be serious. I don't want to do just folk dances and village green stuff.'[44] To venture into the field of musicology for a moment, Britten did of course use the music of the first Elizabethan period as a source of inspiration, notably in the Courtly Dances in 2.iii, where Elizabethan forms, Pavane, Galliard, Lavolta, Coranto, are featured, but Britten specifically asked his music assistant, Imogen Holst – a key figure in helping him compose at the frantic speed that was necessary to meet the Coronation deadline – to warn him if he was straying into pastiche.[45] The most famous number of the opera, Essex's Second Lute Song, 'Happy were he', begins as a quotation from John Wilbye's madrigal 'Happy, O Happy He', but as Christopher Palmer points out in his discussion of *Gloriana*'s music, it recreates the spirit of Dowland, rather than the letter.[46]

The decidedly melancholy leitmotiv of Essex's song is a reminder of something else that may have been overlooked in the enthusiastic planning of the opera. The choice of a book by Lytton Strachey, debunker of eminent Victorians, as the basis of the libretto might in itself have sounded a warning, but the subtitle to Strachey's *Elizabeth and Essex* is 'A Tragic History'. While the Elizabethan period gave an opportunity for the reworking of Tudor music (and the setting gave John Piper the opportunity to create a Tudor décor), the pageantry is undercut by the essentially tragic nature of the story.

Elizabeth is not in her first youth when she is drawn to the charms of the Earl of Essex. Plomer summarizes the opera's theme as 'Queen Elizabeth, a solitary and ageing monarch, undiminished in majesty, power, statesmanship, and understanding, [who] sees in an outstanding young nobleman a hope both for the future of the country and of herself.'[47] She favours Essex, in spite of the advice of her counsellors, and sends him on an expedition to Ireland. But the Queen is made to appear foolish in her attraction to Essex, while Essex fails her in Ireland, turns against her, raising rebellion. In spite of the pleadings of Essex's wife and family, and her own feelings towards him, Elizabeth decides that she must sign the warrant that orders Essex's execution. In its closing moments the opera abandons all pretense of naturalism, and Elizabeth abandons music for speech, as the shades of her own death close about her. Without any change of scene, the epilogue moves on two years, and the opera closes as the Queen herself is dying – though still very much a Queen.

It was too late for the suitability of such a serious work – for all of its opportunities for pageantry – to be questioned when it was submitted for both official and unofficial Royal approval. Britten and Plomer played over the score

---

[43] Peter Alexander, *William Plomer* (Oxford: Oxford University Press, 1990), 272.

[44] Interview with the author, 24 July 1991.

[45] Christopher Palmer, 'The Music of *Gloriana*', in *Peter Grimes, Gloriana*, ed. Nicholas John, 93.

[46] *Ibid.*, 95.

[47] William Plomer, 'Notes on the Libretto of *Gloriana*', in *Peter Grimes, Gloriana*, ed. Nicholas John, 99.

to the Queen and Prince Philip less than a month before the première. As a new work, the opera also had to be submitted to the Lord Chamberlain, the Royal official then responsible for licensing the performance of all new theatrical works. The only change demanded was that a chamberpot should not appear in a London street scene. It was explained: 'There just happens to be a rule of long standing, and the Lord Chamberlain has had to set his face against chamberpots.'[48]

* * *

I suggested at the beginning that responsibility for the first night disaster of *Gloriana* lay not with Britten, but with his audience. By this I mean that he showed a more profound understanding of the realities of the new Elizabethan age than they did, but for the audience at Covent Garden at the opera's gala première their inability to understand was quite literal. Lord Harewood recalled, 'It never occurred to me that it would be other than a salutation on the part of the arts to their sovereign.'[49] But the people who might be said to have represented the arts had not been invited to the gala; instead the house was filled with dignitaries, both British and foreign, unprepared for a piece of new music. Lord Drogheda, who was to become chairman of the Royal Opera House in 1958, described the evening.

> Long remembered it was, but as a fiasco. The music was not remotely difficult to music-lovers, but much of the audience were not in the habit of attending opera at all. *Gloriana* was quite long, the evening was warm, the intervals seemed endless, stick-up collars grew limp, and well before the end a restlessness set in. 'Boriana' was on everyone's lips. Most distressing was that in one scene the elderly Queen Elizabeth I removed her wig from her head and was revealed as almost bald: and this was taken, for no good reason at all, as being in bad taste.[50]

What little enthusiasm there was in the house was further muted by the white gloves worn by the audience, which muffled their applause. The professional critics were inevitably influenced by the atmosphere of boredom, distaste and embarrassment around them.

Had Britten simply provided 'lovely pageantry', he might have got away with it, indeed he might have caught some of the more reactionary aspects of the New Elizabethanism of the time. William Plomer's recollections of that disastrous first night make the point.

> Were these chatterers interested in anything beyond a plenteous twinkling of tiaras and recognizable wearers of stars and ribbons in the auditorium? Did they perhaps expect some kind of loud and rumbustious amalgam of *Land of Hope and Glory* and *Merrie England*, with catchy tunes and deafening choruses

---

[48] P. Alexander, *op. cit.*, 278; see also p. 109 below.
[49] Interview with the author, 24 July 1991.
[50] Lord Drogheda, *Double Harness* (London: Weidenfeld and Nicolson, 1976), 239–40.

to reproduce the vulgar and blatant patriotism of the Boer War period? If so, they didn't get it.[51]

What they did get was something altogether more thoughtful, and possibly more prescient about the problems that Britain, diminished in majesty, power and statesmanship, would face in the coming years. With hindsight, it seems that Britten may have been equating the difficult decisions facing Queen Elizabeth I with the difficult decisions facing the country as it sought refreshment in the youth of Queen Elizabeth II.

As I indicated earlier, I would argue for an essential continuity between the Festival of Britain and the Coronation. Both were concerned with national identity, both were celebrations of renewal, to the extent that the Coronation could be said to have finished the work that the Festival began. I asked Lord Harewood how genuine the spirit of 'New Elizabethanism' had been – not in any reactionary sense – but in terms of a new start. He said, 'We felt we were on the crest of everything going right, with a young Queen, looking to the future, not looking back. The feel of it was very real, but in the end it lacked substance.'[52] Writing at the end of 1953, the sociologists Shils and Young concluded: 'The central fact is that Britain came into the Coronation period with a degree of moral consensus such as few large societies have ever manifested.'[53] But did that consensus, which essentially preserved the old cultural order and the old cultural values manifested in the lovely pageantry of the Coronation, actually serve the best interests of Britain, or did it merely mask long-term problems with complacency? How substantial was New Elizabethanism by the end of 1956?

For an alternative view of the period I turn to Raymond Williams, who wrote in 1981 that the key changes in post-war life occurred between 1947 and 1953, 'cultural changes, affecting very large numbers of people, though less evidently recorded in particular commercial and artistic successes. Indeed that is probably the point, that what mainly happened in those years was a sequence of failures, after which, at different levels, new moods and adaptations, new kinds of break and attempted break, and eventually new kinds of misplaced confidence came through.'[54] Thus the darkness at the close of *Gloriana*, even the failure of the first night, shows that Britten was more in touch with his time than the pomp and circumstance of a Royal gala might lead us to suppose.

The *Gloriana* story demonstrates the sense of blockage in public cultural life in the early 1950s. It certainly blocked Britten's career, and there was an envious backlash against the favour he had been enjoying. In spite of singing the part of Essex, Peter Pears had never been enthusiastic about the project, and he urged a further retreat into the more private world that Britten and Pears were creating for themselves in Aldeburgh. Britten did not write another large-scale opera for

[51] William Plomer, 'Let's crab an Opera', *London Magazine* 3/7 (October 1965), 101.
[52] Interview, 24 July 1991.
[53] E. Shils and M. Young, *op. cit.*, 77.
[54] Raymond Williams, '1956 and all that' (see fn. 27).

seventeen years, and then it was for television. However limited the actual extent of royal patronage, the reception of the piece cannot have encouraged the Royal Household, which was reported not to have liked the opera, to favour the arts in future. The music critic David Cairns argues that the fiasco helped to discourage public patronage in general: 'The particular nastiness of the *Gloriana* episode lay in the unholy alliance that was forged between traditional British philistinism, in one of its most reactionary periods, and forces within the musical profession activated by prejudices of a scarcely superior kind. In opposing state-subsidized opera, and Britten as the pampered symbol of it, traditional British philistinism was only acting according to its sad lights.'[55]

* * *

Britten is not the only composer to have had a disaster with a coronation opera. Mozart's *La Clemenza di Tito* was considered boring when it was first played in Prague on the Coronation of Franz II. (Nor should we overlook the tones of melancholy and introspection to be found in some of Elgar's public works, including the *Coronation Ode* for Edward VII and the *Coronation March* for George V.) The score of *Gloriana* lay unused for ten years, until a concert performance at the Festival Hall.[56] Sadler's Wells revived the opera in 1966. Lord Harewood kept faith with the theme of national identity by presenting it with the English National Opera at the time of Britain's entry into the European Community. But, if not entirely lost, *Gloriana* has not established itself.

Until, that is, this year. For the good news is that Decca are about to fill the glaring gap in their catalogue with a recording of the work with the Welsh National Opera under Sir Charles Mackerras. Josephine Barstow takes the part of Elizabeth and Philip Langridge that of Essex. It is hoped that the recording will be released in time for the fortieth anniversary of that disastrous first night, 8 June 1993. Not only that, a new production of *Gloriana* is planned by Opera North for 1993/4, directed by the distinguished young director, Phyllida Lloyd. It is to be hoped that this rare attempt at British 'national expression' in opera will now receive the recognition that the audience of dignitaries – or, if you prefer, the representatives of traditional British philistinism – so churlishly refused to give it in 1953.

---

55 David Cairns, 'Gloriana' in *Responses: Musical Essays and Reviews* (London: Secker and Warburg, 1973), 79.
56 But music from the opera was heard in non-operatic contexts, in various choral and instrumental adaptations; see List of Sources.

2

The Creative Evolution of *Gloriana*

PHILIP REED

Although William Plomer (1903–1973) and Britten probably first met in February 1937 on the occasion of the opening night of W.H. Auden's and Christopher Isherwood's play, *The Ascent of F6*, for which Britten had composed a remarkable incidental music score, like E.M. Forster (who was also present at the *F6* première), it was not until the post-war years that a friendship with Britten was to develop more fully. Like Forster, Plomer was invited to participate at the first Aldeburgh Festival in June 1948, when he lectured on the Suffolk man of letters Edward Fitzgerald, translator of *The Rubaiyat of Omar Khayyam*, and thereafter he became a regular and much valued contributor to the annual Festival programme.

Britten's choice of Plomer as the librettist of *Gloriana* in 1952 had its roots in two earlier operatic libretti, both of which remained unachieved projects. It had been Plomer's edition of Herman Melville's *Billy Budd*[1] that had inspired Britten's opera, with a libretto by Forster and Eric Crozier, and in the summer of 1951, while casting around for a new subject suitable for children (in fact while still working on the full score of *Budd*), Britten alighted on Beatrix Potter's *The Tale of Mr Tod* and invited Plomer to collaborate. Although some progress was made – for example, a draft scenario in Britten's hand survives – the project had to be abandoned when copyright difficulties with Potter's publishers arose.[2] Britten and Plomer were not, however, to be thwarted by this setback and after the première of *Billy Budd* in December 1951 (which Plomer attended) they began to plan a new and original children's opera on the subject of space travel, entitled *Tyco the Vegan*. It was with Plomer's draft libretto of *Tyco*[3] in his suitcase that Britten and Peter Pears set off for the Continent in February. After a recital in Vienna where they were joined by their friends the Earl and Countess of Harewood, the party of four embarked on a skiing holiday at the Austrian resort of Gargallen. It was from Gargallen that Britten wrote to Plomer with his

---

[1] See Mervyn Cooke and Philip Reed, *Benjamin Britten: Billy Budd* (Cambridge: Cambridge University Press, 1993), 47.

[2] See also Peter Alexander, *William Plomer: A Biography* (Oxford: Oxford University Press, 1989), 268–70.

[3] The draft survives at *GB-ALb*.

latest criticisms of the *Tyco* draft, but while on holiday a new and more topical idea emerged which forced the abandonment of the children's opera.

In his memoirs, *The Tongs and the Bones*, Lord Harewood has recalled how one day at Gargallen their discussion centred around the 'national' expression in opera and the particular 'national' operas of other countries – Smetana's *The Bartered Bride* (an influential model for Britten's *Albert Herring*), Musorgsky's *Boris Godunov*, Wagner's *Die Meistersinger von Nürnberg* and Verdi's *Aida* were all mentioned. But when faced with the question of what might be thought appropriate for England nothing sprang immediately to mind, and the suggestion arose that Britten ought to write one in time for the forthcoming coronation of Queen Elizabeth II in June 1953. Various subjects were proposed, including the Tudor period, and Henry VIII was suggested and rejected. (Perhaps he would have been too Falstaffian a figure.) But the idea of basing an opera around the figure of Queen Elizabeth I was found to be attractive, particularly as obvious parallels with the new Queen and the prevailing concept of the dawning of a second Elizabethan age could be made.

Lord Harewood had recently read Lytton Strachey's *Elizabeth and Essex* and this was taken as a useful starting point. But there were objections to the project even at this early stage from Pears, who was rightly concerned about the concert plans he and Britten had already laid for the rest of 1952 and 1953. (Pears's negative feelings are interesting in the light of his subsequent view of *Gloriana*, coloured by his discomfort at playing the role of the ardent young lover, the Earl of Essex.) In addition, Britten would have to postpone a commission from the Venice Biennale Festival for a new opera – *The Turn of the Screw* – in order for his desk to be clear for work on the Coronation opera.

According to Lord Harewood, ideas for what was to become known as *Gloriana* germinated throughout the remainder of the Continental trip. When the inevitable question was raised about who should write the libretto for the new opera, Britten, at that stage uncertain of Plomer's co-operation (Plomer may, after all, have been unwilling to undertake such a large-scale project for his first libretto), agreed to Harewood's suggestion of Ronald Duncan. However, because of the composer's uneasy relationship with Duncan – they had hardly collaborated since *The Rape of Lucretia* in 1946 – Britten persuaded Harewood himself to become involved as an assistant to Duncan and a neutral liaison between composer and librettist. On their return to London, Harewood set about dividing a copy of Strachey's novel into operatic scenes (L1.1).[4] When questioned about his annotated copy Lord Harewood replied:

> I probably still have my copy of Lytton Strachey's 'Elizabeth and Essex' but of course I only annotated it for my own purposes when Ben was uncertain whether William Plomer could be persuaded to divert his attentions to writing the libretto. If William had refused, he wanted me to collaborate with

---

[4] These reference numbers refer to items in the List of Sources, pp. 101–170 below; unless otherwise indicated they refer to material listed under (A).

Ronnie Duncan – or at least, that's what he said when he was making up his mind to undertake the work.

I don't know though whether it would be of the slightest use as it was my notions – indeed, first notions – about what would be suitable, not Ben's.[5]

When discussing the project, one thing was most certainly decided by Britten at the outset: that if he were to compose a Coronation opera, the work would have to be part of the official celebrations and, as Harewood recalled, 'not quite commanded but at least accepted as part of the celebrations'. Although Lord Harewood is quite certain of the possibility of Duncan's involvement, on his return to Aldeburgh Britten soon contacted Plomer, inviting him to a meeting at his London home: 'So very sorry to be so vague & hectic . . . but I think I can explain it if & when we meet.'[6] One or two days after their meeting, Britten travelled to Henley-on-Thames to visit the artist John Piper, who had designed most of his operas since *Lucretia*. He was evidently lining up his collaborators for *Gloriana*.

In the meantime Lord Harewood had been in touch with his cousin, Sir Alan Lascelles, the Queen's Private Secretary, in order for the idea to be placed before the Queen. Her consent was forthcoming as Britten reported in an undated letter to Plomer, probably written towards the end of April 1952:

The Queen has graciously given her O.K. to the scheme I told you about – there is a slight money difficulty, but I've had a word with David Webster [General Administrator] of Covent Garden who says that that is no obstacle as far as they are concerned (i.e. If the Treasury does not fork out direct, Cov. Gard. will find the money). Everything seems set, therefore; only with the librettist, there is a doubt still . . . ? I hope not, & that those days' silence means an agreement. I want to go to my agent to-day or to-morrow to cancel every-thing for the year (till April) . . .

Sorry to bother – but the matter is now really urgent, & also, I feel very exciting too.

Plomer's agreement was forthcoming and both he and Britten began to think about the subject-matter in a more disciplined fashion. By now both had read through Strachey's text and decisions were being made about the opera's shape. Plomer, for instance, wrote to Britten on 8 May:

I am posting you to-day Neale's book about Q. Elizabeth wh[ich] is a sort of corrective to Lytton Strachey. We must if possible have the moment when Essex, back from Ireland, bursts in upon the Q. en deshabile at Nonesuch. And we must have her feeding the dying Burleigh with her own hand. I begin

---

[5] Private communication to the author, 17 July 1992. It has not been possible to examine this source text.

[6] Letter from Britten to Plomer, 27 April 1952. Quotations from Britten's correspondence are © 1993 the Trustees of the Britten–Pears Foundation and may not be further reproduced without written permission. They appear here by the Trustees' kind permission.

to think we must have Burleigh & Cecil as benevolent beings, if not 'heroes'. Dialogues are visiting me in my dreams, wh. I take as a hopeful sign.[7]

Britten responded a few days later, on 11 May, after receiving Neale's biography of Elizabeth:

I am deep in it, & enjoying it thoroughly. I haven't got on to the later bits, so I haven't yet felt the 'corrective' to Strachey; but I am learning alot about the extraordinary woman & times.

I long to start planning with you. My feelings at the moment are that I want the opera to be crystal-clear, with lovely pageantry . . . but linked by a strong story about the Queen & Essex – strong & simple. A tall order, but I think we can do it!

In fact, J.E. Neale's 1934 biography of Elizabeth I proved to be an important source text for Plomer's libretto, though Britten's copy is unmarked (see L2).[8]

Plomer visited Aldeburgh for a few days from 30 May; two days earlier a press release had announced the Coronation opera project to the general public.[9] The title of the new work was yet to be finalized, and Pears, in a letter to Mary Behrend on 3 June, reported: 'Ben's back & hard at work discussing "Elizabeth (& ?Essex)" with William Plomer!!'[10] On his return to London, Plomer wrote to Britten on 4 June: 'I am very happy to think that we have made such a hopeful beginning with out great proceeding.' He ended with a humorous postscript, as if to show his prowess as a versifying librettist: 'The rose is red, the leaves are green: Long live Elizabeth, our noble Queen!'[11]

* * *

The first of our commentaries on the *Gloriana* source materials is concerned with those surviving documents which, although we are unable to date them with absolute confidence, undoubtedly belong to the earliest period of discussion between Plomer and Britten.

A copy of Strachey's *Elizabeth and Essex* has survived, signed by Britten on the flyleaf (L1.3). It is surprisingly unmarked considering Strachey is the

---

7 All extracts from William Plomer's letters are © Sir Rupert Hart-Davis and are reproduced with his permission.

8 I am grateful to Antonia Malloy for drawing my attention to the hitherto unrecognized role played by Neale's volume: many of the incidents in *Gloriana*, and in some cases actual words and phrases used in the libretto, can be traced back as much to Neale as Strachey.

9 Early press announcements are listed in section 3a of the Bibliography, pp. 173–74 below.

10 Quotations from the letters of the late Sir Peter Pears are © 1993 the Executors of Sir Peter Pears and are not to be further reproduced without written permission. They appear here by the kind permission of the Executors.

11 Oddly enough, an echo of one of the opera's recurring motifs (both musical and verbal) symbolizing national pride and loyalty to the monarchy: 'Green leaves are we, / Red rose our golden Queen' (see below, pp. 28–30, 80–82).

acknowledged source of the opera, and it may be possible that another copy, now missing, was more fully used. The only passage in the volume marked with what may be one of Britten's pencil annotations – a vertical line in the margin adjacent to the text of interest or importance – can be found on page 4 against a paragraph describing conflicting elements of Essex's personality:

> The youth loved hunting and all the sports of manhood; but he loved reading too. He could write correctly in Latin and beautifully in English; he might have been a scholar, had he not been so spirited a nobleman. As he grew up this double nature seemed to be reflected in his physical complexion. The blood flew through his veins in vigorous vitality; he ran and tilted with the sprightliest; and then suddenly health would ebb away from him, and the pale boy would lie for hours in his chamber, obscurely melancholy, with a Virgil in his hand.

This is an exceptionally interesting passage to find highlighted by the composer in the light of how Essex's – and for that matter, Elizabeth's – character is portrayed in *Gloriana*, and, as Donald Mitchell has shown, casts new light on how we might interpret the operas that precede and succeed *Gloriana*, *Billy Budd* (1951) and *The Turn of the Screw* (1954). The essentially dual nature of Strachey's Essex is enhanced by Plomer and Britten as a theme for the whole opera, namely the conflict between public duty and private passion (a dilemma which also confronts both Vere and the Governess).[12] (With the Strachey volume is an invitation card addressed to Lord Harewood (dating from 1951), the *verso* of which has been used by Harewood to demonstrate by way of a family tree his own descent from Robert Devereux, Earl of Essex.)

Two draft scenarios in Britten's hand survive, one incomplete (L3), the other complete (L4). L3 peters out in Act 2, although the essential elements of Act 1 are present and in an order which conforms to the final version of the opera. Act 2, however, is a little confused. Elizabeth's 'Progress at Norwich', described by Britten as a 'Diversion' (it is not given a scene number here), is sited not at the beginning of the act but after the conspiracy scene in the garden of Essex House (2.ii in the published version). The draft scenario breaks off abruptly with the heading 'Scene II', which was presumably intended to be the ballroom scene which now concludes the act. The simple yet effective pattern to be found in the final version of the work, in which scenes of public and private concerns are alternated, is not fully present in this incomplete scenario. It was perhaps the realization that this scheme might be of significant dramatic and musical interest that Britten broke off from making this first scenario to begin again.

---

[12] See Donald Mitchell's comments below, pp. 74–5, and his 'A Billy Budd Notebook', in Mervyn Cooke and Philip Reed, *op. cit.*, 122–34.

L4 reads as follows:

Act I

Scene I   Tiltyard. Quarrel between Essex & Mountjoy – Arrival of QE reconciliation

Scene II   Private ['Interior' crossed through]   QE & Cecil   Arrival of Essex – Love scene   QE Alone (Song?)

Act II

Diversion ['Scene' crossed through] – Progress at Norwich

Scene I   Essex House. Essex with P. Rich, Mountjoy & Lady Essex in conspiracy

Scene II   Richmond Palace
Ballroom Scene   Episode of Lady E's dress   Essex is sent to Ireland

Act III

Scene I
Essex arrival from Ireland   As before

Diversion?
Proclamation of Essex death?

Scene II   Elizabeth's death
as before

In the second draft the Norwich progress is now to be found in its correct position, although it is still described as a 'diversion' rather than as a scene proper. The notion of the diversion was probably bound up in the composer's mind for *Gloriana* to include examples of 'lovely pageantry'; a parallel diversion was to be included in Act 3 in which the death of Essex would be related. (The idea of a blind Ballad-Singer had apparently not yet occurred to Britten and Plomer.) The swapping around of the order of the components of Act 2 now allows the juxtaposition of public/private concerns to continue uninterrupted to the end of the work; extremely revealing in this context, and surely unequivocal in its demonstration of Britten's preoccupation with this important theme, is the substitution of the single word 'Private' for 'Interior' in 1.ii. The musico-dramatic possibilities of the alternation of these themes – redolent of Verdi's *Don Carlos*, a work set in roughly the same historical period as *Gloriana* – were evidently uppermost in Britten's thinking about the piece. In the same scene we should note '(Song?)', the first indication of that crucial and memorable moment of repose when Essex sings to Elizabeth his two lute songs.

Of the materials in Plomer's hand surviving from this formative period, there is a scenario, more detailed than those by Britten, for Act 2 only (L5); similar scenarios by Plomer must have once existed for the other acts but these have apparently not survived. The level of detail given by Plomer in his scenario, in which the action of each scene is summarized in a succession of smaller units, includes indications of the formal musical devices to be employed – recitative, duet, quartet – and suggests that the librettist used this structural groundplan when drafting the libretto proper (see L6, and pp. 28–33 below). Both the scenarios for 2.ii and 2.iii follow, in principle, the course of events unfolded in the version of the text as set by Britten. For example, the progression from, and contrast between, the duet sung by Lady Rich and Mountjoy and that by Essex and his wife, leading ultimately to their quartet of agreement, can be seen in Plomer's scenario; not present at this stage, however, is the concept of the 'double duet' (largely a musico-dramatic feature) in which the pairs of characters present not a unity of purpose but conflicting motives. The final quartet proper is where dramatically (and therefore musically) they reach their point of agreement, expressed (rather crudely) in Plomer's scenario thus: 'If we four stick together, we can manage the Queen all right, & feather our nests.'

Scene 3 likewise offers a typical encapsulation of the narrative thrust of the ballroom scene, albeit in an embryonic state:

1. Dances. The Q. taking part.
2. recit: The Queen says she must go and change her linen.
3. solo dancer, or tumbler.
4. The Q. returns, wearing Lady Essex's too fine dress. Murmurs of amazement, enquiry, explanation, among the courtiers, towards Lady E. on far side of stage.
5. recit: taunting Lady E. and exit.
6. quartet. Outburst of rage from the four plotters (Essex, Lady Essex, Penelope Rich, & Mountjoy). Essex's 'crooked carcass' remark.
7. The Q. returns in a third dress, accompanied by Raleigh & Cecil, & makes a gracious little speech telling Essex she is giving him the command in Ireland.
8. Sceptical asides by Raleigh & Cecil.
9. Dance. The Q. gives her hand to Essex, who, leads her out in the dance.

Already in the above outline it is apparent that dance is to play an important structural role in the formal balance of the scene, and that maximum irony will be sought by the juxtaposition of Essex's insulting comments about Elizabeth, culminating in 'Her conditions are as crooked as her carcass!', and Elizabeth's appointment of him as her Lord Deputy in Ireland, charged with crushing the rebel Tyrone.

One further point of interest about Plomer's scenario is that it contains nothing to indicate the nature of the proposed diversion destined for 2.i except the single sentence 'Act 2. Scene 1. The Q. on Progress at Norwich.' This scene was clearly yet to be finalized and would remain in a state of limbo for some time to come.

* * *

After the 1952 Aldeburgh Festival, during which Plomer had stayed at Crag House and given a lecture on his forebears, Martin Folkes and Martin Rishton, Britten was anxious to make further progress with *Gloriana*. He wrote to Plomer on 29 June inviting him to visit Aldeburgh for a few days in early July, 'because

I go off abroad for 5 weeks after that, & hope to be able to carry something of Elizabeth in my head abroad, to cogitate on, & perhaps even to start sketching.' Among the scenes discussed during this second working visit at Aldeburgh was the opening tournament. After his return to London, Plomer wrote to Britten on 10 July:

> I feel, & I hope you do, that that was a fruitful visit . . .
>
> Since I got back I have revised the whole of the first scene. It seems much improved, & I mean to have a fair copy of it for you to take away with you on Monday, when I expect you at one o'clock here for lunch. Afterwards, all being well, we'll go off to the Portrait Gallery.

After lunch on 14 July Plomer and Britten made a research trip to the National Portrait Gallery where they hoped to imbue some Elizabethan atmosphere for the opera by examining portraits of the historical figures from the period destined to feature in *Gloriana*. Accompanying the libretto materials in the Britten–Pears Library are five monochrome postcards of portraits, published by the Gallery, of Elizabeth I, Essex, Cecil, Raleigh and Philip Sidney (who does not appear in *Gloriana*), each with an outline biography printed on the verso; the thumb-nail life of Elizabeth is by Lytton Strachey. Britten's need to be able to visualise his characters and their setting was a characteristic trait of his working methods when writing stage works, and the purchase of these cards entirely in keeping with his practice elsewhere. For example, the draft libretto materials for *Peter Grimes* and *Billy Budd* both contain examples of early drawings of their respective stage sets; Britten needed a tangible reference point to how an opera might appear while working on the composition.[13]

Accompanied by Lord and Lady Harewood, Britten and Pears sailed for France on the night-boat on 15 July, travelling by car – according to Lord Harewood, Britten and Pears in Britten's Rolls, and the Harewoods in their Austin Princess – to Ménerbes, near Aix-en-Provence, where they stayed with Tony and Thérèse Mayer (Tony Mayer was the French cultural attaché in London). Britten and Pears were to give a recital on the 24th as part of the Aix-en-Provence Festival. After nearly two weeks at Ménerbes they travelled to Menton on 31 July where Britten conducted a concert given by the Hamburg Chamber Orchestra, with Pears as soloist, on 5 August. On 14 August Britten and Pears left for Salzburg where they gave a concert on the 18th; they returned to England by way of the night-boat from the Hook of Holland on the 21st.

In spite of these recitals, the trip was really by way of a vacation; but a holiday for Britten was a characteristic opportunity to think about composition and the time in France was no exception. The subject of *Gloriana* inevitably came up and Lord Harewood has indicated in his memoirs some aspects of the work that were raised at this time, in particular Pears's attitude to the project:

---

[13] See Philip Brett, ed., *Benjamin Britten: Peter Grimes* (Cambridge: Cambridge University Press, 1983), 43, 49, and Mervyn Cooke and Philip Reed, *op. cit.*, 47.

Peter had taken up a glum position over the whole thing, hating the cancellations, disliking the disturbance of his routine, the official nature of the affair, the risk involved in the venture into international waters, and perhaps too of playing a young, ardent lover in the shape of Essex . . . He preferred to sing Cecil.[14]

According to Harewood, Britten even began to consider other singers for the role – Boris Christoff or Nicolai Rossi-Lemeni, for example – although these were soon dismissed. But when asked about the role of Essex by John Evans, in an interview thirty years after the first performance of *Gloriana*, Pears remarked: 'I adored the lute songs, of course, and there are two wonderful duets with Elizabeth, but I think that in many ways in the rest of the part I was wrongly cast. I'm not sure, but I think somebody else should have done it rather than me.'[15]

Despite these doubts and worries, Britten was able to make considerable progress on the libretto while abroad. He wrote to Plomer from Aix-en-Provence on the 24th, the day of his and Pears's recital there, a letter in which all of Britten's enormous experience as an opera composer can be felt and which must have been very helpful to his relatively inexperienced librettist. Moreover, the letter clearly indicates how much of the libretto was completed in draft form.

. . . inspite of the travelling, I've done alot of reading & thinking about Gloriana, & here are some random remarks about the new version of Act I.

Terribly good. I am delighted with it & ideas come fast & furious. I'd like to start the tournament earlier, so, in fact, that practically the whole of it could be described by Cuffe. Could Essex have some more asides – such as 'Hearuss' – 'I can't bear it' kind of thing? Which leads to one general worry . . . I think that metre & rhyme (especially the latter) may make the recitatives very square, & unconversational. Can we take out a word here & there to break them up?

Could Essex (& Mountjoy perhaps) have a reaction (an aside even) to Raleigh's little song in the 1st scene – it will pave the way for the later outbursts. Similarly there could be generally more reactions from the crowd, through this scene.

Could Essex, in the final ensemble have a more personal couplet? I don't think this need be regarded as realistic – just his thoughts.

I am thrilled with Act I Scene II. It is a lovely, a really lovely scene. One comment – wasn't Essex called Robin, by the Queen? It would be nice & tender I think, & also prevent confusion with Cecil.

Britten continued:

---

[14] Lord Harewood, *The Tongs and the Bones* (London: Weidenfeld and Nicolson, 1981), 136.
[15] See Nicholas John, ed., *Peter Grimes, Gloriana*, Opera Guide 24 (London: John Calder, 1983), 68.

One or two general remarks on future scenes. I still don't like the reference to Lady E's dress in Act 2 Scene 2 – it seems quite against the mood of the moment, & anyhow she wouldn't be wearing her glamorous ball-gown in the garden, would she? <u>Couldn't</u> she come in in it at the beginning of the Ball-room scene, & then when the grand ladies retire to 'change their linen', Elizabeth could snoop the dress & come back in it. It would be more fun to have it more closely in the audience's mind.

And I've had a big idea about the end of the opera, which I'll hint at, only, now. After the great discussion, & the deputations about Essex's execution, & the signing of the Warrant – could we make a quite unrealistic slow flow out of the Queen? Like this. Signing of warrant. Take lights down except for a spot of Elizabeth. Then, so as to suggest her mind is on Essex, play an orchestral version of the 'Bramblebury' [sic] song [i.e. Essex's Second Lute Song, 'Happy were he'],[16] while people come & hand her documents to sign, consult her on matters – to which she replies automatically or not at all. Then finally, perhaps one might suggest she's dying; some doctor tells her to go to bed – she won't, but continues to stand there gauntly, like some majestic fowl, & slow fade of all lights to show the end. Could you think about this?

Plomer responded to Britten's letter on 2 August, addressing each of the points in turn:

I was very glad to get your letter from Aix and to see in the paper on the same day a good account of your concert and of your & Peter's accomplishments. I am not less glad to know that you have not been prevented from thinking about Gloriana. It is a great comfort to me to feel that you're pleased with the way Act I is shaping. I am sure the first scene can be improved on the lines you suggest, and the recitative <u>throughout</u> can easily be loosened up & freed from the harness of metre and rhyme, as seems best. I will see what I can do and will confer with you as soon as we meet.

Yes, I like the idea of the Q. calling Essex "Robin" in Act I, Scene 2.

I've been working on Act II, Scene 2. I am still inclined to think that Lady Essex <u>ought</u> to stroll in the garden in her "too fine" dress. I will explain why when we meet, but I won't be obstinate about the point. We must simply search out always what is most effective and appropriate to our purpose.

I like <u>very much</u> your suggestions about the final scene of the opera.

Plomer reported to Britten on his meeting with John Piper, who was to design the décor and costumes for the new opera:

I have had him here & given him a conspectus of our proceedings. He took some notes, and of course showed himself thoroughly imaginative & understanding & full of good ideas. I feel very contented at the prospect of his collaboration . . .

---

[16] Britten and Plomer referred to it as the 'Brambleberry' song presumably because of one its lines: 'Content with hips and haws and brambleberry'.

Clouds of dust rush up and down in this town, & the grass is bleached and pulverized: but in the garden of Essex House it is evening, and a distinguished couple, obviously in love, have just caught sight of another distinguished couple strolling on a terrace . . .

In the same letter Plomer reports on a meeting he had had with the Queen Mother and Princess Margaret which evidently touched on at least one issue of common public interest:

To the Q. Mother – but not to her daughter – I was able to talk about the opera. She has such charm that it was difficult to tell whether she was as interested as she seemed to be. I found myself talking about Elizabeth I rather than about the opera, & she then raised the question of the prospects of a "new Elizabethan Age". At least one can hope that she has really filed away in her mind & memory a reminder about the opera.[17]

After Britten's return from Europe he and Plomer met once again at Aldeburgh, between 28 August and 1 September. This visit gave Plomer the opportunity to see for himself the kinds of alterations and improvements Britten was suggesting and allowed him to show Britten what else he had achieved. Evidently one of the areas under discussion was 1.ii, when Essex sings his so-called 'lute songs' to Elizabeth. Originally only one (now the second song) was included; but on 4 September, having now returned to London, Plomer wrote to the composer:

Here is a little song for Essex to sing before the Brambleberry Song. It is intended to be light & slight, & relevant to his immediate purpose of cheering & diverting the Queen, and I hope it may lend itself to a lively tempo before the elegiac mood of the Brambleberry. The phrase "Quick music's best" comes from John Hilton (d. 1657), from a rather suggestive little madrigal by him: the rest from my noddle . . .[18]

And of course let me know if you don't like the Essex song that I enclose, so that I can get busy on other lines.

*   *   *

---

[17] See also Robert Hewison, p. 9 above.

[18] Plomer probably found this text in E.H. Fellowes, *English Madrigal Verse 1588–1632*, first published in 1920, the second edition appearing in 1929. The line appears in 'You lovers that have loves astray', the third of the *Ayres, Or Fa Las for Three Voices* published by John Hilton in 1627. Fellowes presents the text as paired with that of the second; Plomer's characterization of their content seems apt:

II–III   My mistress frowns when she should play;
             I'll please her with a Fa la la.
             Sometimes she chides, but I straightway
             Present her with a Fa la la.

             You lovers that have loves astray
             May win them with a Fa la la.
             Quick music's best, for still they say
             None pleaseth like you Fa la la.

Britten appears to have had with him in France all of Act 1 and 2.ii of Plomer's draft libretto (L6); scene 1 from Act 2 was in abeyance at this time. This document is exceptionally complex in that it contains several layers of comments, corrections and revisions, and, because of the very necessary speed at which the opera was written, overlaps with other later stages of source material related to the opera's genesis (chiefly L10.1 and H1/H2). These layers of annotations demonstrate unequivocally the care which both composer and librettist lavished on the text and can be roughly sorted chronologically by the types of writing implements used. Plomer's first draft is written throughout in violet ink (sung text) with all stage directions, character names and page numbers inscribed in a red-orange ink; by ignoring all subsequent accretions it is possible to reconstruct his original versions of each scene, both their textual matter and the narrative sequence of events. Britten's pencil annotations – chiefly terse reminders to himself about how Plomer's draft might be improved – are confined to the scenes known to have been written by July 1952 and which provided the basis for his comments on the draft of Act 1 and 2.ii in his letter of 24 July. The final level of material relates to the revisions undertaken by Plomer in response to Britten's criticisms and takes the form of interpolated folios of new or substantially revised material, some in the ink colours of his initial draft, some in blue ballpoint (which may date from a different occasion), and ballpoint revisions made on the original folios.

Plomer's original version of 1.i began thus:

> *Outside a tilting-ground, at the conclusion of a tournament. Essex, attended by Cuffe, is listening to the proceedings within. Cuffe, at an opening in the wall, reports on what he can see.*

CUFFE: There, now, the tourney's done:
        The mob have all gone wild
        Because Mountjoy has won.

CHORUS: Mountjoy! Mountjoy!
         Mountjoy has won!

CUFFE: See the champion
        Lift the lance,
        With pride advance,
        Dismount with joy!

CHORUS: Mountjoy salutes the Queen

CUFFE: Before the Queen
        In strength and beauty
        Now he makes
        His humble duty:

ESSEX: In strength and beauty?
        What beside?
        Mine the task
        To break his pride!

CHORUS: Mountjoy! Mountjoy!

CUFFE: Now from the royal hand
            He takes a golden prize!

CHORUS: O Gloriana, golden Queen,
            O royal rose, our evergreen!
            The rose is red, the leaves are green!
            Long live Elizabeth,
            Elizabeth our Queen!

Even from this very brief excerpt it is possible to recognize immediately the basic style of the tournament scene as it was eventually to be set in the final version. The descriptive phrases from Cuffe, Essex's jealousy of Mountjoy's success and the interjections from the off-stage chorus are all successfully preserved and improved in the later revisions of the scene. Moreover, after providing Britten with a new start to the opera in which, as Britten suggested, the tournament itself is described, Plomer adapted his original opening and dovetailed it into the revised narrative sequence. Plomer's revised opening was probably ready by the time of Britten's return from abroad; it corresponds, with relatively few amendments, to the version as set by the composer, but with notably more evocative interpolations from the chorus: 'Mountjoy! Mountjoy!' is replaced for a more poetic play on his name 'He mounts in hope, / With joy we cheer: / Mountjoy!'

Plomer's original draft of this opening passage is important too for containing a version of a text, the musical setting of whose revised format was to form one of the most memorable musical images of the entire piece. It is the exhortation of homage to Queen Elizabeth (and by implication to Queen Elizabeth II) after Mountjoy receives his prize. This passage was in fact redrafted by Plomer in blue ballpoint, probably after a discussion between himself and Britten. The revision reads: 'Green leaves are we, red rose our golden Queen, / O crownèd rose among the leaves so green!' Against the original draft of the chorus's words Britten has placed a single pencil cross, suggesting that he recognized something here of dramatic importance and worthy of further exploitation. This may indeed be the case. Plomer's original draft of scene 1 ended in a rather downbeat manner:

       Mountjoy and Essex rise, approach her side by side, and kneel at her feet.

QUEEN: Fail not to come to court
           In fine or dirty weather,
           And I will not neglect you –
           But see ye come together!

           And now I give you both
           My hand, for your obedience

           She removes her glove, and gives her hand to Essex, who kisses it.

CHORUS: And now she gives to both
            Her hand, for their obedience.

She gives her hand to Mountjoy, who kisses it.

QUEEN: To reconcile your quarrel,
And so to end this audience.

A fanfare is sounded. Essex and Mountjoy embrace.

At Britten's request this whole passage was subsequently redrafted. Most significantly from a musico-dramatic point of view was the repetition of the 'Green leaves' idea to bring the scene to a wholly more positive conclusion and one, moreover, in which Elizabeth is depicted most strongly as a well-loved and deeply respected monarch. Musical and dramatic considerations apart, Britten had not lost sight of the occasion which his new opera was celebrating.[19]

Plomer's draft and its various layered revisions bears out Britten's remaining criticisms of this scene. An interpolated page includes Essex's and Mountjoy's reaction to Raleigh's song: 'I curse him for his insolence, / And some day I will hurl him down.' In the redrafted conclusion to 1.i, Plomer also provided the 'more personal couplet' Britten sought in an aside for Essex: 'If Gloriana gives me armies to command, / More than a subject's love will ripen here!'

Britten's letter from France suggests that, apart from Elizabeth calling Essex 'Robin', he was satisfied with the shape of 1.ii. But his pencil annotations to Plomer's draft reveal at least one crucial addition to the scene which seems to have been his own idea from a structural point of view. The passage in question concerns Essex's pair of lute songs, sung to the Queen to divert her mind from the cares of State. The original version ran as follows:

QUEEN: Your Princess thanks you, trusty elf.

CECIL: Now if I may obtrude myself,
The new ambassador from Spain –

QUEEN: Is at the old one's tricks again!
With one care ended, others are begun.

A stir at the door.

PAGE: My lord of Essex!

Essex enters, kneels, and rises.

QUEEN: Welcome, my lord. Sir Robert here,
So wise in counsel, will return anon.

Cecil bows himself out.

Cousin, I greet and bless thee
But cares of State oppress me.

ESSEX: Your liege-man would relieve you.

QUEEN: Good Robert, I believe you.

---

[19] For a further discussion of its musical and dramatic significance, see below, pp. 80–82.

ESSEX:	Cares most to lonely hours belong, And Majesty's perforce alone Raised high and dazzling on a throne: Pray let me speak in song.
QUEEN:	Ah yes, divert me with a song.
ESSEX:	Happy were he could finish forth his fate . . .

This transition into the lute song (there originally was only one) was too abrupt for Britten, particularly when one recalls the importance of the associations that 'Happy were he' has elsewhere in the opera (his letter of 24 July when discussing Act 3). It evidently required greater care in its placing. Britten's pencil annotations 'More? / – leading to song & depression' before Essex's entry in the passage above, and at the lead into the 'Brambleberry' song, 'Another song / gay' paved the way for Plomer's interpolation of some new material and a revision of the original text in which another song for Essex was to be included. Plomer's revisions, in blue ballpoint and dating from his and Britten's Aldeburgh meeting in late August/early September, mark the position of the new song; the text, however, was to arrive by post enclosed with Plomer's letter of 4 September:

QUEEN:	Your Princess thanks you, trusty elf.
CECIL:	Now if I may obtrude myself, The new ambassador from Spain –
QUEEN:	Is at the old one's tricks again! With one care ended, others are begun.
CECIL:	The newest is an old care now renewed.
QUEEN:	What new old care is this?
CECIL:	Word has been brought The King of Spain designs A new Armada to be sent –
QUEEN:	How soon? How nearly can they guess, Our faithful eyes and ears?
CECIL:	Perhaps before the spring.
QUEEN:	God's death! What lives, What money must be thrown Into the maw of cannon! Treasure and blood!
CECIL:	Madam, we are in the hands of God. He at a breath can melt the steel of Spain: We can but watch and wait.
QUEEN:	We can but watch and wait.
	A stir at the door.

31

PAGE: My lord of Essex!

Essex enters, kneels, and rises.

QUEEN: Welcome, my lord. Sir Robert here,
So wise in counsel, will return anon.

Cecil bows himself out.

Cousin, I greet you.

ESSEX: Queen of my life!

QUEEN: Cares of State eat up my days.
There lies my lute:
Take it and play.

ESSEX: (song)

QUEEN: Too light, too gay:
A song for careless hearts.
Turn to the lute again,
Evoke some far-off place or time,
A dream, a mood, an air
To spirit us both away.

ESSEX: Happy were he could finish forth his fate . . .

Plomer's new lute song for Essex appears in the draft on an interpolated sheet:

> Quick music heals
> When the heart is distressed,
> Then one moment reveals
> That quick music's best:
> Hallalloo, hallallay.
>
> Quick music's best
> For the pipe or the strings
> When the heart after rest
> Upriseth and sings:
> Hallalloo, hallallay.

There are no pencil annotations in Britten's hand on the draft text for 2.ii. There are, however, examples of the ballpoint revisions undertaken by Plomer in which parts of the text are resited and the references to Lady Essex's dress are removed in deference to Britten's request. The original version is perhaps less taut than the text as set, with too much dialogue for Mountjoy and Penelope Rich and a more extended conspiratorial exchange at the end of the scene. It concludes with an interpolated passage that echoes the sentence to be found in Plomer's draft scenario for this scene and in which all the political tensions of Elizabeth's succession and the conspirators' treacherous pact can be felt:

> Whether the coming King of England reigneth
> As King of Scotland now, or King of Spain,

One thing above all remaineth –
We four must maintain
Our love, our faith, in our ordainèd fate
Ourselves to seize and hold the helm of State.

* * *

On 8 September 1952, a week after Plomer's second visit to Aldeburgh, Britten reported to Eric Walter White that he had written the 'first notes' of *Gloriana*. On the 14th he wrote to his librettist:

> Your letter [4 September] & the very nice little song for Essex is days old, but we've had the house full of Harewoods & what little spare time has been at work on Gloriana. I think it is <u>excellent,</u> & it'll go in very well . . .

> I've written the first section – the tournament & got Mountjoy on to the stage. But I await your next visit here with impatience, because I have had to make drastic changes in the form of this part (I have been searching for ages for the correct form for the music for it, & <u>think</u> I've got it at last), & I hope & pray you'll approve . . . In the meantime I'll go ahead & hope we can sort out any difficulties later.

Plomer returned to Aldeburgh the following week, bringing with him the drafts of 2.iii and 3.i. While staying at Crag House he and Britten discussed various points in connection with the first two scenes of Act 2 and undertook the necessary revisions to 1.i hinted at in Britten's letter. Britten had also evidently played over to his librettist what he had so far composed: on his return to London Plomer wrote to him (25 September), 'The Prelude is ringing most spiritedly & excitingly in my ear & bosom: my untutored ear has a more precise memory than I should expect.' The same letter also included a reference to a press report 'to the effect that I handed over the finished libretto to you a fortnight ago. How they lie & invent.'[20]

After Plomer's visit Britten wrote to Basil Coleman, who had produced the première of *Billy Budd* in 1951 to widespread acclaim. His letter (25 September) indicates that there had been some difficulties in resolving Britten's commitments to the English Opera Group because of the need for his time to be fully occupied with *Gloriana*. The most pressing problem was Britten's acceptance of a commission from the Venice Biennale Festival for a new opera (in fact, *The Turn of the Screw*) to be presented by the EOG and, because of the intervention of *Gloriana*, the need for this première to be temporarily postponed. Britten confessed to Coleman that 'the problem of writing a good opera is more in my mind than anything else', and that the libretto was progressing very well, with the whole text 'sketched out fully . . . except the last two scenes'. Britten was generous about Plomer's abilities – 'He is a great sweet, & fine to work with; reasonable & skilful' – and told Coleman that the Pipers were due in Aldeburgh

---

[20] This report has not been traced.

33

the following weekend to discuss *Gloriana* and *The Turn of the Screw*. He concluded: 'It's lovely to think you'll be in on it with us all – our team is now complete!'

One piece of information contained in Britten's letter to Coleman was to be of considerable significance to the whole creative process of *Gloriana*, although in his letter the context is in connection with the administration of the Aldeburgh Festival: '. . . dear Imo Holst is taking up residence next week to help straighten things out.' Britten and Imogen Holst had already known one another for almost ten years. For most of that time she had been Director of Music in the Arts Department at Dartington where she built up a remarkable and unusual training school. Pears and Britten had often given recitals there, and in 1951 Pears taught at Dartington at Miss Holst's invitation. Attending some of her classes, he had been enormously impressed by her abilities and was determined that he and Britten should find a niche for her at Aldeburgh. A gifted composer, conductor and teacher, 'Imo' visited Aldeburgh on 4 September (according to Britten's engagement diary) for what was probably a preliminary discussion during which Britten most likely told her about *Gloriana* and asked her to act as his amanuensis, chiefly responsible for the vocal score and the initial preparation of the full score (i.e. the ruling up of the bar lines, the drawing of the clefs and instrument names, etc.). In addition to her duties as Britten's musical assistant, Imogen Holst kept a private diary during her first years in Aldeburgh which provides an amazing perspective on Britten's day-to-day working life and in particular on the progress of *Gloriana*.[21]

Miss Holst's diary records that scene 1 was finished on 30 September – 'It was pouring with rain and he said he'd got very wet indoors because he hadn't noticed that the rain was coming in on him while he worked' – and in a letter to Basil Coleman (6 October) Britten reported that he was 'well on with the 2nd'. In a postcard to Plomer on 17 October Britten told his collaborator that Act 1 was completed 'roughly . . . & am starting on Act II Scene II'.

While progress on Act 1 seems to have been fairly straightforward, Act 2 was full of difficulties that would not yield to a satisfactory resolution. The choreographic dimension of 2.i was the cause of major problems upsetting Britten's compositional flow. Imogen Holst noted in her diary for 14 October: 'He said he was depressed about the Masque scene in Gloriana because he had absolutely no idea what to do with the Masque.' Moreover, the Royal Ballet were deeply unhappy that they were not presenting the Coronation Gala, a subject which Britten related to Coleman in a letter (6 October) which barely disguises his impatience with the situation and their attitude:

> They forget that if we'd not had the idea of the new Opera & George H. [Harewood] hadn't bullied the Queen there wouldn't have been a gala at all – & they forget that they've had the other two galas there have been since the

---

[21] All passages from this unpublished diary quoted here are © 1993 the Estate of Imogen Holst, and may not be reproduced further without written permission. They appear here by kind permission of the Estate of Imogen Holst.

war. But still, there it is, & they are jealous. I've said that if they want there are two little ballets in the opera where they can hop around & make their little bows . . . further than that I can't go. When the situation calms, we can possibly discuss with them & you who should collaborate in the ballets. It must be someone you like, respect & can work with. Freddy Ashton??

In the meantime Britten proceeded with what he could of Act 2. On 30 October Imogen Holst wrote in her diary:

Ben rang up and said would I go round in the middle of the morning because he was stuck with the problem of the dances [in 2.iii] in Gloriana. When I got there he began talking about the orchestra on the stage for the ballroom scene: what instruments would they have had; he'd decided to have violas for viols, so as to get away from the 'sloppy brilliance' of the violins! He also talked about woodwind and suggested 2 flutes in unison, high up, with the slight out-of-tuneness adding to the ⊂===⊃ loudness. Then he talked about trumpets in Gloriana – he was enviously reading the lists of the numbers they'd had in 1600. I asked him how many he'd got on the stage and he said only three because he didn't think in all conscience he could ask for more, and I said of course he could, what else were the taxpayers paying for, and he said 'Well perhaps I could', and I said yes, for the Gala night, and then be able to have fewer when necessary, and he said 'Yes, I think I'll have <u>twelve</u>'! (This is so far my only tangible contribution to Gloriana.)

That evening, when Britten was 'quite mystified about speeds and lengths of dances', Miss Holst volunteered to go to Oxford the following day 'to have lessons on the Pavane, Galliard, Coranto and La Volta'. Three days later she returned and 'went round directly after breakfast and made Peter do the La Volta straight away!' She spent over two hours demonstrating the various dance steps she had mastered. Her diary contains a vivid account of Britten's progress on 2.iii on 4 November:

Ben walked in about 4 o'clock and said he was stuck in the dance tunes and would I go down and hear them. When we got in he played over the two tunes – the Pavane very lovely; there was one new attack on a forte chord which cut across the middle of a double bar and wouldn't do, so he's going to get a gradual crescendo up to it. Galliard, which he'd only just written that moment, was excellent, with Dowland-like scale passages, but thoroughly Ben. There was a cross-rhythm which made the ordinary coming to rest on the sixth beat very difficult in the middle: at first I thought it wouldn't do, but decided the choreographer could wangle things round it. Then he asked about the tumbler, and in the same breath talked about the morris, so I leapt at it, and he showed me a paragraph in Arbeau which mentioned a small boy dancing a morris jig in aristocratic circles! So I showed him some steps and told him why they painted their faces black.

On 5 November Britten wrote to David Webster, General Administrator at Covent Garden, about the importance of choosing a choreographer for *Gloriana*; at this stage it was not finally decided that the ballet would not make their own wholly separate contribution to the gala evening. Britten told Webster that he had been forced to omit 2.i for the time being 'because before writing it I must be able to discuss in detail the shapes and styles of the dances'. If a ballet programme was indeed to be a feature of the gala night then Ashton would be 'all-absorbed in it', in which case Britten proposed John Cranko, who had already worked with Coleman on the EOG production of *Love in a Village* at the 1952 Aldeburgh Festival. As Britten remarked, 'Being young and enterprising, he will not feel that collaborating in an opera with a producer is a rather dull job (as I feel his seniors might)', and pleaded with Webster 'for a decision on this immediately, because this gaping void of the Progress Scene is awkward to say the least.' Moreover, he warned Webster of the nature of the third scene from this act:

> I have been studying the Elizabethan dances for which I am now writing the music . . . It seems to me fairly clear that we shall need a corps de ballet to dance these dances. However simplified they may be, I do not feel that any <u>chorus</u> could cope with them. I hope you will not mind this.

Two days later Britten sought Imogen Holst's opinion on the dances from this scene, and wrote to Plomer to let him know about her idea of a morris dance by a small boy (with a blackened face) – 'the music is excellent and a complete contrast to what's gone before . . . a little creature hopping around the place would look lovely after the La Volta'. On the 17th Britten played to Imogen Holst as much as he had written of 2.iii: 'it was just right: the morris superb and the continuity between the dances and the agonizingly embarrassing bit with Q. Elizabeth and the borrowed dress.' On the 19th she records that Britten had decided to include a coranto at the end of the scene, and on the next day 'told me about the ironical march he's writing for the Queen's second entry in the scene'.

On 18 November Britten wrote to Plomer, who was recovering from an operation, that the end of 2.iii 'was in sight', but two days later he wrote again to Plomer with a new suggestion for the act's conclusion:

> I'm having quite a struggle with the end of the Act which won't go right. But I have had an idea to-day which may improve matters . . .

> Essex, & rightly, takes no part in the great 'ensemble' after the Queen's proclamation of his Ireland job. Could he have a shortish heroic reply to all the exhortations "Go into Ireland" saying he'll have a smash at them etc. etc.?? It'll round off the scene well, & should I think have a somewhat characteristic & ironic flavour considering what's just gone before & what's coming next. You write 'too overcome to speak' but although dramatically that is right, operatically (espec. <u>this</u> kind of opera) I think those rules of realism don't apply . . . It can be in prose if you wish – to balance the Queen's speech.

Plomer responded immediately and the new speech – 'Armed with the favour of our gracious Empress . . .' – was slotted into place in Britten's composition draft. Britten thanked him on 23 November:

... the lovely Essex speech ... fits what I'd planned (& even sketched in!) like a glove. A lovely case of thought transference! The other bits are fine also although I haven't actually fitted them in yet ...

I finished Act II (except the Masque scene) last week, & tomorrow start Act III which I look forward to greatly. I played the whole of what I've done through to Peter this morning & we were both pleased – remarkably so for this uncomfortable middlestage of the work. (He's beginning to like his part.)

Miss Holst's diary offers a more detailed account of the day's events:

Ben had asked me to go round with the [vocal] score of Gloriana after breakfast, and to stay to hear him play it through. Ben had begun rewriting the new recitative in Act II Scene III – he told me how he'd decided that Essex <u>must</u> have something to say after the announcement that he was to go to Ireland – he couldn't just remain in a stupefied silence. He'd been so full of what he wanted to write that he did the music before the words, and when the words came from William they fitted <u>very nearly</u> perfectly, with one or two tiny adjustments. The new bit is superb – wonderful ironic march, and parody of an official announcement; terrifyingly agitato bits for Essex – then a wonderful recitative with comments from the chorus – leading up to the final coranto with the full orchestra drowning it at the curtain. Then he played the second scene in the second act which gets more and more beautiful at every hearing. He said he'd give anything not to have to write the Masque for Scene I – and he thought Scenes II and III would make a complete Act in themselves.[22] But obviously this is because he's still weary with the effort of having written the dances in Scene III, and dreads having to do it all over again. Peter very insistent that Scene II isn't right for the beginning of the Act.

Peter very much moved by the second lute song, and obviously longing to begin work on his part, and Ben terribly happy that he should be so thrilled by it.

* * *

Our commentary is forthwith made more complicated because for the period covered by Chronicle III there were at least three types of material circulating at once – draft libretto, typed libretto, and composition draft – all of which reflect different, sometimes overlapping, stages of the opera's genesis. Unusually for Britten he began work on his composition draft before the libretto had been

---

[22] This was in fact tried out during the revival of *Gloriana* conducted by Reginald Goodall during January and February 1954. Britten wrote to Plomer on 31 January 1954: 'Everyone missed "Norwich", but many agreed the work gained in dramatic intensity, if it lost in open-airness or splendour.' A further production change, the omission of the procession of ghosts at the conclusion of Act 3, according to Britten, 'worked well'. Lord Harewood gave his reaction to this alteration in a letter to the composer (19 April 1954): 'I very much regret the loss of the Norwich scene, but it does give the opera more tension, and tips the balance towards the private, and necessarily more moving side of the opera, and away from the public side of it.' See also pp. 62–4 below.

completed, sometimes using Plomer's ink draft (L6) rather than the subsequently typed version (L10.1).

It has already been mentioned that in September 1952 Plomer brought with him to Aldeburgh drafts of 2.iii and 3.i in readiness for detailed discussions with the composer. In fact, Plomer's draft contains not one but two versions of 2.iii, neither of which includes any annotations in Britten's hand or revisions by Plomer so typical of the drafts of earlier scenes of the opera. It is not, alas, clear which of the versions Plomer brought for Britten's scrutiny – perhaps he offered both? – but there is no doubt that it is the second version which moves closer to the text as set to music.

The earliest version of the ballroom scene opens with an exchange between Essex and his wife, Frances, in which he asks her why she is not wearing 'that dress you wore to court last week' (a reference also to the previous scene where Plomer originally had her wearing the fine dress in the garden). The stage directions are not specific about the kinds of dances in progress: this was evidently a matter for Britten to settle and, as we have seen, one over which he exercised an enormous amount of care. The opening of the scene reads as follows:

> *A great room in Whitehall Palace at night, with assembled courtiers and their ladies in all their finery. A dance is in progress, led by Mountjoy and Lady Rich. Presently Essex draws his wife aside. She is dressed in grey, and looks conspicuously modest beside the other ladies.*

ESSEX: Frances, among these jewelled butterflies
I see you dressed too plainly, like a moth.
Where is that dress you wore to court last week?

FRANCES: I feared the Queen would disapprove:
I saw her fix me with her coldest look:
She likes to shine alone. I fear her eye.
I fear her vengefulness.

ESSEX: Frances, you are my wife.
I love your beauty,
And I would have you fine,
Finer than all at court.

FRANCES: Even so, my lord,
I could not wear that dress to-night,
Even at your command.

ESSEX: Even at my command?

FRANCES: Robert, it hangs no longer in its place!
It is not there!

ESSEX: Not there!

FRANCES: My maid came running, saying
'Twas nowhere to be found!

ESSEX: A thief at work?
           Under my roof?

FRANCES: I fear some grievous mischief –
           Here's the Queen.

Plomer's opening is self-evidently less pregnant in terms of dramatic flair than the subsequent text in which, the ladies having retired to change their linen after the exertions of the lavolta, Elizabeth steals the dress for herself, and because she looks so ridiculously grotesque in it, completely humiliates Frances. The text for this particular passage appears virtually intact in all later drafts of the scene. The response of the conspirators to Frances' humiliation by Elizabeth is more verbose here than in the later versions but, as with the overall structure of the scene, the basic framework is recognizable in the final version.

The second draft of 2.iii may have been written while Plomer was staying with Britten in September 1952: an immediate response to the composer's dissatisfaction with the initial text. Plomer now specifies the dance types – pavane, galliard, etc. – presumably after discussion with the composer, although Britten was not averse to revising this scheme when composing the music; after the Queen's entrance she originally commanded not a lavolta but a coranto (the coranto was displaced to the end of the scene). The second version now has Lady Essex already wearing the dress that Elizabeth will steal. This far more dramatically incisive idea was presumably included as a result of discussions between composer and librettist. Neither draft of 2.iii includes Raleigh's and Cecil's comments at the announcement of Essex's Irish appointment, or the choral interjections.

Plomer's ink draft of 3.i was submitted to revision after discussion with Britten, as evinced by the librettist's ballpoint revisions and the inclusion of revision leaves on a different paper type to the first draft. The opening conversation for groups of Maids of Honour (drawn from the chorus) was formerly divided among four Ladies-in-Waiting, an alteration which reflects purely practical concerns in not overstretching available resources. Much of the interview between Elizabeth and Essex appears on interpolated leaves, with Plomer expanding and subsequently discarding his earlier draft. It is clear that at least two leaves from Plomer's original draft of this scene, his pages 6–7, are now missing, having been replaced by the interpolated new pages 6, 7, 7a and 8. Moreover, as its 'a' suffix suggests, page 7a (the duet 'O, put back the clock') was an additional layer of redrafting. Its inclusion provides a convincing musico-dramatic climax to Essex's encounter with the Queen, as well as a foil to the duet in 1.ii. The Dressing-Table Song remained intact from the earliest draft until the libretto as set: as a closed number it provides a much-needed moment of repose between the highly-charged atmosphere of the preceding duet and the succeeding interview with Cecil. Plomer redrafted his first thoughts on Cecil's audience with Elizabeth (revision leaves are present), originally concluding (in both the first draft and its initial revision) with Elizabeth's 'I have failed to tame my thoroughbred'. Elizabeth's declaration that Essex is to be restrained is not present; however, a draft survives on a separate leaf (L9), with a minor revision by Britten, virtually as it appears in the opera.

Much of the typed, second draft libretto (L10.1) had been generated by the end of November 1952: i.e. all of Act 1, Act 2 with the exception of the opening scene in Norwich, and most probably 3.i as well. Under normal circumstances it would have been from this layer of libretto draft that Britten would habitually work when actually writing down the music of the opera. However, as we have already observed, the stringencies of the composing schedule for *Gloriana* placed constraints on Britten's normal working practice and he was forced on occasion to work not from a clear typescript copy of Plomer's text, as revised by composer and librettist, but from the considerably annotated versions of the initial draft. As a consequence, two effects may be observed on the surviving principal documents (L6 and L10.1): a profusion of layered annotations on L6, contrasting with a relatively small number of changes to the latter.

Britten's copy of the Act 1 typescript is entirely carbon copy with very few alterations in Britten's hand; the top copy, typed by Elizabeth Sweeting (General Manager of the EOG), has not been located, nor is it known how many carbons were generated (but see, for example, L12 and L13); and it seems improbable that Plomer did not retain a text, either the top copy or another carbon, for his own use). L10.1 was typed from Plomer's revised first draft, with its many interpolated leaves. The redrafted clean version of the opening Tournament was possibly made specifically for the typist to work from. The significantly small number of changes suggests that Britten did not work from this libretto when composing Act 1; many of the alterations that can be found in the text are typical of those Britten would make while writing the music, e.g. the unavoidable transposition of lines as dictated by musical needs.

As the collation for L10.1 shows, 2.i belongs to a different paper type and is a blue rather than black carbon: this scene was yet to be composed in November 1952 and was evidently typed at a later date. The remainder of Act 2 however matches the Act 1 typing. Scene 2 includes a number of insignificant annotations; but the changes between the revised draft and the typescript may be too radical for Plomer not to have supplied some (now missing) intermediary handwritten draft. Scene 3 was typed after the decision to include a morris dancer had been made and the re-ordering of the dances established. Added in pencil in Britten's hand are the choral interjections describing each of the dances, the text for each having been transcribed from lines drafted by Plomer after this scene had been written (see L8). From Plomer's suggested lines,

1. Pavane so grave and dignified,
2. Virtue sounds thus, and so decorum moves.
3. Slow and solemn, too slow for the young,
4. The very step of honour, harbinger of state.
5. Majestic music majesty obeys.

Britten selected fewer than half to produce:

> Pavane so grave & dignified!
> Slow & solemn!
> Too slow for the young!
> The very harbinger of state!

Scene 3 was typed without Essex's final comment, 'Armed with the favour of our gracious Empress . . .', but with enough space left for Britten to make a handwritten insertion of the text after Plomer had supplied it (see Imogen Holst's diary entry above). As in the previous scene, the level of changes involved in L6 makes one doubtful that it was possible for a typist to work from the much annotated handwritten copy.

One general point about Britten's typescript copy: Britten has throughout added in pencil the titles of the musical numbers as they subsequently appeared in the published score (i.e. 1 Prelude; 2 Tournament; 3 Recitative and Fight, etc.). These titles – which, ironically, emphasize the closed-form tradition in opera even when Britten's compositional practice in *Gloriana* blurs the edges of such divisions[23] – do not appear in the published librettos. It is, of course, not known when Britten inscribed them onto the libretto draft – before, during, or after writing the music – but their appearance at this stage in the work's genesis points perhaps to their musical origins rather than to some predetermined structure in Plomer's text.

A few general words on Britten's composition draft (H1) and its related discarded leaves (H2) are necessary, although it is impossible in the context of the present discussion to explore these documents in any real detail. The pattern of Britten's working methods hardly ever varied and the disciplined routine adopted in early adulthood was maintained, with only very few exceptions, with unfailing regularity. Britten's business-like timetable for the working day is well attested: two main periods of composition at his desk (not his piano), one in the morning, the other in the late afternoon/early evening, framed a long 'thinking' walk after lunch. He always mistrusted working at night, although scoring might be undertaken then if a deadline were fast approaching. By adhering to this rigorous schedule, Britten was usually able to gauge the amount of time needed to complete a major composition with unnerving accuracy.

As with the vast majority of Britten's output, *Gloriana* took shape on the manuscript paper as a (more or less) through-composed short score draft written in pencil throughout, with the orchestral texture reduced onto two, three or perhaps four staves and the vocal lines occupying their own staves. At first glance the draft resembles something approaching a vocal score and was certainly used as a guide by Imogen Holst when she prepared the vocal score (under Britten's supervision) for Boosey & Hawkes. The instrumentation is indicated by verbal abbreviations – 'str.', 'trbn', 'ww' – at the time of composition, ready for instant retrieval when the time came for the full score to be made. This simple technique was effective in allowing Britten to press on to the

---

[23] This feature is discussed by Peter Evans in chapter 5.

end of a work before making the full score, safe in the knowledge that the piece was in effect written; in the case of complex stage works, such as *Gloriana*, it also allowed an assistant to follow behind the composer using the draft as a basis for the all-important vocal score from which the principal singers and chorus would learn their roles. Once a new piece was complete in draft form, the business of making the corresponding full score was largely a calligraphic labour; the majority of the problems had already presented themselves and solutions found.

Throughout his career Britten preferred to work in pencil when composing because of the freedom it offered for changes of mind; the use of pencil was a significantly liberating factor to the composer's creativity since anything that was committed to paper might be easily rubbed out and re-written. Almost every leaf of *Gloriana* shows evidence of the use of the eraser, demonstrating unequivocally how closely Britten tested his original ideas. By and large it is not very easy to read the rubbed-out notes, although occasionally one can discern the impression made by Britten's pencil and decipher something valuable.

Two other, related, methods of making changes to a work can be found on any of Britten's composition drafts. Rather than erasing passages, particularly if they were more than a few bars, Britten would cross-through a section which he wished to delete. Occasionally, if the deleted passage amounted to a full page he might detach it and use the available blank *verso* elsewhere in the manuscript draft. If more than one page was rejected then Britten would almost always remove the offending passage from the main draft and place the particular folio(s) to one side. These discarded leaves form an important category of substantial earlier versions of the music.

Much of the foregoing holds true for Britten's methods while working on *Gloriana*, although the draft (H1) is remarkable in generating a relatively small number of discarded leaves (H2). There are significantly fewer surviving re-drafted passages for the opera than, say, for its predecessor, *Billy Budd*, with the most substantial being for 3.ii, a scene about which, as Imogen Holst testifies, Britten expressed doubts; but even the main draft is fairly free of deleted passages: perhaps Britten simply had to find the right idea first time as the pressures of his composition schedule left little room for the possibility of heavy revision. Unlike *Budd* which may be thought of as a 'symphonic' opera, *Gloriana* largely maintains the number-opera conventions successfully explored by Britten in earlier stage works. The very nature of the opera's formal shape may have a direct bearing on the level of redrafting involved. What is undoubtedly embodied in all the draft pages for *Gloriana*, however, bears testimony to just how remarkably successful Britten was at planning out his music in advance of committing the actual notes to the page: in effect, the long, thinking walks were where much of the compositional thought processes sifted through and refined musical ideas. In H1 and H2 we see the tangible by-products of Britten's art in bridging the differing elements in the complex compositional processes.

* * *

42

Continued steady progress was made on the opera's composition during the remainder of 1952. On 25 November Britten told the schoolboy Steuart Bedford that he expected to finish the composition draft shortly after Christmas, and wrote to Plomer on the 27th: 'Gloriana proceeds: I'm well into Act III & it takes lots of time'. In the same letter Britten invited Plomer – who was convalescing from an operation – to come down to Aldeburgh the following month when Piper and Cranko would also be staying; a few days later he was able to report to Plomer that 'Work is going well – well on with big duet between Eliz. & Ess.' (i.e. in 3.i). In early December Britten told Lady Harewood that Plomer was coming to Suffolk to undertake further work on the libretto, principally 3.iii ('almost from scratch') and to fill the 'hundreds of little gaps'. Plomer was certainly in Aldeburgh 7–9 December when he and Britten worked on the libretto draft for the final scene, the typescript of which was made in Aldeburgh and posted back to Plomer on 10 December. In his letter, Britten remarks that the first scene of Act 3 was now finished and that scene 2 was begun, but that he was 'not very happy about it'. Plomer (and his companion Charles Erdmann) stayed with Britten and Pears during the Christmas holiday period when, no doubt, any additional queries arising from the musical setting of the libretto could be settled.

Imogen Holst's diary for this period furnishes us with many of the minutiae of the opera's day-by-day progress. On 26 November Lord Harewood and David Webster were staying with Britten,[24] who played them Act 1 from Miss Holst's vocal score while she continued work on 2.ii from Britten's draft: '. . . just as he was handing it to me he looked agonizingly doubtful because he wasn't sure about the end of the scene, so I reminded him that my copy wasn't final and was only meant for second thoughts'. On 2 December she records Britten playing as much of 3.i as had been written:

> . . . he obviously hated the idea of bringing himself to having to play it, so I said nothing at all. So he opened the score and sat down at the piano and was in more of a state than I've ever known him before in the way of being nervously wrought up. He stopped after the first dozen bars and shook himself and said "I'll begin again:- it was too fast." This time he played right through as far as he'd worked it out, and he managed to calm down after the voices had begun . . .

> It was quite impossible to tell him of the overwhelming effect of the music, because there were no words for it – but I had to try and break through his depression somehow. After a bit he said "I'm pleased with the silences:- they're the right length anyway!"

---

24 Webster and Harewood were in Aldeburgh not only on matters connected with *Gloriana*: Webster was at that time attempting to persuade Britten to accept the post of music director at Covent Garden in succession to Karl Rankl, a position which Britten most wisely declined. See Humphrey Carpenter, *Benjamin Britten: a Biography* (London: Faber and Faber, 1992), 312–13.

A further play-through of 3.i (as yet unfinished) took place for Pears's benefit on 7 December, now with a 'most beautiful new bit after Essex's last exit, where the ladies-in-waiting soothe her as they finish dressing her [i.e. Elizabeth]' (The Dressing-Table Song). The scene was completed on the 9th when he confessed to Imogen Holst that he was worried because Plomer had to return to London when there was yet more work to do on the libretto of the final scene.

Scene 2 was underway almost immediately, but it is evident from Miss Holst's diary that Britten was far from satisfied with his efforts: 'Went back in the evening and found him more depressed than I've ever known him – really exhausted with the effort of doing Act III Sc. II.' (17 December); 'Ben rang up in the morning. He said he'd been having an awful time with Act III, Scene II; – had gone on working till 9 pm the night before, but he didn't like what he'd written and that he couldn't hear what he'd written' (18th); 'Ben still depressed: said he'd had one of the worst weeks he'd ever known, owing to Act III Scene II' (19th).

Britten stayed at Harewood House, near Leeds, over the New Year and after, where he worked on *Gloriana* each morning in his own room not joining the other guests until midday. To Pears (who was away in Switzerland) Britten wrote that he was writing 3.iii, 'nearing the end' on 9 January. Plomer joined him at Harewood for a few days towards the close of Britten's stay to undertake further modifications to the libretto.

On his return to Aldeburgh on the 13th Britten played over 3.iii to Imogen Holst as well as 'a little bit of Scene II which is absolutely right – can't think why he made such a fuss about being depressed by it'. It would seem that Britten had revised this scene while in Yorkshire (see H2, fol. [6^r–9^v]).

The question of the dance element in *Gloriana* and the wider function of the Royal Ballet at the gala evening planned for 8 June 1953 had always been somewhat problematical and was to reach a crisis at the end of January. In December 1952 Britten had sent a first draft libretto of the Norwich Masque scene (2.i) to Ninette de Valois for her scrutiny (L12). On the basis of the relatively small amount of choreography involved, she was happy to appoint John Cranko (who admired Britten's music and had already worked with Piper on *Pineapple Poll*, and Basil Coleman) to take charge of the ballet company's input to *Gloriana*. It would appear, however, that de Valois agreed because the ballet company were pushing for their own appearance at the gala evening before the scheduled première of *Gloriana*. In a letter to Plomer of 21 January, Britten confidently reported that a meeting at Covent Garden the previous day had resolved that there would be no separate ballet at the gala evening 'if the Ballet people don't tear the place down', and that he was 'trying to get Act III Sc. II into shape. There's not much success in the latter to be reported, alas . . . I've started the Progress [2.i], though'. Two days later de Valois wrote to Britten informing him that the Royal Ballet would make a twenty, or twenty-five, minute appearance on their own because of the little opportunity for ballet in the opera. In addition, she now wished to revert to Frederick Ashton as choreographer in place of Cranko.

The difficulties ensued for a few days more during which Britten, characteristically, reacted by contracting influenza. On the 27th he wrote to Webster:

> I saw William Plomer Saturday morning, and discussed the ballet situation in Act 2 Scene I with him. We will go as far as we can towards meeting the ballet's demands, but as the opera is planned (and the rest of it completely written) we cannot enlarge this scene out of proportion and wreck the work, nor can we do something out of the period and style. The work is a serious one and has never been planned as a hotch-potch.
>
> About the Freddie v. Johnnie battle: I do not see why, if Johnnie were originally good enough to do the work in the opera (and I have Dame Ninette's blessing on his collaboration in it in writing) he should now be inadequate! Anyhow, we can discuss this on Friday afternoon.

While Britten was in London thrashing out the difficulties of the ballet situation the East Coast, including Aldeburgh, was subjected to severe flooding. Britten's home was badly affected but by his return on 2 February the flood waters had subsided and only mud remained. In spite of the inconveniences of such a natural disaster Britten was painfully aware that he still had to keep to schedule to complete his opera. Imogen Holst's diary records the final days of Britten's work on the composition draft. On 4 February:

> Met Ben at the corner of High St. and he asked me to go in. Everything still in a state, and Miss Hudson [the housekeeper] looking weary. Ben had spent most of Tuesday trying to clean out the cellar. He said that after dark (the electricity was off) he went up to the Potters [at the Red House, later to be Britten's and Pears's home] and Mary gave him an extra stiff drink and he managed to write Concord's song "all concords – that's the sort of joke one can make, I think." He was pleased with the scene on the whole; "sometimes God's kind."

The following day Britten played over 'Time' and 'Concord', the two dances he had so far written for the Masque scene. Miss Holst wanted to take away the draft of 3.ii in order to work on her vocal score, but 'he was agonized because he's still got doubts about it'. His doubts about 3.ii continued: on the 8th he told Miss Holst that the only part of the scene he liked was the boys' song ('Now rouse up all the City'). On the 10th, 'he'd reached rock bottom of depression that morning owing to the dance for girls and fisherman' (the fourth and fifth dances, 'Sweet flag and cuckoo flower' and 'From fen and meadow'); and on the 11th, 'he . . . asked my advice about a tune he'd given the chorus sops (!) and then played me the canon between Concord and Time [the third dance, 'From springs of bounty']. He's very nearly finished'. The composition draft is undated but must have been finished around 11–13 February: on the 14th Britten played over the complete work to the Covent Garden directors, members of the music staff and some of the cast.

Work on the full score began immediately. With Imogen Holst's help – she ruled up the pages, added the instrument names and clefs, and entered the voice parts and words – Britten was able to work quickly and methodically from his composition draft, retrieving the instrumentation from his 'shorthand' notation. To save time she was further responsible for filling in any routine doublings. Under such a regime Britten was able to make exceptionally rapid progress on what was, after all, an enormous task, and completed over four hundred pages of full score by 13 March, although it was to be the 29th before Miss Holst had finally brought her work on the score to an end. Astonishingly, it was only a little over twelve months since the idea of a Coronation opera had been first raised by Lord Harewood.

Miss Holst's diary once again proves a fascinating source of information on aspects of Britten's working methods as well as faithfully documenting his remarkable industry. For example, on 16 February Britten wrote twenty-eight pages of full score in a single day's work – 'I suppose I shall learn to be quicker as it goes on, but I hope to heaven I don't keep him waiting' – and on the 17th,

Got to Crag House at 8.45 and began working feverishly to catch up, but was saved by the fact that Ben had to think for nearly an hour about the contra-puntal entries in "Green leaves", because the tune had such a large compass that it ran over the edge of practically every instrument. Owing to this I got enough done to supply him, and began to breathe again.

On the 22nd Britten told Pears that he was 'in the middle of Act I Sc. II', by the following day, 'Act I nearly done, so Gloriana is nearly behind us —!', and on the 25th, 'The score's going well. ½ done!!' On 13 March Imogen Holst wrote in her diary: 'Ben finished Gloriana at 3 o'clock this afternoon!!!'

In July, after the first run of performances came to an end, Britten wrote to Plomer to express gratitude for all his diligent work on the libretto:

Gloriana came to a triumphant, & temporary, conclusion I gather last Saturday. It has been an enormous success, from the box office, having on average beaten all other operas there this season. I expect that you, like me, have felt abit kicked around over it – perhaps more than me, because I'm abit more used to the jungle! But the savageness of the wild beasts always is a shock. The fact remains that I've loved working with you, my dear, & that you've produced a most wonderful libretto, that it is impossible for me adequately to express my gratitude for – Please let us sometime work together again – no hurry – just don't forget me.

Plomer responded by return of post:

V. pleased to hear your news about Gloriana. Well, well, one could write a book about it all, & them all. On the whole I think we have seen a healthy reaction to a new work of art. All the ferocities, the knowingnesses, the super-ficialities, the stampeding sheep-in-wolves'-clothing, the second thoughts, the timidities, the jealousies, and so on, amount, it seems to me, to a real tribute to your powers.

I do much hope that we shall work together again – I feel that we can really make a fire out of the right sort of spark.

That spark was kindled gently into flame after Britten's return from the Far East in 1956, where in Japan he had seen performances of the Noh play *Sumidagawa*. It had been Plomer who had advised Britten and Pears about the Japanese leg of their journey and it was to Plomer that Britten turned when he wanted to adapt *Sumidagawa* as an opera. What eventually emerged in 1964 as *Curlew River* took seven years to refine and reshape, and Plomer's diligence and (not least) his patience were influential in giving Britten enough creative space to make what became the first church parable the substantial artistic statement that it undoubtedly is. All of Plomer's enormous merits as a collaborator had been laid out for Britten on their work on *Gloriana*: it is not surprising, therefore, that having found such a sympathetic librettist, Britten should wish to embark on other projects with him. The sadness is that, in spite of the accepted merits of their first collaboration (and we should perhaps reiterate that it was, after all, Plomer's first libretto), neither he nor Britten lived to see *Gloriana* take its rightful place – as it undoubtedly is now so doing – among Britten's musical legacy.

3

Britten's Major Set-Back?
Aspects of the First Critical Response
to *Gloriana*

ANTONIA MALLOY

Introduction

Gloriana was premièred on 8 June 1953, at a Royal Gala attended by the newly-crowned Queen Elizabeth II. Although it was not officially commissioned by Her Majesty, the opera had been accepted as a 'Coronation tribute', and she permitted Britten to dedicate it to her. This was an important and hopeful sign of renewed patronage for the arts in a Britain only just rediscovering its creative identity after the long years of the Second World War. Britten had been a part of this recovery process from the first. The première of his *Peter Grimes* marked the reopening of Sadler's Wells in 1945, and benefited much from the support of the publishers, Boosey and Hawkes. The old Council for the Encouragement of Music and the Arts (CEMA), with which both Britten and Pears had been associated from 1942, became, with the return of peace, the Arts Council of Great Britain, and was able to make grants to encourage new initiatives. In February 1952 the Earl of Harewood suggested that Britten write 'a national opera in time for next year's Coronation';[1] it is hardly surprising that both Britten and the Queen agreed so readily to the idea. Nor was enthusiasm confined to composer and dedicatee. From the moment of the first official announcement, the press also showed a marked interest in the project, commenting with rising excitement on every stage of the work's progress. Few could have predicted the critical volte-face that took place when *Gloriana* finally emerged.[2]

The rough handling received by *Gloriana* at the time of its première has passed into history as one of the most outspoken expressions of critical ill-will towards an opera. However, although most reviewers concentrated on the less

---

[1] Lord Harewood, *The Tongs and the Bones* (London: Weidenfeld and Nicolson, 1981), 135. See also pp. 11, 18 above.

[2] Virtually the only writer to give any real hint of the adversity that *Gloriana* was to encounter was Scott Goddard, who warned that 'the birth of an opera is often long and painful. The opera's christening, its first performance, can be stormy' (*News Chronicle*, 14 March 1953).

successful aspects of the work, their response was not entirely negative. William Plomer himself was able to collect enough positive comments for his retrospective article 'Let's crab an opera'[3] to answer all the adverse remarks that he cited without having to make an elaborate apologia of his own.

This study examines some of the arguments provoked by the opera at the time of its première, and enters briefly into the critical debate by relating them to the original vocal score and libretto, and also, where appropriate, to the remarks of the librettist and composer themselves, in order to present a more balanced picture of the work and the response that it evoked. For the sake of brevity it has been necessary to limit the discussion to four of the most frequently treated aspects of the opera. These are its generic nature (the problem of combining pageant and opera), its portrayal of character, the contribution of Britten's music to the drama, and the effectiveness of the Epilogue.[4]

Several other commentators have offered brief analyses and explanations of *Gloriana*'s poor critical reception. Of these, only one represents a contemporary viewpoint: Tony Mayer's assessment of 'L'affaire *Gloriana*', published in August 1953,[5] stands alone among the writings of the time in its frank expressions of disbelief at the intolerance and lack of understanding shown at the première by press and public alike. Mayer attributed the opera's initial failure to its predominantly upper-class audience, and pointed out that subsequent box-office figures had shown commoners to be more appreciative. Edmund Tracey's opinion, expressed some eleven years later,[6] challenged this easy explanation: he cited a lack of imaginative staging, Britten's poor choice of librettist, the lack of integration of the festive and the psychological, and the opera's unsatisfactory ending as the main reasons for its rejection. John Klein shared Mayer's feeling of outrage at the ignorant jibes of the first audience,[7] and claimed that 'Far more clearly than his undiscerning critics, [Britten] had fully realised the solemnity of an important occasion and had, on the whole, risen to it with superb dramatic skill and assurance.' Bayan Northcott also took the composer's part,[8] arguing that any unevenness in the work was due to the many and varied demands it was written to meet, and urging that it remain in the repertory. The review made by William Plomer of the press coverage of the première[9] is more substantial, and emphasizes the variety of conflicting opinions, but also exhibits an obvious bias in favour of the work's authors, as might be expected.

These accounts, though they help to confirm the main journalistic themes,

---

3 *London Magazine* 3/7 (October 1963), 101–4.

4 See the Bibliography, section 3 (pp. 173–77) for a list of previews and reviews of the first production of the opera.

5 Tony Mayer, 'L'affaire *Gloriana*', *Opera* 4/8 (August 1953), 456–60. Mayer was particularly well-informed about the work, having acted as host to Britten, Pears and the Harewoods in July 1952 (see p. 24 above).

6 Edmund Tracey, 'London music', *MT* 107/1451 (January 1964), 36–7.

7 John Klein, 'Elizabeth and Essex', *Music and Musicians* 15/3 (November 1966), 16–17, 49.

8 Bayan Northcott, '*Gloriana*', *Music and Musicians* 21/2 (October 1972), 59.

9 William Plomer, *op. cit.*

are selective, and therefore offer what is at best a partial picture of the early critical history. Because of this, and the distance imposed by the passage of time, only Mayer's immediate response has been considered in the present discussion of critical themes.

Before turning to specific remarks on the opera, it is perhaps helpful to outline some of the external factors that may have influenced *Gloriana*'s first audiences. While superficially there were many circumstances in its favour – not least the new Queen's interest, the financial security guaranteed by the Royal Opera House, Covent Garden[10] and the promise of a Royal Gala première – there were other factors that militated equally strongly against its success. Some of them, ironically, were related to these same causes. Martin Cooper drew attention to a number of them and concluded that it was virtually inevitable that Britten should face a critical attack at this time: the popularity he had enjoyed since *Peter Grimes* had provoked a certain amount of professional and private resentment, and, when it was known that he was to compose an opera for the Coronation Gala, accusations of unjust favouritism began to be uttered. Furthermore, the tone of the recently-published Britten symposium[11] had seemed to some to be unnecessarily enthusiastic. Matters, he felt, were bound to come to a head.[12]

The Gala première itself stirred up a certain amount of feeling – the extravagance of the occasion must have struck listeners who were still in the grip of war-time austerity[13] and the 'utility' way of life as spectacular to the point of luxury. Furthermore, the musical cognoscenti were aware that, at the time of the Royal acceptance of *Gloriana* as the Coronation tribute, there were several other British operas not yet assured of a first production.[14] When it failed to live up to expectations, many were quick to blame the Arts Council: if this was the

---

10 The history of *Gloriana*'s financing is complicated. It seems that Britten originally hoped for money to come directly from the Treasury, and in late April 1952 he was assured by David Webster, the General Administrator of Covent Garden, that if these funds did not materialize Covent Garden itself would pay for the opera. The Royal Opera House had received an extra £15,000 to cover the costs of the Coronation season (as well as an unusually large maintenance grant) from the Arts Council of Great Britain that year (see Harold Rosenthal, *Two Centuries of Opera at Covent Garden* (London: Putnam, 1958), 614), and it seems that in the event this Coronation season bonus allowed Covent Garden to accept financial responsibility for the expenses of commissioning and staging *Gloriana*.

11 D. Mitchell and H. Keller, eds, *Benjamin Britten: A Commentary on his Works from a Group of Specialists* (London: Rockliff, 1952).

12 See 'Britten at bay', *Spectator* 6521 (19 June 1953), 783.

13 A certain amount of rationing, for example, was still in force, meat not returning to the open market until the following year. See also p. 10 above.

14 For example, all four of the winning operas in the Arts Council's Festival of Britain competition of 1951 (Arthur Benjamin's *A Tale of Two Cities*, Alan Bush's *Wat Tyler*, Berthold Goldschmidt's *Beatrice Cenci* and Karl Rankl's *Deidre of the Sorrows*) were still awaiting their official premières. Furthermore, Tippett's *The Midsummer Marriage*, Walton's *Troilus and Cressida* (then nearing completion) and Lennox Berkeley's *Nelson* were also in the offing, but were all overtaken by *Gloriana*. *Troilus and Cressida* and *Nelson* were eventually premièred in 1954, while *The Midsummer Marriage* had to wait until 1955, and the Festival of Britain operas were by and large consigned to oblivion without a satisfactory public hearing.

best that the new organization could produce, the intervention of the State in artistic policy seemed a questionable initiative. The anonymous author of an article entitled 'Bill for "Gloriana" '[15] even went so far as to conclude that 'If, as a result of public dissatisfaction over *Gloriana* there arises a determination to abolish all Arts Council activity, then the £20,000 [the sum he believed the opera to have cost] will have been money well spent.'[16]

The very nature of the opera was also partly responsible for the unfavourable press it received. As Andrew Porter pointed out,[17] the amount of historical knowledge assumed by Britten and Plomer in their audience made it a difficult work to appreciate fully at a first hearing, and this miscalculation on the part of its authors had the effect of alienating the average opera-goer. The indistinct delivery of words, to which many critics testify, must only have made the audience more bewildered, though this seems to have been rectified by the time of the second performance.[18] Unfortunately, the excessive compression of the narrative necessitated by the inclusion of purely decorative scenes was not so easily put right,[19] and many critical misgivings arose from poor comprehension of the basic action, in spite of the programme's inclusion of a detailed synopsis by William Plomer.[20]

Finally, and perhaps most necessary to an understanding of the diversity of critical opinions, there was the fact that, as one writer expressed it, the opera 'reached a huge public, which, in other circumstances, would have left it severely alone'.[21] The première was attended by many who were unused to

---

[15] *Evening Standard*, 15 June 1953.

[16] Public feelings were likely to run high, since the Arts Council grants depended on the statutory contributions of the taxpayer, and the resultant distrust of State-controlled arts was also fuelled by a contemporary fear of totalitarianism. In this light, the State control of the arts was seen as a potential threat to the individual both financially and in terms of his personal freedom, and anything resembling an error on the part of the Arts Council was seized upon with glee, in the hope that it might bring about its downfall. In fact, the Arts Council was not directly involved with the production of *Gloriana*. As the annual report for 1952–3 explained, it was concerned only with the financial support of organizations responsible for maintaining the Arts and had no say in the actual material they chose to present: 'The Arts Council's business is to assess the objects, the prospects and the needs of every body it decides to assist and to satisfy itself that the claimants manage their affairs efficiently. It does not decide the repertory of Covent Garden or Sadler's Wells, or the Old Vic . . .'

[17] See 'Britten's *Gloriana*', *ML* 34/4 (October 1953), 277–87.

[18] See the account of 'An improved *Gloriana*', *Star*, 12 June 1953. The Britten–Pears Library holds copies of a recording made from the second radio broadcast (2 July 1953) which confirm the reports of improved diction (see List of Sources, (A)/Rec3.2).

[19] Although the Norwich scene in particular makes little specific contribution to the furthering of the action it is possible to argue, as some did, that the more decorative scenes were vital for the creation of atmosphere and for the correct portrayal of the ceremonial characteristic of the age, as well as allowing the audience to grasp something of the Queen's relationship with her commoners and courtiers respectively, and contributing to the tension between public and private on which the drama relies for some of its momentum.

[20] The libretto had been published by this time, and some, though not all, of the critics had had the chance to read it, as had the Royal family. It is unlikely that the non-professional members of the audience would have had access to a copy.

[21] Desmond Shawe-Taylor, '*Gloriana*, Cheltenham, Glyndebourne', *New Statesman*, 45/1163 (20 June 1953), 729.

opera, let alone modern opera: the Queen, her state guests and several hundred of the great and good; hundreds more must have been attracted to the nine later performances by the exceptional publicity surrounding the occasion. On top of that there was the arm-chair audience listening to the broadcast on the BBC Home Service and the Third Programme, relayed direct from the Royal Opera House on 8 June and again on 2 July.[22] It was therefore highly unlikely that Britten would succeed in meeting the expectations of all his hearers, from the naive and unsophisticated to those experienced in opera; some would have wanted a Coronation Gala of the old concert type with selections from the most popular operas of the day, others a music drama similar in psychological depth and dramatic impact to *Peter Grimes*. The very catholicity of its audience, there-fore, virtually ensured that *Gloriana* would elicit a decidedly mixed critical reception. Tony Mayer stated that 'in many ways to present *Gloriana* at a Gala performance with an audience very largely chosen *intuito officio* was a pity, for a great and beautiful vessel was launched under the worst possible circum-stances with very unpleasant consequences for designer and crew'.[23] One may not agree with his judgement of the opera itself, but his comment provides a fair summary of the extra-musical situation and its effects.

I: *The opera's generic nature*

> The function of an 'occasional' opera poses an immediate question: should it take the form of a pageant especially suitable to a great national event or should it serve as an example of the greatest musical talent the country can produce in the shape of a work which will qualify for inclusion in the perma-nent repertory . . .?[24]

This question summarizes the dilemma faced by *Gloriana*'s first critics; as the more perceptive amongst them pointed out, how the opera was rated depended largely on what type of work it was seen to be. It could either be evaluated solely as a decorative piece of pageantry or assessed as a serious and demanding piece of music drama.[25] The criteria by which it was judged were different in each case, and the conclusions of the various commentators differed widely according to which of these two descriptions they adopted. Those who, like Richard Capell, viewed it as 'principally a spectacular entertainment . . . pageant rather than drama'[26] found most to praise, while those such as Scott

---

[22] Apart from the replacement of Michael Langdon by Marian Nowakowski in the role of Recorder of Norwich, the cast was that of the première.

[23] Tony Mayer, *op. cit.*

[24] George Montagu, '*Gloriana* at Covent Garden', *London Musical Events* 8/8 (August 1953), 10–11, 39.

[25] Britten himself had no such difficulty with integrating the elements of pageantry and drama: his early letters to Plomer make it clear that he intended the opera to be both decorative and narrative.

[26] '*Gloriana* at Covent Garden', *Daily Telegraph*, 9 June 1953.

Goddard who were seeking 'a satisfying musical construction'[27] were less impressed. A third group hovered indecisively between the two, usually concluding that, as one writer put it, 'As a pageant, as a piece of stage colour and production . . . *Gloriana* succeeds. As an opera it is a dead loss.'[28]

Which of these descriptions the critic chose depended largely on the status he ascribed to the Norwich Masque and the Courtly Dances of Act 2. They could, for instance, be seen as pieces of lavish stage and musical spectacle whose lack of significant dramatic action seemed not to matter in a story that was in any case uneventful. To others they seemed irritating and unnecessary interruptions, contributing nothing to the forward movement of the plot and effectively lessening any dramatic tension that had accumulated in the first act. On either side various modifications were possible: Erwin Stein argued in advance that 'the period would not be adequately represented without some of its glamour in masque and dance',[29] while another writer claimed that 'a historical opera . . . can present as integral parts of its action what in other dramas are decorations, so that . . . a masque presented to Queen Elizabeth on a royal progress at Norwich can provide librettist and composer with opportunities for song and dance which are relevant to the presentation of the Queen's personality'.[30]

This debate raises some interesting dramaturgical questions. How far is any inherent drama arrested by these two decorative episodes? Do they, in fact, serve to reveal something of the protagonists' characters, or to illustrate the period or to further the action? A closer examination of 2.i and 2.iii demonstrates that only one of the two makes any real contribution to the development of the work.

The Norwich masque certainly provides an opportunity for that fusion of the arts of which opera ideally consists, making use of dance and a certain amount of scenic decoration in addition to the more poetic diction of the libretto and the unaccompanied choral music to which it is set at this point. However, nothing actually happens as a result of this performance of a group of rustics, and, apart from a few asides which hint at Essex's ambition and jealousy, the audience learns nothing new of any of the characters. It has already been made clear (in the expressions of homage in 1.i) that Elizabeth is the darling of her people, so that the devotion expressed in the masque comes as no surprise. Furthermore, even the asides are likely to prove ineffectual, since Essex's remark that 'Time hath yet to bring me what is due' is too short and ambiguous to strike the listener as significant, and the importance of his hatred of Raleigh does not become apparent until the third act, if at all.

The Courtly Dance scene is far more important structurally. Not only is it almost a convention of opera to set a scene of great drama against a festive

27 'Gloriana', *News Chronicle*, 12 June 1953.
28 'E.S.', 'Gloriana', *Music and Musicians* 1/11 (July 1953), 3.
29 'Gloriana', *The Listener* 49/1266 (4 June 1953), 949.
30 Anonymous review of 'Benjamin Britten's Coronation Opera', *The Times Weekly Review*, 11 June 1953.

background,[31] but it also provides an opportunity for the composer to root the action firmly in its historical period by returning to the dance forms of the time. Indeed, it might be said that the series of dances (Pavane, Galliard, Lavolta, Coranto) offers a mechanically progressing background against which the unpredictability of the Queen and the resultant sudden reversal of Essex's fortunes stand out in sharp relief. Furthermore, the exertions of the Lavolta provide a convenient reason for Elizabeth to command the change of linen that enables her to steal Lady Essex's offensive dress, so that the dances appear integrated into, and an essential part of, the dramatic structure. The return of the Queen at the end of the scene, to appoint Essex Lord Deputy in Ireland, is also a vital part of the development of the plot, showing Essex's commissioning for the task that was to prove his downfall. Without the strong air of celebration that accompanies this moment, the irony of his subsequent tragedy would be less tangible, and the contrast with the following scene, in which his failure is revealed, less effective.

This is also the scene where the most surprising facet of the Queen's personality is shown. Her almost instantaneous change from the willful pettiness that caused her to shame Essex's wife to the queenly benevolence that granted Essex his long-cherished desire to lead the army to Ireland demonstrates the variableness of which she was often accused. Other personalities are also revealed more fully in this scene: the caution that characterized Lady Essex in the previous scene is here developed and her own modesty is seen from her doubts about the finery her husband persuades her to wear. From Essex himself we learn that the Queen once 'struck me with her hand / Before her Council', and it is here that the seeds of rebellion, sown in the previous scene, are shown to be taking root, when, with scant respect for the assembled Court, he proclaims that 'Her conditions are as crooked as her carcass!'

If the validity of the Courtly Dance scene cannot be questioned, it must be admitted that its placing in the same act as the Norwich masque is a little unfortunate since the earlier scene has left the listener with low dramatic expectations of such diversions.[32] The sole function of this first episode seems to be to achieve Britten's desire (expressed in an interview some years later) 'to show off certain facets of English musical life, such as the remarkable ballet and choral singing'[33] – a tactful compliment to British musical life both in Tudor times and as represented by the abilities of the modern ballet and opera com-

---

31 Perhaps the most famous examples of this device (which can be traced as far back as the divertissement in Act 3 of Rameau's 1733 *Hippolyte et Aricie*) are found in Verdi's *La Traviata* (an opera Britten knew particularly well); in Act 1 Violetta is introduced to the besotted Alfredo at a supper party, and in 2.ii her passionate attempt to break away from him is played out against a spectacular ball.

32 One is inclined to agree with Peter Wolfe's verdict that in 1.ii 'Essex sings the odd grouse occasionally, but otherwise this scene has no connection with what had gone before or with what is to come'. ('Facing the music: almost glory', *What's On*, 19 June 1953.)

33 'Benjamin Britten talks to Edmund Tracey', *Sadler's Wells Magazine* 4 (Autumn 1966), 5–7.

panies of the Royal Opera House.[34] In this he was so successful that Peter Wolfe blamed the musical strength of the Choral Dances for the apparent weakness of the rest of the opera,[35] and another critic predicted (accurately, as it turned out) 'a concert suite drawn from the choral and orchestral dances of the second act'.[36]

The effect of having two such scenes in the same act is to create a feeling of disjointedness, on which many critics were quick to comment, and this also contributed to the general verdict that *Gloriana* represented a successful pageant but an operatic failure. One writer even went so far as to suggest that Britten excise the Norwich scene altogether,[37] a suggestion which was taken up in certain subsequent performances.[38] Perhaps the fairest assessment of criticisms relating to the conflict of the decorative with the dramatically functional is that those writers tracing structural weaknesses to an excess of pageantry were in some measure justified, since the Norwich masque is formally unnecessary, but that this in itself is not sufficient ground for dismissing the opera merely as a series of tenuously-related episodes, since the other scene of pageantry is vital to the progression of both drama and characterization.

II: *The portrayal of character*

The Queen and her swashbuckling courtier were once great people . . .[39]

The majority of *Gloriana*'s first critics confined their discussion of characterization to the portrayal of the two principal characters, Elizabeth and Essex. They also shared a common tendency to trace this fault solely to weaknesses of the libretto, which they often implied (inaccurately) that Britten had written himself. Whoever was held responsible, the critics' most frequent complaint was that the protagonists were too lightly drawn to appear credible; on a more specific level, the Queen's role was felt to be the more successful, although this did not necessarily mean that she was seen as a particularly sympathetic character.

---

[34] In the event, Britten had a great deal of trouble from the ballet company. The original intention had been to include a full-length ballet in the Coronation Gala programme, and it was only with difficulty and a certain amount of bad feeling on each side that this idea was dropped to allow *Gloriana* the stage to itself for the whole evening. Because of this the ballet company attempted to withdraw its agreement to allow John Cranko to choreograph the dances and Svetlana Beriosova to take the part of Concord. These problems were not resolved to Britten's satisfaction until early in 1953. See also pp. 34–6, 44–5 above.

[35] *Op. cit.* The Choral Dances' instant and continuing popularity is confirmed by their publication history (see List of Sources, (C)).

[36] Mosco Carner, '*Gloriana*', *Time and Tide* 34/25 (20 June 1953), 818.

[37] Thomas Heinitz, 'The other side (imported recordings)', *Saturday Review* 36/30 (25 July 1953), 58.

[38] John Klein claims that after the première 'the management had quickly begun to mutilate the opera'. By the beginning of the 1954 season (January–April), when *Gloriana* received three performances at Covent Garden and three in the provinces, it had definitely been removed: see fn. 22, p. 37 above.

[39] Anonymous article entitled 'Warm applause for Britten', *Yorkshire Observer*, 13 June 1953.

Martin Cooper's comment that Britten 'has presented isolated moments in the lives of both Elizabeth and Essex with great power, though he has not attempted to portray their characters as a whole or "in the round" '[40] is typical of this first school of thought – typical, that is, except in its implication that the failure to provide rounded characterization was intentional. Most critics regarded this as evidence of weakness on the part of the dramatist or lack of human involvement on the part of the composer. One such was Richard Capell, who felt that 'it was probable that [Britten's] heart was not in the enterprise. Nor can his poet's have been; for his characters are lifeless – puppets and not men and women.'[41]

If it is true that the main characters do not emerge as complete human beings, one reason for this may lie in the economy demanded by the exigencies of operatic portrayal, as Plomer himself claimed. Although he found that Elizabeth I 'was an even more remarkable woman than I had imagined', he could not present a full-length portrait: 'in opera one must simplify everything down to the operatic scale; one can't permit complexities of character and history to get in the way of the musical flow'.[42] Another reason for the protagonists' failure to satisfy may also lie in the difficulty of maintaining the delicate balance between public scenes of pageantry and more private ones in which individual identities are more easily revealed. Joan Littlefield's perceptive remark that 'in such an episodic work it is well nigh impossible to establish the characters of such a complex pair as Elizabeth and Essex'[43] sums up the situation to a nicety. As soon as the audience begins to sense something of the protagonists' interior motivations, curiosities are aroused which there is no time to satisfy; we are tantalized by glimpsing personalities with whom we never become more fully acquainted. A typical example is found in the second scene of Act 1, where, just as we are about to learn to what extent Elizabeth, as a woman at least, actually reciprocates Essex's avowed love for her, Raleigh suddenly arrives and Essex is banished. If the Queen's true feelings were made clear at this point, her later conflicts might appear more convincing.

Of the critics who accepted the reduction of complexity as justifying the sketchy characterization, not all were agreed as to its success. Many who found either or both of the protagonists unsympathetic attributed this in part to their dramatic flimsiness. Richard Capell, for example, felt that although such simplification was 'perhaps inevitable', it 'show[ed] both Essex and Elizabeth in a more or less odious light'.[44]

The treatment of Essex was seen to be less effective than that of Elizabeth. Most were agreed that he lacked clear definition, being at best 'caught, but undernourished'.[45] John Klein gave the fullest report on his character, pointing out that while his more contemplative side found suitable expression in the

[40] 'Gloriana', *Spectator* 6520 (12 June 1953), 755.
[41] 'Gloriana at Covent Garden', *Daily Telegraph*, 9 June 1953.
[42] Quoted by Robert Muller in 'Gloriana is born', *Picture Post* 59/11 (13 June 1953), 67.
[43] 'Britten's Coronation opera', *Canon* 7/1 (August 1953), 19–21.
[44] 'Reflections on Gloriana', *Daily Telegraph*, 13 June 1953.

Second Lute Song, the scenes where he was required to cut a more heroic figure were less successful,[46] and indeed the failure of Britten and Plomer to match the eloquence and form of 'Happy were he'[47] with equally memorable encapsulations of his other moods may account for at least one observer finding him a 'futile, petulant figure'.[48]

Another reason for Essex's lack of appeal may lie in the authors' failure to integrate the two sides of his nature. In the novel on which the opera is based, Lytton Strachey's *Elizabeth and Essex: a tragic history*,[49] the duality of his nature is kept consistently before the reader, in such passages as the following:

> The youth loved hunting and all the sports of manhood; but he loved reading too . . . he might have been a scholar, had he not been so spirited a nobleman. As he grew up this double nature was reflected in his physical complexion. The blood flew through his veins in vigorous vitality; he ran and tilted with the sprightliest; and then suddenly health would ebb away from him, and the pale boy would lie for hours in his chamber, obscurely melancholy, with a Virgil in his hand. . . .[50]

Strachey clearly perceives this as the mainspring of Essex's character, yet in the opera his conduct is rarely explained in these terms. Apart from Elizabeth's 'You man of moods . . . Now up, now down, and cautious never' (1.ii), his double nature is nowhere made obvious.

Had Plomer been able to build such examples as Strachey gave of Essex's complexity into the libretto, the Earl might have emerged as a more convincing character. Alternatively, as Andrew Porter pointed out,[51] he might have gained credibility had he been granted a soliloquy; in fact only the Queen is given the chance to demonstrate her inner motivations in this way. It is possible, too, that Britten had to overcome a certain amount of personal difficulty in portraying Essex, since, according to the Earl of Harewood, Peter Pears, for whom the role was written, was very reluctant to be cast in this part as it was originally conceived.[52]

---

[45] H.G. Sear: 'Needle in a Haystack', *Daily Worker*, 9 June 1953.

[46] 'Some Reflections on *Gloriana*', *Tempo* 29 (Autumn 1953), 16–21.

[47] The words of this number were in fact written by the historical Earl of Essex, which may account in some measure for their success.

[48] 'C.S.', 'Gala Performance at the R.O.H.', *Birmingham Post*, 9 June 1953.

[49] First published by Chatto & Windus in 1928.

[50] This may be found on p. 9 of the 1971 Penguin edition. It is this very passage which is marked in a copy held at *GB-ALb*; see p. 21 above.

[51] 'Britten's *Gloriana*', *ML* 34/4 (October 1953), 277–87.

[52] In his autobiography, the Earl of Harewood recalls discussions with Britten and Pears during the summer of 1952, in which 'Peter had taken up a glum position over the whole thing, hating the cancellations, disliking the disturbance of his routine, the official nature of the affair, the risk involved in the venture into international waters, and perhaps too of playing a young, ardent lover in the shape of Essex, which Ben of course planned to write for him. He preferred to sing Cecil; let Ben find another Essex! . . . But [Britten's] heart was never in this new task. He had Joan Cross for Gloriana, he wanted Peter for Essex, and he was accustomed to getting his own way . . .' (*op. cit.*, 136).

Suspicions that Britten was more interested in the character of the Queen were evident in the writings of several critics. Their reactions to Elizabeth were generally far more extreme, some finding her a 'spiteful, lonely, haunted' creature,[53] while others praised her as 'an intensely human figure'.[54] Even the least satisfied had to concede this humanity, although certain among them would have preferred a less honest portrayal, finding some scenes 'profoundly affronting to the glorious memory of Queen Elizabeth'.[55]

Certain things may be said in the authors' defence. If the less pleasant incidents of the story (such as the Queen's purloining of Lady Essex's dress) had been removed, with them would have disappeared much of the dramatic narrative, as well as any chance of a rounded portrayal of Elizabeth's character; a reviewer in the *Times Educational Supplement* pointed this out, concluding that 'As it is, there emerges . . . a picture of a great Queen that, precisely because it is unsentimental and many-sided, does more honour to her memory than any amount of historical sugar-icing.'[56] Furthermore, it was Britten's stated aim in the opera 'to illustrate the many sides of the great Queen's character':[57] how could he do this if he spurned situations in which she appeared at less than her best? In fact, of all the characters, it is Elizabeth who is at once the most realistic (with paradoxes such as her absolute decorum before the crowd at Norwich and her low cunning in stealing Lady Essex's dress) and the most intriguing (since these paradoxes are never fully explained). Perhaps she too is a victim – though she suffers less than Essex – of the operatic need for concision.

III: *The contribution of the music to the drama*

> As by Britten's other operas, one is left somewhat dazzled: dazed, even, might not be too strong a term, at moments. . . .[58]

Perhaps such impressions made Britten's critics reluctant to make specific comments on the music of *Gloriana*; perhaps, too, the unavailability of scores to the public at the time of the première made them uncertain as to quite what they had heard, and heightened the usual critical unwillingness to commit themselves on the basis solely of aural impressions.[59] Whatever the reason, the fact remains that very few offered more than a handful of adjectives, which were not usually supported by references to specific details. The general opinion was divided, some finding the score uncompromisingly modern and offensively

---

53 Anonymous review entitled '*Gloriana* (Covent Garden)', *Empire News*, 14 June 1953.

54 Roy Sherwood, '*Gloriana*: pathos and pageantry', *Belfast Newsletter*, 10 June 1953.

55 Marie C. Stopes, '*Gloriana*' (Letter), *The Times*, 20 June 1953.

56 '*Gloriana*', *The Times Educational Supplement*, 19 June 1953.

57 Quoted in an anonymous article entitled 'Mr. Britten discusses Gloriana', *Lowestoft Journal*, 17 April 1953.

58 W.R. Anderson, 'Round about radio', *MT* 94/1326 (August 1953).

59 It is possible that some of the hire copies were made available to critics in time for the first performance; see List of Sources, (A)/V6.

harsh, while others, mostly professional musicians, complained that it did not represent the best that Britten could do, being too tame and traditional. There was, however, a certain amount of agreement that the most successful parts were the 'Green leaves' chorus, the Second Lute Song, the Choral Dances and the Courtly Dances. It is interesting to note that all these numbers are cast in fairly traditional moulds and provide the listener with an easily-recognisable melodic line which is organized in clearly apprehensible formal units. In a letter to the *News Chronicle* published two months before the première, a Mr Cross had advised Britten to 'reflect on the fact that the works by which he is best known to the public are his arrangements of old folk songs, which were good tunes even before he arranged them',[60] and it would seem that this claim was proved correct by the critics' later preferences.

The use of traditional forms raised the question of derivation. There was a variety of opinions on the extent to which Britten had allowed his score to be influenced by the music of the era in which it was set. At one extreme, Ernest Newman stated that 'the bulk of the music is hardly more than pastiche, sometimes very clever pastiche, sometimes not so clever';[61] at the other Philip Hope-Wallace applauded 'the way in which the world of the first Elizabeth is echoed without the least recourse to 'olde-tyme' pastiche'.[62] While Britten borrows some Elizabethan forms (most obviously in the Courtly Dances) and quotes one actual phrase of music (the first line of 'Happy were he' is taken from 'Happy, O Happy He' in Wilbye's 1609 collection), it is hardly fair to describe most of the score as pastiche; the music suggests an earlier age for the most part in non-specific ways, adding a strong tendency to modality to the composer's characteristic eclecticism.[63] Britten himself was at pains to point out the non-derivative intention of the music; he claimed in the Covent Garden Press Conference[64] that, although he had 'thought a great deal about [the Elizabethan period] to try to get the atmosphere', he had not 'half-timbered' his music.[65] He had, however, thoroughly investigated the forms he borrowed. Imogen Holst later recalled being sent to Oxford for the day to learn the steps of various Elizabethan dances so that Britten could compose appropriate music for the Court ball.[66] In view of this, perhaps it is fairest to describe these parts of the score as 'revitalizations' of older forms and styles.[67]

[60] Arthur Cross, 'Give us a tune, Mr. B!' (Letter), *News Chronicle*, 18 April 1953.

[61] '*Gloriana*', *The Sunday Times*, 14 June 1953.

[62] '*Gloriana*: Royal Opera Gala at Covent Garden', *Manchester Guardian Weekly*, 11 June 1953.

[63] For a discussion of the various stylistic influences traceable in the score see Peter Evans, *The Music of Benjamin Britten*, 2nd ed. (London: J.M. Dent & Sons, 1989), 200–202.

[64] This took place on 14 April 1953.

[65] Quoted in an anonymous article, 'Mr. Britten discusses *Gloriana*', *Lowestoft Journal*, 17 April 1953.

[66] See Imogen Holst, 'Working for Benjamin Britten', *MT* 118/1695 (February 1977) and p. 35 above.

[67] This term was first applied by 'C.S.' in 'Gala performance at the R.O.H.', *Birmingham Post*, 9 June 1953.

Another feature of the music eliciting frequent comment was its orchestration. Few remained unimpressed by Britten's scoring, though the impression was not always favourable. Britten was particularly praised for his ingenuity. One critic discovered 'orchestral sounds that strike the ear like those of a strange country one is visiting for the first time';[68] and several applauded his orchestration at the start of the Norwich scene (which suggests the pealing of bells) and in the moonlit second scene of Act 2. The main fault was seen to lie in the texture of the score, which was frequently described as thin and unsatisfactory, so that it made at least one critic 'want to cry out for an enormous orchestral noise'.[69] *Gloriana*'s critics were not the first to make such observations; from the very earliest reviews of his works there can be traced a tendency to dismiss the composer as brilliant but superficial.[70] Those writers who attempted to analyze this failing in any depth all agreed that in *Gloriana* the main contributory factor was Britten's 'curious reluctance to wed the sound of violins with that of voices, so that he voluntarily forgoes the lifting power of that alliance'.[71] An examination of the score[72] reveals that, particularly in the Elizabeth-Essex love scenes, the solo voices are rarely doubled by the strings (or indeed any other section of the orchestra). The tendency is for Britten to use the strings to provide a chordal wash against which figuration for wind or harp combines with melodically independent voices, which provides an effect very different from that doted on by the less sophisticated admirers of Puccini.

At times such restraint of texture could be a decided advantage in making the words more audible. However, it could also come near to defeating the librettist's desire for a broad effect. This was particularly felt to be the case in the composer's treatment of the Elizabeth-Essex relationship, which to one viewer 'seemed to be taking place inside a refrigerator'.[73] This impression was not confined to the affair of the principal characters; Martin Cooper complained that the love scene for Mountjoy and Lady Rich was also depicted in 'thin-blooded, nervous, ungenerous music that teases and irritates, instead of satisfying ear and heart'.[74] It is true that Mountjoy's duet with Penelope Rich in 2.ii remains rather too carefully within its stanzaic structure to convey the urgency of burning passion; and although Essex's Second Lute Song suggests some of the poignancy of his doomed affection, the interruption of his potential love scene with Elizabeth in 1.ii by the return of 'cares of state' effectively

---

[68] Andrew Smith, 'Tale of the first Elizabeth', *Daily Herald*, 9 June 1953.

[69] Stanley Bayliss, 'Not a Great Britten', *Daily Mail*, 10 June 1953.

[70] See, for example, the review of *Our Hunting Fathers* that appeared in *MT*, October 1937, in which it is described as 'a clever work, clever almost to a fault . . . teasing, irritating or enjoyable according to the way you take it . . .'

[71] Anonymous article entitled 'Benjamin Britten's Coronation Opera', *The Times Weekly Review*, 11 June 1953.

[72] The 1953 version of the full score has not been published, but the orchestration differs little from that of the 1966 revision, published in the study score (printed 1990, but with the copyright date 1977, (M)/F11).

[73] Anonymous review headed 'Playtime', *Reynolds News*, 14 June 1953.

[74] 'Britten at Bay', *Spectator* 6521 (19 June 1953), 783.

prevents the musical development of his – or her – emotions. It may be concluded that Britten's skill in orchestral effect is not deployed to suggest passionate exchanges of love; he is more at home in its incidental use to portray the picturesque.[75]

IV: *The Epilogue*

> Excursion into melodrama with speech intruding upon what operatic convention demands should be sung is always extremely questionable on the fundamental grounds of the aesthetics of opera . . .[76]

The Epilogue of *Gloriana* drew almost unanimously negative remarks from its first audiences. Even Donald Mitchell, surely Britten's staunchest supporter, admitted that 'this epilogue, with its disruptive spoken interviews, presents the only problematic aspect of the opera'[77] and other writers, less predisposed in Britten's favour, were accordingly less reserved in their condemnation of composer and librettist for what many regarded as a serious breach of operatic convention. Only a handful of critics found it a satisfying and successful conclusion;[78] the rest attributed its failure to a number of different causes, ranging from the inclusion of the words of the historical Elizabeth to the musical disintegration perceived in their accompaniment.

A contributor to the *Monthly Musical Record* noted that Elizabeth's words in this last scene were taken from the recorded speeches of the Queen; he then went on to distinguish them from what had gone before by virtue of their 'memorable prose' which he claimed rendered them doubly difficult for the composer to set.[79] One need hardly add that he felt that Britten had failed in this task. Other critics who agreed with him went on to discuss the musical weakness of the close in more detail. Most of them took issue with the change to speech at this point. Stanley Bayliss's remark is typical: 'just as the music was at last taking charge of things and building up to a magnificent climax, we were suddenly brought down to earth with a bump by a spate of spoken words'.[80] Most serious of all were the allegations that Britten had abdicated his responsibility as a composer in refusing to set these words; this was put down either to willful perversity[81] or to technical deficiency.[82]

---

75 The sounds of the 'blue fly' and the bee in 1.i and the lark in 3.i provide the most striking instances of this type of depiction.

76 Anonymous review of 'Benjamin Britten's Coronation opera', *The Times Weekly Review*, 11 June 1953.

77 'Some observations on *Gloriana*', *Monthly Musical Record* 83/952 (December 1953), 225–60.

78 Roy Sherwood, Andrew Porter and Philip Hope-Wallace were the main advocates in its favour.

79 'Notes of the day', *The Monthly Musical Record* 83/949 (September 1953), 169–72.

80 'Not a Great Britten', *Daily Mail*, 10 June 1953.

81 See, for example, Sidney Harrison, 'Homage to Queens', *John O' London's Weekly* 62/1511 (26 June 1953), 573.

82 See, for example, Noël Goodwin, 'Music', *Truth*, 19 June 1953, 751.

While it is true that the sudden change of vocal medium seems incongruous as the only use of speech in the entire opera, it need not necessarily be seen as an admission of defeat on the composer's behalf. Other composers had succeeded in blending spoken with sung lines, as one critic pointed out: 'This [writing for the spoken voice] can be justified when it is used with discretion, as when in *Der Rosenkavalier* the Marschallin whispers almost to herself 'Gar nix' . . .',[83] and it was a device that Britten himself used in other works.[84] In fact, Elizabeth's reversion to speech in her final scene is entirely appropriate to her declining state, where a full-throated operatic climax might have posed too great a challenge to the suspension of disbelief. However, it must be admitted that the lyrical interpolations of the Second Lute Song contrast oddly with the spoken lines of the Queen, and the preponderance of speech in the closing moments of the work leaves a feeling of bleakness inappropriate to the festive intention at least of the première. Even the reprise of 'Green leaves are we' with which the opera concludes cannot dispel this chilliness.

What music there was in the Epilogue also came in for attack, Mosco Carner, for example, finding Britten's restatement of the Second Lute Song inadequate, since its lack of symphonic development belied the tragic alteration of its author's circumstances.[85] A consultation of the score reveals that the melody is not, in fact, quoted directly at this point, but is instead fragmented, only some of its associated words actually being articulated. Such phrases as are actually sung are inserted at dramatically appropriate moments; the spectral procession of monarchs is heralded by the words 'In some unhaunted desert', and the thought of the 'winding-sheet' in which Elizabeth's dead body will soon be wrapped recalls the line 'There might he sleep secure'. Between these two lines the implication is that the intervening phrases continue to resound in her mind. This does not seem ineffectual: the lute song grows in its new situation and serves to highlight the dramatic ironies of the close.

Another criticism levelled at the Epilogue was that most of the Queen's ghostly visitors remained unidentified to the audience, so that any significance they had was lost. As John Klein pointed out, 'about this finale there is something indeterminate and just a trifle mystifying . . . At such a crisis, who cares about a routine visit of the French Ambassador? . . . Even the undoubtedly moving and significant reference to the meeting between Essex and his old enemy Tyrone is inopportunely introduced . . .'[86] This is surely one of the

---

[83] Anonymous article entitled '*Gloriana*', *The Times Educational Supplement*, 19 June 1953.

[84] Edmund Tracey, in an interview conducted some thirteen years later, questioned Britten on his tendency to entrust climactic moments to speech or orchestra, citing Balstrode's last words to Grimes (in *Peter Grimes*), the chords following Budd's trial (in *Billy Budd*), the finale of *Gloriana* and Miles's cry 'Peter Quint, you devil' (in *The Turn of the Screw*). Britten replied that 'in each of the cases . . . I felt, after reflection, that the silence of the singing voice would be more effective than the voice continuing to sing' ('Benjamin Britten talks to Edmund Tracey', *Sadler's Wells Magazine* 4 (Autumn 1966), 5–7).

[85] '*Gloriana*', *Time and Tide* 34/25 (20 June 1953), 818.

[86] 'Some reflections on *Gloriana*', *Tempo* 29 (Autumn 1953), 16–21.

moments when only the kind of preparation outlined by Andrew Porter[87] could enable an audience to make sense of the stage action. The score makes it clear that the first apparition is Sir John Harington, the Queen's Godson, the second probably the King of Scotland, the third the French Ambassador, and so on, but to an audience seeing the work for the first time this is not evident, and it is therefore not surprising that so many found the Epilogue unsatisfactory.

In conclusion it should be noted that alteration of the Epilogue constituted the largest change made by Britten when he revised the opera for the 1966 Sadler's Wells production.[88] In this version the irrelevant apparitions were removed, leaving Elizabeth alone with the voice of Essex in her mind (his short speech is relayed from a tape) and with her own reflections on her achievements. The 'memorable prose' disliked by one critic is actually increased by including more of the Queen's original utterances. Only the unghostly Cecil returns (to raise the question of a successor), and the final chorus is preceded directly by Elizabeth's last words; the Archbishop who prayed for her in the earlier version has also been excised. In its later form the Epilogue is more satisfactory from the point of view of an uninformed audience, but the original objections to the use of speech at this point may still stand.

Conclusion

The fact that Britten did subsequently alter the Epilogue, and also authorized performances in which the Norwich scene was removed, suggests that he took at least some of the critics' comments to heart.[89] No doubt he was also personally affected by the hostility of their response. John Klein's subsequent claim[90] that the failure of *Gloriana* had caused the composer to abandon large-scale operatic composition for chamber opera was clearly an overstatement: chamber opera had long interested Britten, who had founded the English Opera Group precisely in order to develop the medium. Nevertheless, in later years he was to refer to *Gloriana* as his 'slighted child',[91] and he must have been gratified by the more favourable response it received at the time of the 1966 production; though the range of critical coverage was naturally much smaller, the assessors looked at the work without the distracting considerations attending its première.

The large number of writers who took it upon themselves to offer opinions

---

87 See '*Gloriana* and Lytton Strachey', *Opera* 4/8 (August 1953), 464–7.

88 The ghostly episode was evidently modified during the 1953/4 season (see fn. 22, p. 37 above); see also p. 150 below.

89 The removal of the Norwich scene (2.i) in some of the later performances of the first production may also have been the result of far more pragmatic decisions: in any case it was restored in the 1966 production and retained in all publications.

90 See 'Britten's major setback', *Musical Opinion* 90/1069 (October 1966), 13, 15.

91 'Benjamin Britten talks to Edmund Tracey', *Sadler's Wells Magazine* 4 (Autumn 1966), 5–7.

on the first production of *Gloriana* is indicative of the unusual amount of public interest it received.[92] The variety of opinions these writers expressed, and the diverse aspects of the work on which they commented, cannot claim to be exhaustively treated in a study such as this; the criticism of *Gloriana* is a subject for study in its own right. It is hoped that this brief account of some of the issues it raised has served to illustrate a little of the breadth and complexity of its problematic première, and to offer a deeper insight into the widely accepted view of the work as the least successful of all Britten's operas.

[92] Another sign of this concern is seen in the large and inconclusive body of correspondence relating to *Gloriana* that was published variously in *The Times*, the *Daily Telegraph*, *Music and Musicians*, *Musical Opinion*, and even in the *Radio Times*.

4

The Paradox of *Gloriana*:
Simple and Difficult

DONALD MITCHELL

May I begin by throwing a little explanatory light on the title of this paper? 'Simple and Difficult' appears as part of it because, in 1953, Hans Keller and I had managed to get into the rehearsals (with some difficulty, I must tell you) of *Gloriana* at Covent Garden. We were not made particularly welcome by the Royal Opera House. The composer was there. We didn't know him at all well at that stage. This was just in the wake of our symposium – our *Britten Commentary*, which had been published early in 1952.[1]

We sat in the stalls, and in the middle of one of the scenes Britten walked over and standing over us from the row behind, said, 'You know, the more simple I try to make my music, the more difficult it becomes to perform.'

I've remembered that ever since; and it is very relevant to *Gloriana*. *Gloriana* is, from one point of view 'simple', intentionally so, if by that one has in mind its directness of utterance, at which, I have no doubt, Britten worked particularly hard in this particular work. Hence his disconcertedness when the rehearsals threw up all kinds of problems. But if *Gloriana* is and was meant to be 'simple', the opera is also 'difficult', and not just in ways that surprised the composer. There are dimensions, e.g., the psychologies of the principal *dramatis personae*, of Elizabeth, above all, and the organization of the musical ideas to embody the developing individual dramas of those individual psyches in appropriate dramatic forms, which are as 'difficult', that is to say 'complex', as any that we meet elsewhere in a characteristic Britten opera – if there is any such one thing. The – relatively – 'simple' part of Britten's task was to fulfil that part of his mission which was to give an account of established, if highly coloured, historic events in an historic reign. This was the exterior, 'simple' part. But there was the 'interior' part too, made up of a complex texture of conflicts, motives and ambitions, which probably fascinated the composer the more; indeed, without which one wonders if he would have embarked on the opera at all. It is in this pursuit of the 'difficult' *Gloriana* that I believe we shall uncover many remarkable parallels with other operas of Britten's, and be led,

---

[1] D. Mitchell and H. Keller, eds, *Benjamin Britten: A Commentary on his Works from a Group of Specialists* (London: Rockliff, 1952).

possibly, to the conclusion that however hard he may have tried otherwise, what finally emerged in Coronation year was a work entirely characteristic of the composer and revealing a set of marked preoccupations far removed at first sight from costume drama and State occasions.

A gift for dramatic timing and pacing: that comes as no surprise – if Britten hadn't had that, he would scarcely have been the musical dramatist that he was. But there is one example of this skill in *Gloriana* which, I think, is particularly telling, an event of special significance in the opera, the timing and pacing of which, I believe, were to provide an important model for Britten in an opera that he was yet to write.

The event I have in mind occurs in 1.ii, when Essex for the first time reveals *his* 'other self' – I look ahead to the 'Queen's Dilemma' (3.iii.3) – in the justly famous Second Lute Song, 'Happy were he'. I want to give some emphasis to the suggestion that it is for the 'first time' that Essex thus reveals himself to the Queen. As we shall see (p. 69 below), she remarks at the end of the song, 'Tis a conceit, it is not you.' But we have to believe that it is the Essex whom the song defines that she ultimately loves and mourns. By what else – the Second Lute Song – and whom else – other than Essex – is the Epilogue dominated?

It was Britten's original intention that 'Happy were he' should stand alone; but as Philip Reed has pointed out,[2] Britten realised at an early stage that another song was needed, to postpone the revelation of 'Happy were he', to introduce in fact a process of gradual self-revelation on Essex's part: that introspective 'other self' had as it were to be drawn out of him, not immediately vouchsafed. That, surely, is the thinking behind the quick, shallow and unconvincingly gay little song that is the First Lute Song, 'Quick music is best'. Even Essex, we feel, is putting on a show: so much is indicated by the persistent E flat pedal that does not so much underpin as undermine his E major and his empty high spirits. He doesn't concede immediately; and indeed tries to give himself and the song a lift by jacking the song up a semitone, from E to F, only to find himself dogged by that unnervingly stubborn dissonant pedal, which merely follows suit, moving up from E flat to E natural, in the context (now) of Essex's F. 'Too light, too gay', cries the Queen, 'Turn to the lute again, Evoke some far off place or time, A dream, a mood, and air To spirit us both away'. 'Spirit us *both*', one notices. Because that destabilizing pedal not only indicates Essex's need to search for himself, a search – almost literally so – for the right 'note' of genuine self-revelation, of confession even, but also embodies the Queen's need to relieve herself of the oppressive cares of State (of which weary, descending motive the pedal indeed forms an extension: see its origins in 1.ii.4 and cf. No. 5, Fig. 41^{-2} *et seq*.[3]). We are only rid of the pedal when Essex, in 'Happy were he', emerges, unencumbered, as his 'other self' – passionate, poetic, contemplative, solitary, – the self that the Queen comes to love and which he can only occasionally risk uncovering, masked as it is for most of the

---

[2] See pp. 27, 30–2 above.

[3] Note that the rehearsal numbers appear only in the fourth edition of the vocal score and the study score: all previous editions of the vocal score use rehearsal letters.

time by guile, scheming and consuming ambition. Thus at one stroke the Second Lute Song, free of any dissonant pedal, fulfils two sets of needs: the pedal likewise performs a double function. For Essex it is one thing, for the Queen another.

Undoubtedly too there was another tactic involved on Britten's part. To create that moment of stillness that 'Happy were he' represented, it was vital for it to be preceded by a stretch of quick music. 'Happy were he' would not make half its impact if it had been tacked on to the end of No. 4, however skilfully a transition might have been contrived. All questions of psychology apart, timing and pacing demanded a show of vitality before Essex's confession was embarked upon.

It may seem a startling suggestion, but I believe – indeed, I am confident – that when Britten, in 1954, came to write his next opera, *The Turn of the Screw*, this crucial scene from *Gloriana* was very much in his mind, his inner ear, when he conceived the schoolroom scene in the *The Turn of the Screw* (1.vi, 'The Lesson'). Once again he needed to create here an extraordinary moment of stillness – Miles's 'Malo' song – by preceding it with the two children's energetic recital of Latin nouns ('Many nouns in –is we find To the masculine are assigned'). The pace then slows down, and out of the bright chatter – another false show, incidentally, when one takes into account what Miles's and Flora's preoccupations really were – emerges the boy's confession, as much a moment of *first* self-revelation as is Essex's in his Second Lute song in *Gloriana* (and where Miles's harp accompaniment is the equivalent of Essex's 'lute' (harp)). The parallel is striking, not only in timing and pacing, but in confessional character – both Essex and Miles (unusually) are telling the truth about themselves, Miles revealing *his* 'other self' to the Governess, much as Essex does after his pretence at liveliness, to the Queen. In fact there are respects in which the Queen/Essex relationship and that of the Governess/Miles show a similar pattern. It is important not to get bogged down in differences of *style*: clearly the two musics involved in 'Malo' and 'Happy were he' are quite distinct. But it is just that distinction that makes the parallels all the more gripping; and there are others that I shall outline a little later. In the meantime, is there anyone who does not hear behind – just below the surface of – the Governess's exchange with Miles, as 'Malo' and the scene fade:

GOVERNESS: Why Miles, what a funny song? Did I teach you that?
MILES: No. I found it. I like it. Do you?

the Queen's exchange with Essex, as 'Happy were he' fades likewise:

ELIZABETH: Robin, a melting song: but who can this unworldly hermit be?
ESSEX: It might be any man, not one you know.
ELIZABETH: 'Tis a conceit, it is not you.

I want now to look at the final scene of the opera, i.e., 3.iii, which also entails a look at the Epilogue. The scene itself is broken up into numbers – seven in all, including the Epilogue. The number I want to concentrate on is No. 3, 'The

Queen's Dilemma', which, as I see it – or hear it, rather – is one unified number, an elaborate piece of architecture, even though it is laid out as a sequence of individual numbers, i.e., No. 4 'Trio', No. 5 'Lady Essex's Pleading', and No. 6 'Penelope Rich's Pleading', which returns us to the music of No. 3. In No. 3 we have an exposition, which – literally – 'exposes' the Queen's dilemma: shall she sign the warrant for Essex's execution, or shall she not? With No. 6, an impassioned but haughty plea by Penelope Rich – 'You, an unfaithful wife!', exclaims a provoked Queen – we embark on the number that will end with a recapitulation of the opening music, but a recapitulation with a significant difference, dramatically: by the end of it the Queen has resolved to sign – and signs Essex's life away. I think it will help clarify what I perceive to be the function and status of this brilliant number if I drop the numerals and refer to it *tout court* as 'The Queen's Dilemma', the reader bearing in mind that this represents an unbroken continuity until No. 7, the Epilogue, is reached.

Peter Evans draws our attention to the importance of pedals in *Gloriana* in the First Lute Song,[4] and then again in this extended scene of the Queen's agony of indecision. I have already dwelled a little on the role of the pedal in 'Quick music is best', systematically put out of step – or focus – by the dislocating semitone in the bass.

It is again a semitone – this time expressed as a B flat/A sharp–B natural instability – that underpins the extended number of the Queen's dilemma; underpins it, but also simultaneously *undermines* it: the semitonal friction indeed is a concise encapsulation of the conflict by which the Queen is riven. As we shall see, it is a particular semitonal relationship that brings with it resonances from another of Britten's operas, at the heart of which is a comparable moral dilemma and perhaps a similar moral ambiguity.

But it is only by the end of Scene 3 that the element of uncertainty is introduced – what one might think of as a possible contradiction (or mitigation) of the B flat judgement by the Queen's Councillors that Essex 'is guilty and condemned to die' (3.iii.1 'Prelude and Verdict'). Their unanimous verdict is expressed in the unanimity of the unison B flats that we hear intoned in the very first bar of the scene and which establish that pitch as the inescapable resolve of the Court that Essex must die. It is a resolve confirmed by the eruption of E flat minor (Fig. 155^{+3}) in which the Councillors dilate on the impossibility of the Queen extending her clemency – 'Never! Essex can she not forgive' – in the very same fateful key in which he was appointed Lord Lieutenant of Ireland (2.iii, Fig. 101), the mission which has proved to be his undoing.

And it is to the reiterated B flats that the Councillors return after their protestations (Fig. 156), though this time we note, that the Queen, on her entrance, brings with her, as part of the piled up G major wind chords accompanying her – a marvellously conceived orchestral sonority – the B natural that will come to signify her resistance to the Court's verdict, to which B flat the timpani and strings stubbornly cling: these are two bars which vividly represent the gulf which, at this stage of the opera, separates the Queen from

4 See pp. 85–6 below.

her advisers. It comes as no surprise that a few bars later she declines to sign the warrant. She is unmoved by Cecil's attempt to remind her of her duty (No. 2 'Cecil's Warning'), despite – or perhaps because of – the guile he shows in appealing to her, as it were in her own terms, in the G major that accompanied her on her entry. The Queen, in any event, needs no reminder of the 'dreadful duty' that Cecil wants her to expedite without delay: the succession of B flats (timpani plus pizzicato strings) punctuates his G major. It is a brilliant little number this, built out of the tonalities and rhythm of the Queen's entrance music at Fig. 156, and an example – there is to be a further and yet more crucial one – of the skilfully manipulative approaches to the Queen that will be made – couched in her 'own' language. This tiny song is a good instance of both the simplicity of *Gloriana* and of the complexity of motivation that often lies behind it.

The Queen over a sustained B flat dismisses Cecil and the Council, who exit to the music that formed the miniature orchestral prelude to the scene, but this time it ends, ingeniously, with B flat and B natural/C flat in juxtaposition. Whereas until now the music of the whole scene has been organized around B flat as the emblem of execution and vengeance, so that it would not be inappropriate to think of the scene as an invention on a single note (and no doubt Britten was influenced here by Berg and *Wozzeck*), the perspective now widens: will B flat and judgement prevail, or will the Queen permit duty to be overruled by inclination? And along with that confrontation, one pitch becomes two, to incorporate the dilemma. The number which ensues is an invention, on a very large scale, on that semitonal juxtaposition, duty tugging one way, the heart another; and not only an image of public versus private but of the schism in the Queen's own personality: 'I burn', she cries at the end of the exposition, 'Since from myself my other self I turn' (Fig. 160^{-2} *et seq.*).

The use of the two pitches – a veritable *idée fixe* – is so clear throughout the number that it would be a redundant exercise to spell out its every appearance. But one should note that it provides the substance of the Queen's B minor opening solo: all her agitated semiquaver figuration derives from it. A *sforzando* B flat/A sharp ends the solo and initiates the tiny recitative (with Raleigh) which leads into the ensuing trio. Raleigh's one phrase – 'Three persons, in humble duty, Crave audience of their Sovereign' – steers us to the A minor of the trio. His final pitch, A natural, sounds against the B flat of judgement, which is now persistently heard throughout the trio – in which Essex's wife, his sister, and Mountjoy join in a plea that his life should be spared – in this fresh relationship to the lower semitone, A. This same juxtaposition of pitches is sustained throughout the elaborate exchange of Lady Essex with the Queen ('Lady Essex's Pleading'), in which the Queen, moved by a mother's fear for the fate of her children, takes over the music of the trio – after all, she has just been stirred by what has been said to her – and turns it to A major, along with her promise that Essex's children 'will be safe'.

But that proves to be almost the only point of repose in this whole number, and no more than a momentary relief at that; no sooner is A major touched than the fateful B flat cuts it short, in the very next bar, to introduce – again in a tiny linking passage (Mountjoy and the Queen) – Penelope Rich, who is to make the final appeal (Fig. 164^{+5}). While from one point of view she strikes the 'right' note, i.e., F sharp, at the very start of her submission – 'Majestic' is Britten's marking for this release in F sharp major of her inadequately concealed indignation – from another, she could hardly have struck one more wrong. The upbraiding, imperious tone is part of her undoing, as are the contours of her melody, which seem to hark back (as Peter Evans draws our attention to on p. 84 below) an earlier motive associated with Essex – ('A favour now for every fool!': 1.i, Fig. 14) – but one that reflects the most unattractive, indeed, dangerous, features of his personality – jealousy and ambition. Yet more perilous are the implications of the F sharp tonality, which, one feels, if Lady Rich had been aware of them, would have led her to choose another key! For F sharp incorporates A sharp/B flat as part of its established hierarchies. It is of course a continuous presence throughout Lady Rich's harangue, but an integral presence, not an interruption, not a dissonant reminder of what *still* has to be decided, not, as in its earlier relationships to B flat or A natural, a signifier of the Queen's indecision. Indeed, there is nothing indecisive about the Queen's interjections (not interruptions) – 'He touched my sceptre', etc. – delivered as they are over an A sharp/B flat *tremolo*. The more Lady Rich indulges her fiery protest in F sharp, the more clearly we hear that now the moment of possible reversal has been passed: there is now no other option but for the decision – the B flat – to be confirmed, which is precisely what happens next. As the goaded Queen gives vent to her final outburst of exasperation – 'Woman! How dare you plead for a traitor's life, You, an unfaithful wife!' – Britten unleashes an abbreviated recapitulation of the music of the Queen's dilemma that opened this epic *dénouement*, the third act's real finale, in which the principal *dramatis personae* are seen in diverse relationships to the Queen and when we overhear the Queen's analysis of herself. The absentee is Essex. But then Essex has – and haunts – the Epilogue, still to come.

But to return to the recapitulation, to B minor, to the agitated semitonal figure alternating B natural and B flat. What is the justification for Lady Rich taking over the Queen's opening music when, by the time we have reached this critical point, the two women are, so to say, at each other's throats? Why doesn't Lady Rich have – sing – her own music? Interestingly, this was something that troubled Imogen Holst when, before the première, she was working as Britten's music assistant on *Gloriana* and, as her diary shows, she took the matter up with the composer. This is what she wrote, which reveals the sharpness of her critical intelligence (who else has even questioned this crucial passage?):

July 28th [1953]

. . . Ben suggested that we should work at *Gloriana* in the garden. The sunshine was lovely. He was very patient about the mistakes I'd let through and made a good many suggestions for improving things in the second edition.[5]

---

5 Imogen Holst is referring here to the error-ridden first edition of the vocal score, rushed through the press in time for the première (see List of Sources, (A)/V7.1), and her work with Britten to prepare the corrected second edition, eventually published at the end of the year.

But when I told him my doubts about quoting from Q.E.'s dilemma in Act II Sc. III he said I'd missed the overall drama of the music in that section but I said that he'd created such characters that one couldn't forget their personalities and that Q.E.'s cry from the heart was a very different sort of heart from P. Rich's. The food arrived so we had to stop arguing. Lovely picnic in the garden.[6]

Lunch, as we can see, put an end to the cross-examination (no doubt to Britten's relief). But perhaps it is possible to enlarge a little on what he might have said if it had not been left at the 'overall drama of the music' stage. This in any event is very true so far as it goes, and if in fact what Britten had at the back of his mind was the 'overall architecture' of the number – which seems to me highly probable – it is surely a convincing response to Imogen Holst's complaint. Because of the musical extent of the 'Dilemma' and the tangle of interpersonal relationships, there was clearly a need to impose on it a form that would stake out the perimeters, make audible a beginning and end, and – above all – bring us back to the 'Dilemma' itself for its now irreversible resolution. But why is Lady Rich singing back to the Queen what the Queen had been singing to herself in her opening soliloquy, when there was no-one about to hear her, but for ourselves the audience – in the theatre? What we hear, and yet more importantly, what the Queen hears, in Lady Rich's immediately preceding F sharp major solo, is not what Lady Rich herself would necessarily have recognized as the case she was making for Essex. In other words, we hear her as the *Queen* hears her, not – we must suppose – as she hears herself: for Lady Rich to have made a different impression she would have required a different composer to write her brief.

This is surely yet more true of the moment of recapitulation, where once again what matters is how the *Queen* hears Lady Rich's final appeal, who makes the lethal error of formulating it in terms – 'He most deserves Your pardon, Deserves your love!' – which, tragically (for Essex), confront the Queen with that 'other self' the Queen has no other course but to reject. What could be more subtly and psychologically right, then, that the Queen should hear herself appealing to herself, embodied in a reprise of her own music? Her dialogue, such as it is, with Lady Rich, is a dialogue with herself, that same dialogue we have heard earlier; and it is herself, that 'other self', she banishes when the strain becomes intolerable.

The very last straw, the last turn of the screw, is Lady Rich's playing the card of 'love', which we notice, with awful, suicidal logic, is allotted to a top B flat. Small wonder that the Queen responds with a ferocious 'Importune me no more! Out!', which, with a final reference to the basic semitonal figure that has embodied the 'Dilemma' from beginning to end, leads to the signing of the warrant and to the Epilogue, with its massive resurrection of C minor and

---

6 Imogen Holst's unpublished diary, © 1993 the Estate of Imogen Holst. This and all other quotations from Imogen Holst's diaries may not be reproduced further without written permission.

'Happy were he', emerging climactically in full orchestral dress for the first time.

I have already mentioned one instance in *Gloriana* where a later opera is anticipated – the link between Essex's 'Happy were he' and Miles's 'Malo' – and alluded to a further anticipation by an earlier opera, in fact *Gloriana*'s immediate predecessor, *Billy Budd*. It is the great 'Dilemma' number which inevitably calls to mind the agonizing indecision of Vere, when faced with Billy's inadvertent slaying of Claggart. Other writers have commented on the remarkable parallels here between the two operas, Christopher Palmer[7] and Arnold Whittall[8] among them, while Peter Evans[9] has focused our attention on one of the most significant parallels of all: it can surely be no accident that in both operas it is B flat and B natural that have a critical role to play. In *Billy Budd*, Vere's tragic fate, to sacrifice Billy on the altar of 'duty', is embodied in the semitonal juxtaposition and/or conflation of the two tonalities. In *Gloriana*, the selfsame pitches, as I hope I may have sufficiently demonstrated, represent the Dilemma of the Queen, one no less cruel than Vere's. Is she too not required to sacrifice Essex, as her public duty dictates, to the needs of the State?

There are, of course, differences too, for the discussion of which there is no room on this occasion. I have attempted to examine them in greater detail elsewhere.[10] But even the differences might be thought to point up the bond between the two operas. After all, one of the features of *Billy Budd*, and one endlessly speculated about, is the rapidity with which Vere concludes that he has to follow the rulebook. There is a sense of terror at what he has to do – convict Billy – but no 'dilemma': there can be no question of his bending or circumventing the rules. It is otherwise, as we have seen with the Queen; and it seems not far-fetched to suggest that the 'dilemma' Vere was unable to have – and which perhaps Britten might have wished he could have had – came to be composed, finally, in *Gloriana*, where the Queen is able to give vent to her indecision on a scale and in a spirit denied Vere. There was never a possibility of reprieve for Billy: but for Essex, yes, there is, until that fateful last B flat strikes home. *Gloriana*, from one point of view, completes what in *Billy Budd* was left incomplete, albeit necessarily so.

The more one considers the three operas in succession, *Billy Budd* (1951), *Gloriana* (1953), *The Turn of the Screw* (1954), the more one becomes aware that all three of them share common preoccupations and common *dénouements*. For example, all three end with epilogues, in which the music associated with the three 'victims' – Billy, Essex, Miles – takes the shape of a lament sung – ironically – by the agents of their various deaths; for what else but an epilogue is the

---

7 Christopher Palmer, 'The Music of "Gloriana" ', in *Peter Grimes, Gloriana*, ed. Nicholas John, Opera Guide 24 (London: John Calder, 1983), 85–6.

8 Arnold Whittall, *The Music of Britten and Tippett*, 2nd ed. (Cambridge: Cambridge University Press, 1990), 145–9.

9 Peter Evans, *The Music of Benjamin Britten*, 2nd ed. (London: J.M. Dent & Sons, 1989), 197.

10 Donald Mitchell, 'A *Billy Budd* Notebook' in *Benjamin Britten: Billy Budd*, Mervyn Cook and Philip Reed, (Cambridge, Cambridge University Press: 1993), 122–34.

Governess's outpouring of grief over Miles, a recapitulation of his 'Malo', like Vere's of Billy's 'But I've sighted a sail in the storm' and the Queen's of Essex's 'Happy were he'. Each 'victim', so to speak, furnishes his own musical obituary. The more we hear *Gloriana* in the 'frame' provided by its predecessor and successor, the more clearly the work emerges as wholly characteristic of its composer. The opera, with its spectacular and festal dimension, was certainly faithful to the occasion that was its stimulus. But more interestingly, at the heart of it, the composer remains stubbornly faithful to ideas that were central to his creative life.

But all this perhaps begins to take us rather far outside the parameters of the topic of this paper. Relevant considerations none the less. Because they help us to understand why it is that the most important musical and dramatic events in *Gloriana* are charged with such overwhelming power and intensity: they are fuelled – inspired – by passionate preoccupations and concerns shared, incontrovertibly, by all the major theatrical works of Britten's from these years. Or to put it another way, they unveil the complexities that lie behind the simplicities of *Gloriana*.

5

The Number Principle and Dramatic Momentum in *Gloriana*

PETER EVANS

In honouring the Queen's Coronation with an opera based on events in the life of the first Queen Elizabeth, Britten was departing significantly from the paths he had followed in his earlier operas. However difficult the decisions to be made in reducing a fictional narrative to the space of an operatic cycle of incident, the shaping of events has already been contrived so as to tend inevitably towards *dénouement*: librettist and composer must agree on the means by which substantial paragraphs of description or reflection can be excised, and on the kind of encapsulated statement (often approaching banality when simply read) that invites the lyrical setting in which a composer offers a reading of the emotional situation; yet the dramatic scaffolding is already there, so that music's unique enhancement of our sense of time as an onward flow of linked events is ready to make its effect.

But the peculiar untidiness of history is less helpful in shaping the dramatic sequence that completes itself in a relatively restricted span (restricted above all in the number of words that can be used) and that captures in some measure a feeling of period and place without rejecting opera's chief glory, its illumination of human character. In two Russian operas with a basis in history (albeit subjected already to some literary ordering), *Boris Godunov* and *War and Peace*, we can observe the alternations between these two functions, but we see that it is Prokofiev, placing greater reliance on fictional constructs, who ties the neater dramatic knots, despite the jolt of his midway shift from a drama of individuals to one of nations. Musorgsky is subtler in his cross-cutting between psychological and epic drama, but precisely because his scenes from Russian history convey so powerfully a sense of their being prised from the continuum of events, the emotional unity of our experience has to be imposed, notably by the poignant commentary of the idiot's final song.

Britten's Elizabethan opera, to be appropriate to the celebratory occasion for which it was written, had to include grand scenes that showed the Queen in the context of those she ruled, yet to secure a convincing dramatic shape a drastically selective narrative would have to accommodate these. It remains debatable how much Plomer and Britten drew upon Lytton Strachey's *Elizabeth and Essex* in designing a plot for their opera, though the particular cross-section they chose to treat, from a long and intricately compounded reign, was obviously comparable to that which Strachey had made his central theme. If the dramatic cycle was based upon this limitation, at the same time the opera should offer a broader view of Elizabeth's times and the influence she exercised on them. The alternation of, roughly speaking, public and private events articulated the musical sequence of three acts into eight self-contained scenes, but within these the same contrasts might persist (for example, when the final scene progressively reduces its focus from the Queen with her council, through her interview with the suppliants for Essex, to her final isolation, when she is attended only by spectral figures), and it seems likely that, the more detailed the plans for the libretto became, the more logical it became for Britten to conceive its musical realization as a mosaic of individual pieces, rather than as a few through-composed entities.

It could be said that Tippett's *King Priam* is a mosaic structure, one containing many more pieces than *Gloriana*, but its point lies essentially in the effects produced by the juxtapositions, often of musical units that are in themselves almost inert – that is to say, non-developing and certainly non-concluding. Britten's own interest in such methods can be seen to grow out of the experience of the first church parable, *Curlew River*, and achieved its most ramified expression in *Death in Venice*. As reference to those works reminds us, beyond a certain point the effect of fragmentation may be to emphasize continuity, but clearly *Gloriana* is to be apprehended as a precisely articulated structure, and to make his point unequivocally (perhaps even ostentatiously) Britten revived not only the principle but the literal practice of the 'number' opera, which so much nineteenth-century activity had sought either to eliminate or to conceal by sophisticated arts of transition. His labelling is not entirely consistent – neither the separate dances of the Norwich Masque (2.i) nor the various components of the Ballad-Rondo (3.ii) are numbered individually – but, as shown in the score, some 54 numbers represent the segmented experience of this opera.[1]

The music in *Gloriana* most generally familiar is from scenes blatantly composed of separable units, for both the choral dances that begin Act 2 and the instrumental dances that end it have often been performed out of context. The court dances in particular make their effect by the expressive distortion they impose on still recognizable historical types – pavane, galliard, coranto and so on. Given also the role that a highly flexible but evidently quasi-archaic modality plays throughout the opera, we might conclude that the belated restitution of the number principle is another conceit. Today one no longer has to argue for the cumulative dramatic power that can be generated from a succession of events as contrived as the alternation of compressed action or narrative in recitative and luxuriously protracted emotional consequence in aria; a principle so convincingly vindicated by so many masterpieces needs no defence. Any doubts we may entertain turn rather on the conviction likely to be brought to such a structural method by composers whose concepts of musical

---

[1] For the complete list, taken from the published vocal score, see pp. 102–3; as is recorded there, the five verses of the Ballad in 3.ii are labelled as such.

unity and continuity cannot easily recapture a pre-Wagnerian innocence. *The Rake's Progress* is the pre-eminent example of an opera that survives the precarious minefield where historical conventions are placed in the foreground and are then negotiated so as to create by deviations of syntax an entirely modern sensibility, inevitably heavily dependent on irony.

Britten's use of the number principle in *Gloriana* is not an essay in musical historicism, and I hope to show that the opera is as much concerned as are any of his others with the building of embracing dramatic spans. Conversely, this reminds us that his recognition of the principle, while more overt in *Gloriana*, is scarcely less influential in much of the rest of his operatic output. Indeed, it was in writing about *Peter Grimes* in 1945[2] that Britten stressed how much he conceived the greater rhythm of an opera as depending upon a succession of discrete musical organisms rather than the blurring that helps to suggest endless flux. It would not be difficult to number in our scores the constituent units of *Grimes* scarcely less definitively than Britten did in *Gloriana*. In *Lucretia* the effect would be still more underlined by the tendency to give an almost Baroque unity of affective instrumental colouring to each unit, and in a pioneer essay on *Albert Herring*[3] Erwin Stein clarified similar structural principles. The set-piece articulation is no less obvious if we look at *Billy Budd*; but if we listen to it, the quasi-symphonic structures into which the units are bound create an entirely different impression, of Britten's broadest operatic canvases. After *Gloriana*, we can see in *The Turn of the Screw* a new approach to the greater unity, where again the isolable nature of the brief scene is a vital part of our experience, yet the pattern to which it belongs is now very palpably the entire work.

In such a study of obsession as *The Turn of the Screw*, this sense that every musical diversion must be discovered to lead us back to an unyielding central predicament is suffocating. In *Gloriana*, the diversion, such as the Queen's Progress at Norwich, broadens the historical conspectus, and the entirely fresh tone of its music is appropriate and welcome. The Norwich masque is not, however, a *divertissement* in the common sense of offering spectacle (and an enlarged cast) to enhance the entertainment without significant propulsion of dramatic issues: we learn much about Elizabeth in this scene which is nowhere else revealed, and without which the opera's closing homage, 'Green leaves', could seem hollow. Even so, the succession of choral dances presented by the citizens make up a deliberately slightly stiff tableau, whereas the court dances become enmeshed in the dramatic action, so that musical shapes acquire associations that draw them out of the neat frames in which they first appear. The use of motives that give more than the superficial meaning to later contexts is one obvious device by which Britten spurns doctrinaire adherence to construction by 'numbers', but there are many others, ranging from the retention of one musical element across the join between successive pieces to the planning of a

2 Benjamin Britten, 'Introduction', in *Benjamin Britten: Peter Grimes*, ed. Eric Crozier, Sadler's Wells Opera Book, no. 3 (London: John Lane, 1946 [1945]), 8.
3 'Form in Opera: *Albert Herring* examined', *Tempo* 5 (Autumn 1947), 4–7; reprinted in *The Britten Companion*, ed. Christopher Palmer (London: Faber and Faber, 1984), 127–32.

considerable sequence of numbers as parts of a greater musical whole, unified by recurrences of material and by purposeful tonal divergence and convergence.

Some of the motivic usages are perhaps more accurately regarded as reminiscence themes, cited to make a point rather than intensively worked out. Yet if there is no shape as pervasive in *Gloriana* as is Grimes's 'and God have mercy upon me' (to say nothing of the *Screw* cell, or 'Marvels unfold' in *Death in Venice*), at least half the eight or so migratory shapes in the opera, whether or not they are literally quoted elsewhere, can be found operating at a relatively submerged level, so that we sense the congruity without necessarily recognizing the device that produces it. The most memorable theme in the opera, since it closes it with so affecting a fade-out, is no doubt 'Green leaves are we, Red rose our golden Queen', her people's homage to a well-loved monarch.[4] First appearing in overt form at the end of the tournament we overhear but do not see in Scene 1, it may then seem a little too statuesque in its balanced disposition of wide intervals (see Ex. 1), but its true character emerges in the close

Ex. 1   Britten: *Gloriana*, 1.i.2

overlapping of imitative statements that follows in the orchestra. Transferred to the chorus, this achieves its most glowing form at the end of the Reconciliation scene, when Elizabeth's skill in drawing the best from those around her elicits the myriad tributes of a contrapuntal web rather than a regimented paean.

In fact, the 'Green leaves' shape has been foreshadowed before it emerges in this definitive form. The orchestral prelude to Act 1 is a playing-out in advance, but without vocal parts, of the tournament. Its opening bars, in both rhythm and modality (here a Lydian that persists throughout this piece), epitomize the special sound of this opera, adapting patent archaism to the service of an idiom that is evidently not pastiche. They also vividly convey an excitement that we can only later make specific to the events on the tilting ground. So, for example, the sporadic interruption of a musical alternation of chordal fanfares and brilliant, headlong two-part counterpoint by percussive interludes is explained when, in the scene that follows, Cuffe provides a commentary on the joust between Mountjoy and an unnamed opponent for his master Essex, who is too jaundiced to attend in person: in these percussive bars Essex's resentment of

---

[4] For a history of the text of this passage, see above, pp. 28–30.

Mountjoy's success is graphically conveyed by his vocal lines, adding an element missing in the prelude that consistently contradicts by its flattening inflexions the optimistic buoyancy of the prevailing Lydian. Another feature of the prelude clarified is the striking bass shape of one of the two-part contrapuntal sections, for it now prompts Cuffe's report on the competitors – 'They both salute the Queen' (see Ex. 2). Only after the tournament has ended and the

Ex. 2   Britten: *Gloriana*, 1.i.1

victor, Mountjoy, has received his prize from the Queen's hand is this bass theme developed and moulded into the hymnic 'Green leaves', taken up by the crowd.

This is a simple example of a technique by which the apparently disjunct musical statement is given a greater expressive weight than its face value would suggest, and it shows Britten from the outset of *Gloriana* thinking in dramatic spans that render subservient the articulation of the number principle. Of course, 'Green leaves' is so idiosyncratic a melodic line that, once the progress to complete definition has been completed, it is irreversible: none of the subsequent references to this shape is in any way concealed, though considerable distortion may be applied to the intervallic values; the orchestral punctuation of Elizabeth's soliloquy leading up to the Prayer that ends Act 1 provides a good example. The theme is little heard in Act 2: the citizens of Norwich are intent on their distinctive tribute, and only at the end of this scene is the drooping sixth of their final dance of homage converted into a single line of 'Green leaves'; the courtiers who dominate the other two scenes do not express themselves with the unaffected warmth that this shape now embodies, though the chorus, 'Victor of Cadiz', makes a reference at the words 'for Gloriana, go'. But after Essex's departure in 3.i we hear it again very plainly. And now its distortion, after two literally recurrent pitches, is particularly telling, for it betokens an affection gone awry. Essex has returned from Ireland, having failed in his appointed task to quell Tyrone's rebellion, and has attempted to protect himself against the Queen's displeasure by parading the warmth of feeling both have acknowledged in happier times (see Ex. 3).

Ex. 3   Britten: *Gloriana*, 3.i.3

Even after the soothing attentions of the Dressing-Table Song, distortions of 'Green leaves' disturb the following interview with Cecil, creating an obsessive preoccupation with the betrayal of affection that prepares us in some measure for Elizabeth's decision in the agonizing clash between personal loyalty and political expediency after Essex has compounded his offence. It is worth noting that the first reference to 'Green leaves' in this Cecil scene was not in the D major of its original and its closing appearances in the opera, where it symbolized her bond with the common people, but in E flat, the key associated with her sovereign authority (Britten's later revision of these bars dulls the reference). And it is in E flat that she touches on the theme as she replies to Lady Essex's plea for her husband's life – 'A Prince is set upon a stage, Alone in sight of all the world'.

But if the various modifications of this central theme are intended to be instantly recognized and unambiguously related to dramatic events, there are at least two other shapes in the opera that, while not conspicuously derivations from 'Green leaves', quite potently resemble it in contour. The more short-lived is the angular outburst with which Essex vilifies the absent Queen before the courtiers, after Elizabeth has ridiculed Lady Essex by appropriating her excessively grand dress (see Ex. 4). The contour is altogether more bizarre, but

Ex. 4   Britten: *Gloriana*, 2.iii.10

in its return to the original pitch area and in its constituent intervals this uneasily jolts memories of 'Green leaves', in relation to which it is already an act of treachery. And, in the orchestra at least, it reverberates on with ironic effect in the following number, 'The Queen's Announcement', when Elizabeth appoints Essex to the office he has been seeking, the Lord Deputyship of Ireland.

The other related shape has more extensive dramatic consequences, for it provides a thread connecting Essex's overweening ambition to his downfall. It is the phrase, 'A favour now for every fool', with which Essex pours his ready contempt on the 'golden prize' Mountjoy has received from the Queen. The contour is a drastic simplification of the 'Green leaves' curve, almost a reductive analysis of it (see Ex. 5), and it follows so quickly upon the dying strains of

Ex. 5   Britten:*Gloriana*, 1.i.3

the crowd's tribute that the association can be readily made. The new motive and its inversion are then made familiar, bandied about in the fight between Essex and Mountjoy which the insult provokes, and still audible in the string theme (see Ex. 6) punctuating the fanfares of the Queen's entry that halts the

Ex. 6 Britten: *Gloriana*, 1.i.4

fight. This cell of pitches, B flat E flat G B natural, remains active in the bass throughout the processional music, heard last to words that reinforce the point – 'Rivals for a lady's favour'; as the processional march returns after the reconciliation to end the scene, the reverberations of the motive continue. Thereafter it disappears until Elizabeth herself restores it, to the words 'Lord Deputy in Ireland', in 2.iii, when she bestows on Essex the favour he has been coveting with a furious impatience. The explosive impact of this moment owes much to the long F pedal that sets in towards the end of the quartet, 'Good Frances, do not weep', continues throughout the March to which Queen and Council enter, and rumbles on in the timpani during 'The Queen's Announcement'. Raleigh gives a hint of what is to come when he sings 'a matter of great moment', but it is with a fundamental shift from that pent-up F to E flat minor, the key of royal authority coloured ominously, that Elizabeth releases one cumulative dramatic tension and prepares the build-up of another. Her charge to Essex, 'Go into Ireland, and bring back *victory and peace*' stamps crucial new words upon the 'favour' motive, a phrase made still more specific by all the court in the chorus and ensemble that follow, 'Victor of Cadiz, *overcome Tyrone*'. The Coranto danced by the courtiers to end the act is in the opera's most affirmative key, D major, but the little stage band that plays it is intruded upon by faint stirrings in the pit orchestra, which well to the surface and finally overwhelm the celebratory stage music (the curtain falls slowly on the continuing dance) with a gargantuan unison version of the 'Victor of Cadiz' music in A minor. Even before the consequences of Elizabeth's decision have begun to unwind in Act 3, there seems a chilly foreboding here, and the musical shape we must still relate back to its origins as 'A favour now for every fool' has already acquired a haunting irony.

A nightmarish version of music from the 'Victor of Cadiz' ensemble, in clipped rhythms and with strings *col legno*, is heard (still in A minor) behind Elizabeth's reproaches 'Were you not required to break his power down?' in 3.i, when Essex has returned from Ireland with no more than a truce to show for his campaign. But the decisive re-emergence of the 'favour' motive comes after Essex has broken free from imprisonment and stirred up rebellion, has been recaptured, found guilty of treason and condemned to death. His wife's plea for mercy has touched the Queen and ensured at least that Essex's children will be spared, but the intervention at this point of Lady Penelope Rich, Essex's sister, is fatally maladroit. To a brazenly unapologetic version of the 'favour' motive (see Ex. 7), she argues that Essex's inherent greatness is still needed by

Ex. 7 Britten: *Gloriana*, 3.iii.6

the state and, moreover, that it owes nothing to his preferment by Elizabeth: 'Still great he would have been / Without the grace and favour of a Queen'. Carried away in a frenzy of indignation, Penelope is swept into uttering the unutterable: 'He most deserves your pardon / Deserves your love', this last to an inversion of the 'favour' motive which reaches up to a shrill B flat – a pitch that, as will be seen later, has been touching a raw nerve for Elizabeth throughout this scene. In a cold fury she signs Essex's death warrant, and the action of the opera is completed, even though its most penetrating summary of Elizabeth's character remains to be made in the Epilogue.

Three further thematic shapes, all introduced in 1.ii, are no less closely associated with each other in the subsequent action than the group discussed above; the full chapter and verse can be reduced here to some of the principal contexts that involve them. The first shape is an orchestral motive of rising fifth (with connecting slide) followed by whole-tone descent (see Ex. 8(i)). This occurs first as the constant background to a discussion between Elizabeth and Cecil of the threat from Spain, and can best be summarized to words Elizabeth sings against it – 'cares of state'. However, this explicit meaning comes only after Cecil has left, to allow entry to Essex. And Essex has led off with motive (ii), a gesturing exclamation, 'Queen of my life', founded on an orchestral appoggiatura harmony that, even without hindsight, we may feel a shade

Ex. 8(i)   Britten: *Gloriana,* 1.ii.4

Ex. 8(ii)   Britten: *Gloriana,* 1.ii.4

Ex. 8(iii) Britten: *Gloriana,* 1.ii.7

too studied in its Romantic fervour. These two shapes are so often juxtaposed that it is not too pat to see embodied in them the struggle between the gnawing preoccupations of high office and the need for reciprocated affection that the ageing Elizabeth must seek to resolve.

Indeed, almost immediately after their first presentation, a conflation of the two themes leaves a heavy undertow in the orchestral bass, which shows us that Essex's attempt to cheer the Queen with the dancing music of his First Lute Song is not penetrating beyond the surface of her attention – and the recalcitrant pitch emerges at the stanza ends as the root of 'cares of state'.

(This provides a particularly clear first example of a musical overlap that leaves the numbered piece identifiable, yet sweeps it into a continuing musical process.) But Essex cannot be neatly relegated to the one part of Elizabeth's life; characteristically, a scene that begins as a conceit, a delicately veiled protestation of love, mounts in ardour until, at the approach of a political adversary, Raleigh, Essex switches instantly to a fury that prompts his direct appeal for the Irish mission. Seeing Raleigh's silhouette, he sings 'The jackal, lurking by the wall / How vain his hope, *the lion will fall*'. This is motive (iii) of this group; its melodic descent echoes the whole-tones of 'cares of state' (see Ex. 8) and it ends with an orchestral dissonance. With or without its scalic preparation, this chord (prompting comparison with the *Grimes* 'storm' chord) is to become an ever more insistent omen of the lion's fall; thus, it penetrates the orchestral prelude to Act 3 even before we have heard the frustrating news from Ireland. At the end of that magnificently organized scene (discussed in full below), it is heard for the last time but now to Elizabeth's words, 'It is I who have to rule' (Ex. 9),

Ex. 9   Britten: *Gloriana*, 3.i.8

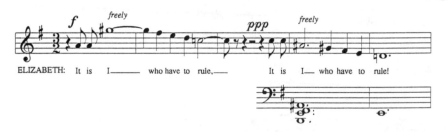

her magisterial whole-tone descent making unequivocal the relationship to the 'cares of state' motive, and thrusting home her inevitable acknowledgement of political rather than personal priorities. Earlier in this scene she has similarly appropriated, and defused, Essex's insidious appeal to her emotions. His 'Queen of my life', brandished to support the argument he is losing about his handling of the Irish campaign, is wrenched by Elizabeth out of its sharp-key context and developed into a valedictory line, over a funereal pedal in C minor; this represents with extreme power the critical breaking point in their relationship, and in the brief recall that follows of the Second Lute Song they both recognize its finality.

It was noted earlier that Britten's numbering of the constituent pieces in *Gloriana* is not entirely consistent. A single 'number' as shown in the score may contain several pieces far more distinct in their musical function than, say, the complementary pairing of cavatina and cabaletta that an aria might once have comprised. Conversely, several 'numbers' may be apprehended by the listener as one span not because the music is uniform but because its components follow in unbroken dramatic sequence. A simple example was seen in the bass undertow that takes us into, and beyond, Essex's First Lute Song. The link into the Second Lute Song is still simpler – a series of minor-mode I–V progressions in the brass, becoming less predictable in their sequence until, magically, the I–V of C minor is discovered, on muted strings, as the opening of the song itself. A common element in the accompanying figuration may serve the same purpose, as when the Queen in her early-morning interview with Essex (on his unauthorized return from Ireland) sings 'Because you're here / When larks alone have right of audience' and the flute's lark figures, apparently a rather glib response, prove to be a rearrangement of the notes of the orchestral motive that has dominated the whole scene. Thus an apparent lightening of the mood has not deflected Elizabeth from the question at issue. The central scene of the opera (2.ii), placed between the two great tableaux of the Norwich progress and the court dances, is for four characters only – Essex and his wife; his sister, Penelope Rich, and her lover, Mountjoy. The cross-cutting between the two pairs before the culminating quartet (much of it in fact a 3 + 1 disposition, since Lady Essex cannot share the others' treacherous sentiments) tends inevitably to break this scene into evidently disjunct episodes. Britten tightens it up musically by deriving both the accompanying shake F–E and the splenetic ninths of Essex's outbursts from a characteristic feature of the Penelope/Mountjoy duets that frame them, creating the effect of parenthesis within one paragraph.

But the most embracing device in the opera, one that impels the action forward and heightens our expectancy whatever the changes of foreground musical detail, is the pedal-note. Britten's mastery of composition around a fixed pitch was shown as early as 'Jesu, as thou art our Saviour' in *A Boy was Born*, and its dramatic potentiality was tapped in *Peter Grimes*, where the pitch F, established quietly with Ellen's word 'peace' ('What aim, what future, what *peace* will your hard profits buy?'), is taken up as the monotone of the Creed in the offstage church service but in the foreground action seems an immovable obstacle to agreement between Peter and Ellen as they offer conflicting interpretations of the pitch's tonal meaning – F in G flat Lydian, in F Lydian, in E flat minor. And, of course, it is this monstrously threatening F that, suddenly exploding as a dominant ('so be it, and . . .'), releases Peter's fateful 'God have mercy upon me', from which the rest of the tragedy unfolds.

We have already noted an F pedal in *Gloriana* too, that which in the court scene preceded the Queen's Announcement. But a far more momentous pedal is the B flat which persists, heard or apprehensively awaited, throughout the first six of the seven numbers which make up the final scene; in that the seventh number, the Epilogue, is no longer dominated by it (though its two brief recurrences are telling), we recognize, if only subconsciously, that *dénouement* is complete; we have moved beyond the tensions of time into Elizabeth's fantasies as she nears death.[5] Though the scene (see Ex. 10) begins with the

---

5 For another account of this scene, see pp. 69–74 above.

Ex. 10

Nos: 1   2   3   4   5   6   7

B flat, against which the theme of Essex's death-sentence is first heard, it functions as a dominant to E flat as the scene begins with the councillors endlessly rotating the musical symbol of their verdict. E flat minor, familiar from earlier events as the key of Elizabeth's authority in its most autocratic form, gives weight to their conviction that 'Essex can she not forgive', but now the Queen enters, and it is from this point that the pedal B flat takes root; it is inescapably brought to our attention by the conflict it creates with the G major triad above. Whatever their deflections of harmonic progression, or even of wholly incompatible tonal shift, all the subsequent musico-dramatic events cannot expunge for Elizabeth that fateful B flat, token of the terrible responsibility thrust on her by the death warrant of her beloved Essex, now branded a traitor. Cecil's advice that she must act quickly goes by in a G that is entirely tangential to the stabbing B flats, but in 'The Queen's Dilemma' (only the second moment in the opera at which we hear her in soliloquy) Britten makes the crucial pitch a pivot in one of those studies in semitonal ambivalence by which he so often represents polarities. As in much of *Billy Budd*, a predominant key of B minor (in which, however, the A sharp of the timpani pulls constantly against the bass strings' oscillations that are trying to tip it back to a stable B) is supplanted from time to time by B flat major. The violent antitheses ('I love, and yet am forced to seem to hate') of this desperate little aria are finally epitomized in Elizabeth's closing phrase, 'Since from myself my other self I turn', twisting between the two keys but ending hopelessly with the B flat. The pitch is again foreign to, but a baleful intruder upon, the A minor (recalling 'Victor of Cadiz') of the Trio in which Lady Essex, Penelope and Mountjoy plead for Essex's life. It comes more into focus as the A sharp in the F sharp major of Penelope's assertive plea; as the Queen's anger mounts, this F sharp becomes a dominant that swings back into the B minor music of the 'Dilemma' piece, with its attendant B flat tensions. As we have seen, it is Penelope's own hectoring high B flat that snaps Elizabeth's irresolution, and in a highly controlled B flat major phrase she signs the death warrant. The final scurrying scales of the 'Dilemma' figuration quickly lose all B minor potentiality, but by their peak B flat too has been exorcized, in favour of the C minor that controls the Epilogue. Transparent though the device of one insistent pitch serving as *idée fixe* may be, this long span of music is handled with much subtlety of detail which ensures that the dramatic momentum never falters.

In an earlier commentary on *Gloriana*,[6] I tried to show that one of the factors which give a distinctive tone to the opera is its use of archaic (and especially modal) reference, and that the unifying effect is not at all qualified by the wide historical spread of the background sources, since reconstruction of specific period styles is not to the composer's purpose. That the three trumpets in C which play the processional music in 1.i are actually restricted to the pitches available to natural trumpets in E flat invests the sound with a token antiquity, but in no way denies Britten a panache derived from no historical models; the court dances in 2.iii offer a delightful study in archaisms creatively misappropriated. Our present topic is not the vivid colourings which Britten brings to many of the individual pieces, but rather the means by which he secures a sense of forward movement in the dramatic action. Modality is not necessarily irrelevant to this, since it can be given, if less assertively, the same kind of ambivalence as key relations, and so suggest a friction or a gulf between characters more fundamental than their words may convey. We noted the extraordinarily bilious tone Essex's comments on the tournament acquire when they consistently swing the bright Lydian G tonality into the flat territories of his obsessive pride. In contrast to this, we find in the duet for Elizabeth and Essex that follows his two lute songs in 1.ii that it is Essex whose melodic lines eagerly reach out to sharpened degrees while Elizabeth's ruefully incline to flattened alternatives. The whole passage (from 'O heretofore') is no more than the embellishment of one chord, but the contrast in the reading of its emotional value revealed by these modal divergences is powerful and, of course, prophetic: even when Essex's protestations are most ardent, Elizabeth is troubled by the shadow of her advancing years.

My chief concern is with questions of continuity, means by which the brusque articulation of successive pieces can be smoothed over so as to concentrate our attention on the flow, as well as the nature, of events. But in an opera whose action includes songs and dances, the effect of musical *closure* may be not only plausible but essential at many points: even Wagner's endless melos is conspicuously broken up by the pieces of music-as-music placed within the music-as-drama of *Die Meistersinger*. And it is not only the choral dances of the Norwich Masque, the instrumental dances of the court and the lute songs of Essex which have this status in *Gloriana*. The Dressing-Table Song is an aubade that we surely take to be literally sung to the Queen; indeed, its self-conscious beauty of sound sets it apart from everything else in the opera. The central scene of the last act is set apart in quite another way. For the whole episode of Essex's escape and revolt is viewed, not from the court, but from the streets of the city, and as reports filter through or the mutinous rabble is glimpsed, events are interpreted by a ballad-singer. Sophisticated musical structures could be incongruous here, and the Ballad-Rondo (Britten's title) is strung together on

---

[6] Peter Evans, *'Gloriana'*, in *The Music of Benjamin Britten*, 2nd ed. (London: J.M. Dent & Sons, 1989), 188–202.

the successive stanzas of the Ballad-Singer's improvised narrative; the rondo's episodes are formed of the intrusions of Essex's followers and finally of the City Crier, proclaiming Essex a traitor. There is a driving orchestral motive that creates an excitement the more tense for the Ballad-Singer's studiously measured, even lugubrious, delivery. Not only does this scene give us our only view of the common people (and the prevailing tonality of D accurately reflects their instinctive loyalty to the Queen), but its stark change of musical manners intensifies the sense of crisis.

We saw how one of the rigidly delimited pieces, the Coranto at the end of the court's dancing, could be swept into a dramatic confrontation (with the 'Victor of Cadiz' music in the main orchestra) that breaks the mould; as it fades behind the curtain, the dance seems to have become endless. A still more momentous conversion of a fixed form into a free is to be heard in the return as the Epilogue of Essex's Second Lute Song. That it should return at all already sets a momentous stamp upon it, for, whatever the threads of motivic reference and the recurrent phrases of 'Green leaves', there has been no substantial recapitulation of material beyond (at most) the confines of a scene. In the changes that were made after the first performances to the spoken interludes in this orchestral version of the song, the voice of Essex was introduced, reproaching the Queen with her rejection of him and asking for release in death. It seems to me regrettable that this focus on Essex can narrow the implications of this remarkable scene, for although the song we mentally reconstruct, with the odd phrase brought to the surface by Elizabeth herself, is Essex's, it is rather the whole of her life that is passing in review before the dying Queen.

Coinciding with Penelope's scream from top C as Elizabeth hands the signed death-warrant to Raleigh, the Epilogue version of the lute song 'Happy were he' quickly loses contact with actuality. Opening as an overpowering tutti, it is a bizarre distortion of the delicately whimsical original, and phrases undergo gargantuan expansion before they subside into the sustained backgrounds against which we hear, in the speech of melodrama, the Queen and those apparitions that intrude upon her reverie. The piece retains the C minor – C major – C minor (brief reprise) shape of its model, but in this monumentally protracted delivery all sense of balancing phrase is lost. The interlude in which Essex's voice is heard comes after a cadence on to B flat (see the diagram, Ex. 10), stirring up memories of all that pitch has symbolized in the earlier part of the scene. But when Britten chooses to modify a later phrase so as again to close on B flat (coloured now by tam-tam, wind-machine and *ponticello* double-basses), the phantom that confronts Elizabeth is not Essex's death but her own, and the words she haltingly sings are no longer those of the song, but 'Mortua, mortua . . . sed non sepulta!' The return to C minor is not inflated, and it fades without completing the route to cadence; instead a transitional phrase on flute, then solo violin, separated by the Queen's last words, 'I see no weighty reason that I should be fond to live or fear to die', transports the music out of its funereal C minor into the D major in which the offstage chorus with harp sing 'Green leaves are we, Red rose our golden queen' (a tonal rise prefigured at the close of Act 1), fading into a silence that coincides with darkness. This boldly imaginative Epilogue came in for much criticism at the first production,[7] and it is probably true that the original melodrama, introducing figures like the Queen's godson, Sir John Harington, and the French Ambassador, who have taken no part in the earlier action, was confusing. The conversion of a decorous lyrical conceit into an awesome vision of Elizabeth's death that is also a celebration of her life may be seen to be Britten's most powerful adaptation in *Gloriana* of the set piece to a long-term dramatic purpose.

It will be clear by now that set pieces, pieces that we apprehend as musical entities, may vary greatly both in the freedom or rigidity of their internal structure and in the means by which they are absorbed into their context. The rather complacent strophic design of Raleigh's song in the first scene matches the cut-and-dried nature of the judgment he pronounces, whereas we detect in Cecil a more intelligent and politically shrewd character, because his through-composed song, 'The art of government', finds such circumspect routes to such unexpected tonal destinations (all three Cecil pieces are dominated by conjunct lines). As for the linking material itself, Britten acknowledges at times in his section-titles the use of recitative, and there are a few points at which the job of bridging in this way the gap between two major pieces seems to have been done rather mechanistically: the recitative between 'Green leaves' as it ends the Reconciliation Ensemble and the E flat ceremonial exit music always strikes me as such a join. But at few moments in *Gloriana* are we likely consciously to note that we are listening to recitative for, like Purcell, Britten moves so smoothly from etched declamation into arioso phrases. And since his orchestra remains available to sustain musical threads, however functional the vocal enunciation, Britten has no scruples about drawing on methods that range from Baroque to Wagnerian.

Finally, it may usefully tie up some loose ends to trace the complete shape of a scene, one to which several references have already been made. We looked at the last scene of Act 3 and sketched the ground plan of the Ballad-Rondo, scene 2; 3.i will provide a final case study. Though we cannot know at once that the agitated fugato of its prelude represents Essex's flight back to England in disarray, the chords that punctuate it clearly enough relate to Ex. 8(iii), 'the lion will fall', as the whole-tone approach confirms. This big orchestral paragraph builds up in textural density, and strains against its initial E minor, yet it is held firmly to an E centre by a tonic pedal. Only when the paragraph begins again, now to the chatter of the maids of honour who are preparing for the Queen's levée, does a series of bass progressions relieve tension (the moves are essentially traditional ones – to V, IV and III). But an abrupt disruption of texture underlines the agitation which a disturbance outside creates, and Essex bursts in, demanding to see the Queen; the stalemate as he is refused admission corresponds to the return here of the prelude's pedal-bound music, its abandonment, for an assertive augmentation of the fugato motive, to his aggressive intrusion upon the Queen at her dressing table. Thus far the impetus of the

---

[7] See above, pp. 62–4.

music has derived entirely from the driving figurations of the fugato, but here, after a loaded silence, the patterns are broken up and retarded, and E minor is quickly lost. Instead the dialogue between Elizabeth and Essex is articulated by all the other eleven minor triads (i.e, making twelve in all), as dry interjections at first, but as Elizabeth probes further into Essex's strange behaviour, their tone changes. So, for instance, the ninth triad, of F minor, is sustained by muted brass, a coincidence of harmony and timbre that awakens memories from Act 1, where she asked him to 'evoke some far-off place or time': now her words disown such illusions – 'But the years pursue us / And the rose must feel the frost.' From recitative she passes into the little piece, 'Because you're here / When larks alone have right of audience', where the fugato motive is reshaped into the flute's lark figures. The G minor of this duet (for Essex replies in the same manner) is displaced by a return of the prelude's version of the theme and of its E minor, so that a ritornello marks off a major structural division.

The interview continues with two new tonal spans, A minor and C minor; as the themes they restore bring home forcibly, these are the appropriate keys in which Elizabeth must settle her account with Essex on respectively the office entrusted to him and their emotional relationship. So 'Victor of Cadiz, overcome Tyrone' and its sequel in that ensemble, 'Exalted high among his peers', underlie her accusations that he has proved himself unequal to his mission. Essex's incredulous response to this charge comes in hasty, repetitive little stanzas, still mechanically traversing tonic to dominant patterns of A minor. But his trump card goes awry when he launches histrionically into 'Queen of my life', and in that crucial twist noted already the Queen seizes upon it in C minor to her own words – 'Dear name I have loved, O, use it no more! The time and the name Now belong to the past: They belong to the young, And the echoes are mute.' The phrases of the C minor lute-song into which this leads (now 'Happy were we') are valedictory, and as she dismisses him, the appeal of 'Queen of my life' in the orchestra is stifled by 'cares of state'. There follows the Dressing-Table Song of the ladies-in-waiting and maids of honour, set apart as a necessary interlude in this emotionally as well as structurally complex scene, not only by its seductive beauty of sound but also by a key colour, C sharp minor, heard nowhere else in the opera. The formality of its lay-out, solo stanza followed by women's chorus, and repetition in which the soloist adds a descant to the chorus, aptly conveys familiar duties soothingly done, and the piece affords Elizabeth the respite she needs before addressing the political implications of the foregoing action. Cecil's entrance finds her ready to lead in the denunciation of Essex's wilful behaviour, though Cecil skilfully gives an analysis of the situation apparently so measured that it encourages the Queen to a greater decisiveness. In a scene almost consistently dominated by a chain of minor keys (see Ex. 11), Cecil's Report (like his suave advice in Act 1) is supported on a series of major triads: only his final understatement, 'I see a certain danger', reinstates the minor as a cue for Elizabeth's indignation. Their discussion of the steps to be taken to curb Essex is in G minor, but as Elizabeth becomes more emphatic in her pronouncements, the bass slowly rises by degrees, until the initial E minor of this scene is regained; this is the last of the

Ex. 11

minor-third tonal shifts that provide the structural foundations of the scene. With E minor there returns also the unifying music of the opening fugato, but now its figurations are repetitive, not expansive, and the only appearance of the chord that had presaged Essex's downfall is subdued by Elizabeth's final phrase, 'It is I who have to rule' (Ex. 9).

In terms of Britten's numbering there are eight units in this scene, while in terms of its tonal scheme (summarized in Ex. 11) one elaborate circuit connects the opening to the closing E minor. Our experience in the theatre is likely to be of neither of these extremes, but of a cycle of urgent musico-dramatic events, retarded at one point by a lyrical interlude. To dub this scene a 'typical' structure would be misleading, for no two scenes of *Gloriana* are shaped in remotely similar ways, but it serves rather to show the typical versatility with which Britten, having set out the groundplan of a 'number' opera, is able to reconcile this with his concern for dramatic exigencies and cumulative impact.

6

Gloriana: A List of Sources

PAUL BANKS AND ROSAMUND STRODE

BACKGROUND

To accompany the Britten–Pears School Study Course on *Gloriana* the Britten–Pears Library mounted an exhibition of material relating to the opera. This was prepared by Rosamund Strode and Philip Reed, with a photographic display by Pamela Wheeler and was open to members of the course on 7 September 1991. The exhibition, consisting of 32 items, was introduced by Miss Strode, and gave a brief glimpse into the work's compositional history. This talk and the exhibition were the starting point for the present list of sources, and some of the captions and notes in the *Handlist* which accompanied the exhibition have been incorporated into the descriptions of the sources.

However the present list had another important predecessor. In October 1991, at a Conference *The Thematic Catalogue of F. Liszt's Musical Works* at the Liszt Memorial Museum, Budapest, Paul Banks presented a paper on the problems of preparing a thematic catalogue of Britten's music. As an example embodying some of the issues posed by such a project, a draft catalogue entry for one work, *Curlew River*, was prepared.[1] Since the main problems are not so much concerned with the organization of the catalogue as a whole, but rather with the layout of individual entries, *Curlew River* offered an excellent illustration. The task was to arrive at a design which would present bibliographic information about the extraordinarily numerous and varied sources for the work in a way which was accessible both to the general user and the specialist. The basic model was that of Kern Holoman's magisterial *Catalogue of the Works of Hector Berlioz* (Kassel: Bärenreiter, 1990) but increasingly modifications were adopted to handle the complex array of sources for *Curlew River*.

The experience gained with this first attempt at a catalogue entry for a major Britten work was invaluable, and encouraged the idea of expanding the

---

[1] See 'Encompassing a plenitude: cataloguing the works of Benjamin Britten', *Studia Musicologica Academiae Scientiarum Hungaricae*, xxiv (1992), forthcoming. These issues were treated at greater length at a meeting of the Royal Musical Association on 28 November 1992 at which Philip Reed and Paul Banks presented interlinked papers: 'The compositional history of Benjamin Britten's *Curlew River*' and 'A Britten thematic catalogue: *Curlew River* as a test case.'

material prepared for the *Gloriana* exhibition into another trial entry. This opera offered a new set of challenges: a large work, but one for which the surviving sources were a less complete record than for *Curlew River*. But more significant was the fact that whereas the church parable inspired no 'spin-offs', *Gloriana* itself exists in two versions, and also provided material for at least fifteen other works, or arrangements completed during the composer's lifetime, all of which had to be included in a single, accessible entry. In addition the opportunity has been taken of providing more extensive bibliographical information than was attempted in the *Curlew River* list.

The description which follows is a user's guide to the list, but not a detailed account of the descriptive and organizational conventions employed – the Britten–Pears Library cataloguing manual has a 40-page section covering the processing of printed and manuscript music.

SCOPE OF THE LIST

The list makes no claims to comprehensiveness, but it does seek to include descriptions of all the relevant musical and literary sources in the most significant collections of material relating to the work and its history up to Britten's death: the Britten-Pears Library (*GB-ALb*),[2] the material held by Boosey & Hawkes (*GB-Lbh*), the Music Library of English National Opera (*GB-Leno*), the Holst Foundation Collection (*GB-ALhf*), the British Library (*GB-Lbl*), and the private collection of Rosamund Strode (*GB-ALrs*). Two other, potentially important, collections (the Plomer Collection at Durham University Library, and the music library of the Royal Opera House, Covent Garden) hold no primary source material for the opera.

So many of the sources for *Curlew River* survive that it was possible to include entries for most of the lost material in the source list for that work. In the case of *Gloriana* unlocated and lost sources are included less comprehensively, and only where their existence can be inferred with some certainty, and to clarify entries for material which does survive. Thus the present list does not offer an exhaustive account of the stemmatic relationships between the sources it records, though it does offer a considerable amount of information about the main connecting patterns.

A complete discography is not offered in this list,[3] but recordings of textual or historic importance are included, e.g. recordings of first performances and of performances under the composer's baton or supervision. Material relating to set and costume designs has not been included in the list. Although it is envisaged that a Britten thematic catalogue would contain bibliographic references, none are included here, but have been incorporated into the separate bibliography prepared by Antonia Malloy (see pp. 171–81).

---

2 See pp. x–xi for a list of the library sigla employed.
3 A basic list of published recordings is offered by Charles H. Parsons, *A Benjamin Britten Discography* (Lewiston: The Edwin Mellen Press, 1990).

ORGANIZATION OF THE LIST

As in the trial entry for *Curlew River* the predominant principle of organization is chronological, so the list is divided into seventeen separate sections for each version or derived work, which appear in order of completion. The list begins with the title and sub-title,[4] and a summary of the variants and related works, the latter acting as an index for the list as a whole. The letters assigned to variants and related works in this index are used where necessary in references to individual sources in the form (A)/V10.3.

Sub-entries are divided into two sections. The first presents information about the work, its content, first performance, publication and an outline of its history, all aimed at the general reader. This is followed by a detailed description of the sources. The opening section will thus contain some or all of the following elements:

Author of text
Source of text
Dedication
A list of acts and scenes or movements
Cast and instrumentation
Duration[5]
Date of composition or arrangement
First performance[6]
Publication
Notes[7]

Where there is more than a handful of sources the section devoted to the description of sources begins with a list of the categories of material included in the entry, which acts as an index for what follows. The categories are arranged in a broadly chronological sequence appropriate for the work concerned. Descriptions vary in the amount of information they supply: it has not been possible to examine all the sources listed, and for some material (e.g. orchestral part sets) exhaustive description would have greatly increased the size and complexity of the list. A typical full description of a printed or manuscript source would include:

Item number

This consists of an appropriate letter followed by one or more digits in smaller type. If more than one copy of an item is listed, a decimal point is employed

---

4 Normally from a published source, or from *Benjamin Britten: a complete catalogue of his published works* (London: Boosey & Hawkes and Faber Music, 1973), or (if unpublished) from an appropriate manuscript source. Any significant discrepancies are noted.
5 Normally this could be derived from Britten's own recording(s) of the work; here the Boosey & Hawkes/Faber Catalogue is normally the source. Where that catalogue provides no information, an editorial timing is provided.
6 Includes date, place of performance and a list of performers etc.
7 A brief outline of the work's history.

(see (A)/V10.1–V10.4). The numbering sequence recommences for each sub-entry, except for the two versions of the opera itself: for ease of reference the item numbers for the revised version (M) continue the sequence begun for (A).[8]

Descriptive heading

This seeks to indicate the type of source being described, and in particular to locate it in the appropriate stemma (supplementary information may follow in parentheses).

Description of method of origination and annotations

For manuscripts this element includes details of the implements used and (if non-holograph) the identity of the scribe(s). One terminological usage requires explanation: 'manuscript' is used for arrangements in the hand of the arranger, 'ms. copy' for hand-written copies of any other type of non-holograph manuscript material.

If annotations, revisions or corrections are present in any source, their presence is always noted here, together with details of implements used, and (where possible) the identity of the scribe.[9]

Many processes were used to reproduce Britten's music over the years, and no comprehensive description is yet possible; the terms used here (e.g. printed, dyeline, photocopy) seek merely to distinguish between processes on the broadest level.

Title

Where present in the source, the title-page or equivalent is printed here (in italics) in diplomatic transcription. Capitalization of the original is followed, but no attempt is made to reflect changes in type-face. If transcribed from any part of the source other than the title-page, a note is appended below the main description.

Date

Manuscripts and other unpublished sources: given as stated on the item, or, if none present, supplied in square brackets, if possible.

Published sources: as above, but if none present, the date of copyright will be given (where known), in the form 'c1954'.

In editorially supplied dates a question mark follows any element of the date which cannot be established with certainty.

---

[8] In addition the descriptive headings for published texts adopts a similar procedure: the first publication of the revised vocal score is described as the third edition (not the first edition of the revised version).

[9] It should be noted that the relatively simple form of description does not necessarily establish any connections between a particular type of addition, implement or scribe.

Physical description

Manuscripts:

(a) the extent of the item in numbers of volumes (if more than one) and/or folios, (b) description of the paper(s) used,[10] (c) reference to binding (if present), (d) overall dimensions of the manuscript, (e) description of any additional material, particularly paste-overs.

Printed and other sources:

(a) the extent of the item in numbers of volumes (if more than one) and/or pagination,[11] (b) reference to binding (if present), (c) overall dimensions of the item (for published items the height only is given), (d) description of any additional material.

Analysis

This section indicates how the content of the item is laid out on the constituent folios or pages. The folio numbers (manuscripts) or page numbers (most other sources) for the section concerned are followed by a statement of the content (if editorially supplied it is given in roman, if from the item itself, it is given in italic font); if required, additional information (including an indication of any original foliation or pagination) is supplied within parentheses. For abbreviations, see p. x.

Collation

This section describes the fascicle structure of manuscript items. The folio numbers are followed by an upper-case roman letter indicating the fascicle(s) concerned, and a superscript digit giving the number of leaves (not sheets) present,[12] e.g. A^6. If single leaves are present in the gathering, their presence is indicated in the form A^{6+2} and their precise location specified within the parentheses which follow. If two or more consecutive gatherings share the same structure, this would be indicated in the form $B-G^6$. Additional information follows in parentheses and may include all or some of the following: a statement of paper type used in the gathering, location of single leaves, identity of scribal hands.

Details of printing

For published items this may include some or all of the following elements: (a) the print code as stated on the item, (b) the date on which the printing was ordered, (c) the date on which the completed printing was received by the publisher, (d) the size of the print run. It should be noted that not all printed

---

[10] The elements are (a) number of staves, (b) maker's mark if present and (c) total span from the lowest line of the bottom stave, to the highest line on the top stave. If more than one paper is present, the description is preceded by an upper case letter: these letters are used to identify the paper type in the collation and notes.

[11] Exceptionally foliation may be used.

[12] Letters are not assigned to 'gatherings' consisting of a single folio.

sources were published (i.e. on sale to the public): some were available for hire only.

Contents

Where necessary a summary of the item's contents is given.

Film numbers

The Britten–Pears Library is microfilming its holdings of manuscript and other primary source material as a part of its security and conservation policies. Where appropriate the film and frame numbers are given for items within this collection.

Notes

These elaborate, explain or qualify information given in the description, or supply further details. The entry ends with the appropriate library or collection siglum and a catalogue or shelf-number where available.

Where a text was issued in several editions or impressions, each is assigned a separate entry and number, but only those elements of the description which differentiate the edition or impression from others are included. Similarly repetition of information is avoided in descriptions of additional copies of sources.

Some items are described as 'file copies' and belong to a set of printed copies of most of Britten's music kept at *GB-ALb*. These copies are usually first or early impressions containing corrections and perhaps minor revisions made by the composer, or entered with his authority. Such corrections and revisions were sent to the publishers concerned for inclusion in reprints, and when incorporated into a reprint would be 'ticked off' in the file copy. Any corrections of revisions made subsequently would again be entered and the process repeated. Some file copies were also used by the composer as performance copies. Most file copies are bound in blue cloth, with the composer's initials on the front cover; a few copies bound after his death have these initials enclosed within parentheses.

Descriptions of recordings are broadly similar in organization to those of printed sources, and include matrix and catalogue numbers (if appropriate), details of the sound carrier, performers and the date and place of recording (the date is given in reverse order, i.e. yy.mm.dd.)

Gloriana[13]

An Opera in Three Acts, op. 53[14]

Versions and related works   page

---

[13] There is some evidence that at an early stage the opera was known as *Elizabeth and Essex* (letter from Ernst Roth to Britten, 11 July 1952; see also Pears' letter to Mary Behrend cited on p. 20).

[14] Originally the opus number was to be 52. See the Notes to the original version and (A)/H2.

(A) Original version (1953)

Authors of text: William Plomer; Robert Devereux, Second Earl of Essex.

Source of text: *Elizabeth & Essex, a Tragic History* by Lytton Strachey; *Queen Elizabeth I*, by J.E. Neale.[15]

Dedication: *This work is dedicated by gracious permission to HER MAJESTY QUEEN ELIZABETH II in honour of whose Coronation it was composed.*

ACT I

Scene 1
1. Prelude
2. The tournament
3. Recitative and Fight
4. Entrance of the Queen
5. Recitative
6. The two lords' explanation
7. Raleigh's Song
8. Ensemble of Reconciliation
9. Recitative and Final March

Scene 2
1. Prelude and Dialogue
2. The Queen's Song
3. Cecil's Song of Government
4. Recitative and Essex's entry
5. First Lute Song
6. Second Lute Song
7. The First Duet for The Queen and Essex
8. Soliloquy and Prayer

ACT II

Scene 1
1. Prelude and Welcome
2. The Masque
    First Dance. TIME
    Second Dance. CONCORD
    Third Dance. TIME and CONCORD
    Fourth Dance. COUNTRY GIRLS
    Fifth Dance. RUSTICS and FISHERMEN
    Sixth Dance. Final Dance of Homage
3. Finale

Scene 2
1. Prelude and Song
2. Duet
3. Double Duet
4. Quartet

---

[15] For copies of these books which were, or may have been used during work on the opera, see (A)/L1.1-L2.

102

Scene 3
1. Pavane
2. Conversation
3. Galliard
4. Conversation and The Queen's Entrance
5. Lavolta
6. Conversation
7. Morris Dance
8. Recitative
9. The Queen's Burlesque
10. Quartet
11. March
12. The Queen's Announcement
13. Ensemble
14. Coranto

ACT III
Scene 1
1. Prelude and Chatter
2. Essex's Intrusion
3. The Second Duet of the Queen and Essex
4. The Dressing-Table Song
5. The entrance of Cecil
6. Cecil's Report
7. Discussion
8. The Queen's Decision

Scene 2 Ballad-Rondo[16]

Scene 3
[1.] Prelude and Verdict
2. Cecil's Warning
3. The Queen's Dilemma
4. Trio
5. Lady Essex's Pleading
6. Penelope Rich's Pleading
7. Epilogue

Cast and instrumentation: Queen Elizabeth the First (sop.), Robert Devereux, Earl of
Essex (ten.), Frances, Countess of Essex (mezzo), Charles Blount, Lord Mountjoy
(bar.), Penelope, Lady Rich, sister to Essex (sop.), Sir Robert Cecil, Secretary of
the Council (bar.), Sir Walter Raleigh, Captain of the Guard (bass), Henry Cuffe, a
satellite of Essex (bar.), a Lady-in-Waiting (sop.), a blind Ballad-Singer (bass), the
Recorder of Norwich (bass), a Housewife (mezzo), the Spirit of the Masque (ten.),
the Master of Ceremonies (ten.), the City Crier (bar.). Chorus: Citizens, Maids of
Honour, Ladies and Gentlemen of the Household, Courtiers, Masquers, Old
Men, Men and Boys of Essex's following, Councillors. Dancers: Time, Concord,
Country Girls, Rustics, Fishermen, Morris Dancer. Actors: Pages, Ballad-Singer's
runner, Sir John Harington, French Ambassador, Archbishop of Canterbury,
Phantom Kings and Queens.

---

[16] The five verses of the Ballad are identified as such in the published scores.

3 fls (II, III doubling picc.), 2 obs, english horn, 2 cls, bass cl., 2 bsns, dbsn, 4 hns, 3 trpts, 3 trbs, tuba, timpani, perc., hp, strings. Instruments on the stage: 1.i, trpts (multiples of three); 2.iii, orchestra for dances: five strings and/or five woodwind, pipe (flute), tabor (small side drum without snares); 3.ii, gittern; 3.iii, cymbals, side drum, bass drum, wind machine;[17] on-stage: hp.

Duration: Act I   42 min.

             Act II   50 min.

             Act III 56 min.

Date of composition: September? 1952 - 13 March 1953.

First performance: 8 June 1953, Royal Opera House, Covent Garden (Royal Gala, in the presence of H.M. the Queen). Queen Elizabeth I: Joan Cross; Earl of Essex: Peter Pears; Lady Essex: Monica Sinclair; Lord Mountjoy: Geraint Evans; Penelope, Lady Rich: Jennifer Vyvyan; Sir Robert Cecil: Arnold Matters; Sir Walter Raleigh: Frederick Dalberg; Henry Cuffe: Ronald Lewis; Lady-in-Waiting: Adèle Leigh; a blind Ballad-Singer: Inia Te Wiata; the Recorder of Norwich: Michael Langdon; a Housewife: Edith Coates; the Spirit of the Masque: William McAlpine; the Master of Ceremonies: David Tree; the City Crier: Rhydderch Davies; Time: Desmond Doyle; Concord: Svetlana Beriosova; Morris Dancer: Johaar Mosevaal.
Designer: John Piper; producer: Basil Coleman; choreographer: John Cranko, chorus master: Douglas Robinson; conductor: John Pritchard.

Publication:

Libretto: London: Boosey & Hawkes, Ltd., 1953; 1973 (second impression).[18]

Vocal score: London: Boosey & Hawkes, Ltd., June 1953 (limited edition); November 1953 (second edition); 1966 (second edition, second impression).

Choral score: unpublished; available, on hire only from Boosey & Hawkes Ltd.

Full score: unpublished; available, on hire only, from Boosey & Hawkes Ltd.

Instrumental parts: unpublished; available, on hire only, from Boosey & Hawkes Ltd.

Notes

The early history of the work is recounted in detail by Philip Reed in chapter 2. All that need be added here are two legal details: Britten signed his assignment of the work to Boosey & Hawkes on 15 May 1952, and Plomer his on 15 July.

During the autumn of 1953, after the first run of performances, further work on the opera was undertaken: the second edition of the vocal score was prepared (to replace the hastily-produced and error-ridden deluxe first edition), and the main text of the opera was itself subjected to revision as was recorded by Imogen Holst in a fascinating diary entry for 2 November:[19]

[Ben had] asked me to go round and work at GLORIANA mistakes in the score: — he began by talking about general criticisms. Tony Gishford had felt the character of Essex was incomplete in the libretto. We discussed it and he said again, what he'd said months ago, that Joan and

[17] Though designated as stage percussion in (A)/H3, these instruments were presumably to be placed off-stage.

[18] See (M)/L20

[19] All passages from this unpublished diary quoted here are c 1993 the Estate of Imogen Holst, and may not be reproduced further without written permission. They appear here by kind permission of the Estate of Imogen Holst.

Peter's love scenes were all right for a small theatre but wouldn't do in Covent Garden.

Something of the extent and nature of the revisions is revealed later in the entry:

[Britten] talked of altering several details — the bar before "Love's better than fear" [1.ii.2] — which always hangs fire. He said was it wrong in the music? .... He decided to add horns. He also altered the strings' dynamics at Essex's first entry [1.ii.4], from *sfp* to *f* , and added a perc roll and *cresc* to take out the abruptness of the trumpet's quavers. And he marked down the muted trumpets at the "Jackal" to *pp* from *mf* [1.ii.7] — I was enormously relieved, because it's always been too loud. At the beginning of the Masque scene he took <u>all</u> the strings' *dims* out, saying that it had been an error of judgment, as the wind and brass had the *dims*.

The revisions were completed the following day but for some reason they were not entered into the orchestral parts until shortly before the rehearsals for the 1954 performances: as Imogen Holst recorded in her diary, it was only her valiant efforts, assisted by those of Malcolm Williamson (then working at Boosey & Hawkes), that saved the day:

January 24th 1954

... Went to the V. & A. for Ben and Peter's recital - Sue [Pears] told me there'd been a crisis about the orchestral parts of *Gloriana* - none of the corrections had been put in.... Went round to the artists' room afterwards; Erwin [Stein] with a very long face about the orchestral parts...

January 25th

I rang Ben up just after 9 to ask if I could help with the parts — he asked me to ring Erwin. I went round to Boosey's and Erwin asked me to go with Malcolm Williamson to Covent Garden. We worked in the library all day — terrific hard work and concentration. Got a glimpse of Ben and Peter at the end of the rehearsal while I was collecting the full score from Goodall (even the <u>score</u> hadn't got the corrections in!) ....

January 26th

Went back to the library at Covent Garden.... <u>Finished the corrections</u>, by working non-stop....[20]

January 27th

Orchestral rehearsal at Covent Garden, Acts I and II. V[ery] anxious about having missed mistakes. Some of the things we'd put in were no better....

Alterations to the production of the opera were discussed by Britten and Basil Coleman over lunch on 13 December[21] perhaps including the omission of the Norwich scene and the procession of ghosts in the Epilogue, both of which were effected in the 1954 performances (see p. 37).

One final sidelight on the work: the opera should have been numbered as op. 52, and it is this number which appears on the wrapper to the group of leaves discarded from the composition draft ((A)/H2). However Britten found the appropriateness of '53' for the Coronation opera of that year irresistible, so *Winter Words*, though composed later, inherited '52'.

---

[20] A note in the transcript, edited by Imogen Holst in 1981, adds 'IH remembers how Malcolm Williamson was completely worn out and said "Do you always work as hard as this?"'

[21] Imogen Holst, diary entry.

Sources

Librettos:	Manuscript/typescript librettos	L1-L13
	First edition	L14
Holographs		H1-H4
Vocal scores:	Manuscript/interim	V1-V6
	Printed editions	V7-V11
Choral scores		CS1-CS3
Full scores		F1-F2
Orchestral Parts		P1-P5
Miscellaneous material		M1-M4
Recordings		Rec1-Rec5

Librettos

L1.1   Annotated text source *(Elizabeth & Essex, a Tragic History* by Lytton Strachey (London, Chatto & Windus, 1928)). Printed; with annotations (Lord Harewood). [Item not inspected.]

       Soon after returning from Gargallen, and before William Plomer had been invited to collaborate with Britten on *Gloriana*, Lord Harewood marked up a copy of Strachey's book, dividing it up into operatic scenes.[22]   Private Collection

L1.2   - Another copy (unannotated).   *GB-ALb* 9300226

L1.3   - Another copy *(Elizabeth & Essex : a Tragic History* by Lytton Strachey (London : Chatto & Windus, 1948) (Collected Works of Lytton Strachey)). Printed; with annotation : pencil (Benjamin Britten?).[23]

       Accompanied by the Earl of Harewood's invitation addressed to a private view of the Royal Academy summer exhibition on 4 May 1951. On the *verso* a ms. genealogy in the hand of Lord Harewood shows his descent from Robert, second Earl of Essex.   *GB-ALb* 2-9100092

L2   Text source *(Queen Elizabeth* by J. E. Neale (London: Jonathan Cape, 1950)).

       Although not annotated or inscribed this could be the copy sent to Britten by Plomer on 8 May 1952 'as a sort of corrective to Lytton Strachey'.   *GB-ALb* 9300225

L3   Scenario (unfinished holograph). Holograph: pencil (Benjamin Britten). - *Gloriana*. - [July 1952]. - [1] fol., headed paper of the DET FORENEDE DAMPSKIBS-SELSKAB AKTIESELSKAB ; 21.9 x 13.9 cm.

       CONTENTS: ends after 2.ii.

       This draft probably dates from 1-6 July 1952.[24]   *GB-ALb* 2-9200291

L4   Scenario (holograph). Holograph: pencil (Benjamin Britten). - [Untitled]. - [July 1952]. - [1] fol., headed paper of the DET FORENEDE DAMPSKIBS-SELSKAB AKTIESELSKAB ; 21.9 x 13.9 cm.

       This draft probably dates from 1-6 July 1952.[24]   *GB-ALb* 2-9200292

L5   Scenario (2.ii-2.iii, foliated). Holograph: purple ink (William Plomer). - [Untitled]. - [July 1952]. - [4] fol. : cream, ruled ; 20.3 x 16 cm.

---

[22] See above, p. 18.

[23] For a discussion of this annotation, see p. 21.

[24] Information from Antonia Malloy. Britten was in Copenhagen during this period.

ANALYSIS: [All versos blank.] [1-2] *Act 2. Scene 1.*[sic] ... *Scene 2.* (= fol. 1-2), [3-4] *Act 2. Scene 3.* (= fol. 1-2).
COLLATION: [1-4] single sheets.
CONTENTS: 2.ii-2.iii only.
The leaves have been torn from a notebook and probably date from 7-24 July 1952, with fol. [3-4] pre-dating fol. [1-2].[24]   *GB-ALb* 2-9200296

L6   First draft (various foliations). Holograph, typescript: violet ink, red ink (William Plomer); with annotations, revisions and corrections: blue ballpoint, pencil, blue pencil (William Plomer, Benjamin Britten). - [Untitled]. - [July? 1952 - January? 1953]. - [126] fol. : [A:] white ; 22.7 x 17.7 cm. : [B:] blue ; 25.4 x 20.4 cm. : [C:] white, headed 'Harewood House/Leeds' ; 20.4 x 15.2 cm. : [D:] white, ruled ; 20.3 x 16.2 cm. : [E:] cream ; 25.15 x 20.4 cm. : [F:] cream ; 28 x 21.6 cm.
ANALYSIS: [Unless otherwise indicated the *versos* are blank] [1-20] *ACT I. SCENE 1* (= fol. 1-4, X, 1, 2/1-4/3, 5/1/4, 6, 7/3-11/7, 12, 13/8, 14, 15; [6^v] notes by Plomer, [11^v] note to Act I, sc. 2 by Plomer, [19^v] fol. 6/2, [20^v] fol. 9), [21-35] *ACT 1. SCENE 2.* (= fol. 1-4, 4a, 5, [unfoliated], 6-13; [21^v] music sketch by Britten), [36-46] *Act II, sc. 1* (= tp, 1-10); [47-57] *Act 2. Scene 1.* (= tp, 1-10), [58-67] *ACT 2. SCENE 3.* (= tp, 1-9), [68-78] *ACT 2. SCENE 3* (= tp, 1-10); [79-94] *ACT 3. SCENE 1.* (= tp, 1-5, A, 6-8, 8a/8, 9-11, 12/11), [95-107] *Act 3, Scene 2* (= tp, 1-10, 1-2; [100^v], 101^v, 106^v] = additional text), [108-126] *ACT 3. SCENE 3* (= 1-9, 10/7, 11/8, 6, 1-4, 5/6-6/5, 7).
COLLATION: [Most single leaves:] [1-5] (type A), [6-24] (type B), [25] (type A), [26-56] (type B), [57] (type A), [58-84] (type B), [85-89] (type A), [90] (type B), [91-92] A^2 (type A) [93] (type A), [94-105] (type B), [106-7] (type C), [108-112] (type B), [113-116] (type D), [117] (type B), [118] (type B cut down), [119] (type E, typescript[25]), [120-126] (type F).
This manuscript contains numerous annotations, a musical sketch and a stage-layout sketch by Britten and two versions of 2.iii.
Fol. [36-46, 95-118, 120-126], punched for insertion into a ring binder.
The libretto originally ended on [119^r]. Paper [A] and [D] torn from notebooks.
Because of the speed at which the opera was created, Britten used some sections of this source (which was assembled over several months) while composing, rather than the second, typescript draft.   According to Antonia Malloy, fol. [106-107] were part of a separate working-out of the text, and may even date from the time of revisions to the typescript. Fol. [113-116] were probably inserted to replace a leaf which was discarded and subsequently lost; fol. [119] appears to be the sole surviving page of the top copy of the first layer in L10.1.   *GB-ALb* 2-9200295

L7   Revision sketch (3.i). Holograph: blue ballpoint (William Plomer). - *Act 3: Sc. 1 p 7.* - [late 1952]. - [1] fol. : cream, ruled ; 17.9 x 11.1 cm.
ANALYSIS: [1^r] sketch, [1^v] blank.
COLLATION: [1] single sheet.
Torn from a ring-bound notebook.   Contains additional lines for the Lady-in-Waiting which appear at the foot of p. 7 in the second draft (L10.1), but which do not appear in the first (L6).   *GB-ALb* 2-9200298

---

25 The typeface is that of L10.1, main machine.

L8 Sketches (2.iii, unfoliated). Holograph: blue ballpoint (William Plomer); with revisions: pencil (William Plomer). - [Untitled]. - [after November 1952]. - [3] fol. : cream, ruled ; 20.3 x 16 cm.
ANALYSIS: [all *versos* blank] [1^r-3^r] sketches.
COLLATION: [1-3] single sheets.
The leaves have been torn from a notebook.
Lines to follow the Pavane, Galliard and Lavolta in 2.iii.
GB-ALb 2-9200297

L9 Revision sketch (3.i). Holograph: blue ballpoint (William Plomer); with revision: pencil (Benjamin Britten). - *at end of* / *Act 3* - *Scene 1*. - [November? 1952]. - [1] fol. : cream, ruled ; 20.3 x 16.2 cm.
ANALYSIS: [1^r] sketch, [1^v] blank.
COLLATION: [1] single sheet.
The leaf has been torn from a notebook.
A version of the Queen's concluding lines to the scene expanding the text of the first draft, L6.   *GB-ALb* 2-9200299

L10.1 Second draft (various foliations). Holograph, typescript, typescript (black, blue carbon copy): violet ink (Benjamin Britten); with revisions and annotations: black ballpoint, pencil, (Benjamin Britten). - [Untitled]. - [Autumn? 1952-January? 1953]. - [66] fol. : [A:] cream, wm Kingsclere ; 25.5 x 20.5 cm. : [B:] cream ; 25.2 x 20.4 cm. : [C:] white, wm Croxley script ; 25.2 x 20.4 cm. : [D:] white ; 25. 4 x 20.4 cm.
ANALYSIS: [typescript appears on *rectos* only]. [1^{r-v}] Cast, [2^r-12^r] *ACT ONE* / *Scene One* (= fol. 1-11), [13^r-22^r] *ACT ONE* / *Scene Two* (= fol. [1]-10), [23^r-29^r] *ACT TWO* / *Scene One* (= fol. 1-7), [30^r-34^r] *ACT TWO* / *Scene Two* (= fol. [1]-5), [35^r-41^r] *ACT TWO* / *Scene Three* (fol. [1]-6), [42^r-51^r] *ACT THREE* / *Scene One* (= fol. [1]-10), [52^r-57^r] *ACT THREE* / *Scene Two* (= fol. [1]-6), [58^r-66^r] *ACT THREE* / *Scene Three* (= fol. [1]-9).
COLLATION: [all single sheets]. [1] (type A, holograph: Britten), [2-22] (type B, black carbon), [23-29] (type C, blue carbon), [30-51] (type B, black carbon), [52-57] (type C, top copy), [58-62] (type B, black carbon), [63-66] (type D, top copy, not typed on the same machine as the rest of the text).
Paper punched for inclusion in a ring-binder.
Because of the haste with which the opera was created, this typescript, prepared over several months, was not the only libretto source used by Britten during the composition of the opera; see L6 and pp. 37-8 above.
Much of the typing was undertaken by Elizabeth Sweeting, with revisions prepared by Jeremy Cullum, Britten's secretary.[26] The bulk of the work (Act 1, 2.ii-3.i) was completed by the end of November 1952; 3.iii was sent to Plomer on 10 December 1952.
See also L6.   *GB-ALb* 2-9200304

[L10.2] [Second draft (top copy). Typescript (top copy). - Not located.]
The top copy of the original layer in L10.1 has not come to light, but was probably sent to William Plomer.

L10.3 Second draft, replacement leaves (3.ii, foliated). Typescript (blue carbon). - [Untitled]. - [October? 1952-January? 1953]. - 6 fol. : cream ; 25.2 x 20.4 cm.
ANALYSIS: [typescript appears on *rectos* only] 1^r-6^r Text.

---

26 Information from Antonia Malloy.

COLLATION: All single sheets.

A carbon of the top copy inserted into L10.1 ([52-57]) to replace L11.

GB-ALb 2-9200305

L11 Second draft, deleted libretto leaves (3.ii, foliated). Typescript (black carbon); with revisions: black ballpoint, pencil (Benjamin Britten). - *ACT THREE / Scene Two*. - [October-December? 1952]. - 5 fol. : cream ; 25.3 x 20.4 cm.

ANALYSIS: 1^r typescript, 1^v revisions, 2^r typescript, 2^v revisions, 3^r typescript, 3^v revisions, 4^r typescript, 4^v blank, 5^r typescript, 5^v blank.

COLLATION: all single sheets.

Title from fol. 1^r. Paper punched for inclusion in a ring-binder.

This is an early version of the text and follows closely the revised text in L6. These leaves probably formed part of L10.1, but were replaced by fol. [52-57] in that source.   GB-ALb 2-9200302

[L12] [Incomplete typescript libretto (2.i only). - [before December 1952] - Not located.]

Probably a carbon copy of fol. [23-29] in L10.1. This was sent to Ninette de Valois in December 1952 as part of the protracted negotiations surrounding the involvement of the Royal Ballet in the Coronation Gala.[27]

[L13] [Typescript libretto. - [1952-3]. - Not located.]

On 2 March 1953 Ernst Roth asked Britten to send a copy of the libretto to David Adams at Boosey & Hawkes's New York office. The annotation to the letter suggest a copy was indeed sent.

L14.1 First edition, first impression. - *GLORIANA / OPERA IN THREE ACTS / The music by / BENJAMIN BRITTEN / The libretto by / WILLIAM PLOMER / Price 2/6 net / (1953) / BOOSEY & HAWKES, LTD. / London · Paris · Bonn · Capetown · Sydney · Toronto · New York*. - London : Boosey & Hawkes, Ltd., c1953. - 62, [ii] p., red, stiff paper cover ; 20.5 cm.

ANALYSIS: [fo] *WILLIAM PLOMER / GLORIANA / Music by / BENJAMIN BRITTEN / BOOSEY & HAWKES*, [fi] blank, [1] ht, [2] copyright statement, [3] tp, [4] blank, 5-6 *CHARACTERS*, 7-24 *ACT I*, 25-40 *ACT TWO*, 41-62 *ACT THREE*, [i] blank, [ii], advert (no. 643, dated 11.51), [ri-ro] blank.

PRINT CODE: none   DELIVERED: 3.6.53

PRINT RUN: 2500

The reference to the chamber pot which the Lord Chamberlain required should be removed (see above, p. 14) was printed in this and both later publications of the libretto, and all editions of the music.

L14.2 - Annotated copy. Printed; with annotations: blue ballpoint.

Black ballpoint annotation on front cover (Rosamund Strode): 'Marked on pages 26-29'.   GB-ALb 2-9100238

L14.3 - Another copy.

Initialled on ht (pencil:) 'BB'.   GB-ALb 2-9200206

For further copies of L13 revised in 1966, see (M)/L17-19.

For the second impression of the first edition, see (M)/L20.

---

[27] See p. 44 above.

Holograph manuscripts

H1   Composition draft (signed, various paginations). Holograph: pencil. - *Gloriana* /
[rule] / *BB* / *Act I*. - [September? 1952-February 1953]. - 3 vol. (fol. [1-33],
[34-67], [68-99]) : [A:] 24 staves, [span:] 33.4 cm. ; 36.5 x 27 cm. : [B:] 24
staves, [span:] 32.1 cm. ; 36 x 26.3 cm.

ANALYSIS: Volume I: [1^r] tp, [1^v] blank, [2^r-17^v] Act I, sc. I (= pp. 1-31), [17^r]
deleted sketch (= p. 32), [18^r-32^r] Act I, sc. 2 (= pp. 1-28), [32^v-33^r] blank,
[33^v] sketch.

Volume II: [34^r] tp, [34^v] blank, [35^r-43^r] Act II, sc. 1 (= pp. 1-17), [43^v]
blank, [44^r] sketch for Prelude to Act II, sc. 2, [44^v-52^r] Act II, sc. 2
(= pp. 1-16), [52^v] blank, [53^r-66^r] Act II, sc. 3 (= pp. 1-27), [66^v-67^r] blank,
[67^v] sketch.

Volume III: [68^r] tp, [68^v] blank, [69^r-80^v] Act III, sc. 1 (= pp. 1-24), [81^r-
88^v] Act III, sc. 2, (= pp. 1-[16]), [89^r-98^r] Act III, sc. 3 (= pp. 1-19), [98^v]
sketch, [99^r] blank, [99^v] sketch.

COLLATION: Volume I: [1, 33] wrapper (type A), [2-5] A-B^2 (type B), [6-7] C^2
(type A), [8] (type B = pp. 13-14), [9-16] D-G^2 (type B), [17] (type B), [18-
30] H-N^2 (type A), [32] (type A).

Volume II (all type A): [34, 67] wrapper, [35-42] O-R^2, [43], [44-46] single
sheets, [47-52] S-U^2, [53], [54-64] V-Z^2, [66].

Volume III (all type A): [68, 99] wrapper, [69-98] AA-AO^2.

FILM NUMBERS: A3 (frames 2-201).

Britten's habitual word for such mss was 'sketch' (see the wrapper to H2);
for a notation which might be more conventionally described as a sketch,
see L6.[28]   *GB-ALb* 2-9202574

---

[28]   Britten seems to have begun work on the draft at the beginning of September 1952. By
17 October he had completed Act I, and was starting on 2.ii. The later stages of Britten's work
on this manuscript can be traced in some detail in Imogen Holst's unpublished diary covering
the period September 1952-March 1954.

30 Sep. 1952	1.i completed
1 Oct. 1952	1.ii begun.
8 Oct. 1952	1.ii, no. 3 completed.
9 Oct. 1952	Both lute songs composed.
14 Oct. 1952	Britten 'was depressed about the Masque scene in *Gloriana* [2.i] because he had no idea what to do with the dances'.
19 Oct. 1952	Britten played through the completed Act I.
24 Oct. 1952	Played the beginning of 2.ii to Imogen Holst and William Plomer.
30 Oct. 1952	Britten played through the end of 2.ii to Imogen Holst; he was having problems with the Courtly Dances.
3 Nov. 1952	Imogen Holst showed Britten the Elizabethan dance steps she had learned a few days earlier in Oxford.
4 Nov. 1952	Britten played the Pavane and Galliard to Imogen Holst.
7 Nov. 1952	Britten played 'the first half of Lavolta and the little bit of recit leading up to it' to Imogen Holst.
17 Nov. 1952	2.iii had progressed, at least as far as the beginning of *No. 9 The Queen's Burlesque*.
20 Nov. 1952	Britten was working on *No. 11 March*.
23 Nov. 1952	By this date 2.ii-iii were complete. (A letter written to Plomer on this day indicates that work on 3.i was about to begin.)
26 Nov. 1952	Work on 3.i was under way.
2 Dec. 1952	Britten played the completed section of 3.i (probably to the end of no. 4) to Imogen Holst.
9 Dec. 1952	3.i completed.

H2 Composition draft, discarded leaves (signed, dated). Holograph: pencil; with annotations: blue ink, blue ballpoint (Benjamin Britten). - *op.* 52 [sic] / *GLORIANA* / [rule] / *SKETCHES* / *LIBRETTO BY WILLIAM PLOMER* / *Benjamin Britten* / <u>*ALDEBURGH 1953*</u>. - 1953. - Aldeburgh. - [9] fol. : [A:] 24 staves, [span:] 33.4 cm. ; 36.5 x 27 cm. : [B:] 24 staves, [span:] 32.1 cm. ; 36 x 26.3 cm.

ANALYSIS: [1^r] tp, [1^v] blank, [2^{r-v}] Act I, sc. 1, [3^{r-v}] Act I, sc. 1, [4^r] Act II, sc. 3, [4^v] blank, [5^r] Ballad-singer's melody (3.ii) and unidentified sketches, [5^v] blank, [6^r-7^v, 8^{r-v}, 9^{r-v}] Act III, sc. 2.

COLLATION: [1, 9] wrapper (type A), [2] (type B, replaced by fol. [8] in H1), [3] (type B, replaced by fol. [11] in H1; c.f. [17^v] in H1), [4] (type A, replaced by fol. [53] in H1), [5] (type A), [6-7] A^2 (type A; replaced by [85-6] in H1), [8] (type A).

FILM NUMBERS: A3 (frames 202-217).

The opus number was subsequently revised: see p. 105 above.

GB-ALb 2-9202575

H3 Full score (fair copy, signed, paginated). Holograph and non-holograph ms: black ink (Imogen Holst); with annotations, corrections and revisions, pencil, black ink, blue ink (Imogen Holst, Benjamin Britten). - [Ink, Benjamin Britten:] <u>*GLORIANA*</u> *AN OPERA IN THREE ACTS* / *by* / *William Plomer* / *THE MUSIC BY Benjamin Britten op. 53*. - [1953]. - 3 vol. (fol. [1-61], [62-125], [126-207]) : 34 staves, [maker:] SCHIRMER / IMPERIAL BRAND / No. 14-34 Staves / [rule] / Printed in U.S.A., [span:] 45.15 cm. ; 50.8 x 34 cm.

ANALYSIS: Volume I: [1^r] tp, [1^v] blank [2^r] *CAST*, [2^v] blank, [3^r] Act I tp, [3^v] blank, [4^r-35^v] *ACT I SCENE I* (= pp. 1-64), [36^r-61^v] *ACT I SCENE II* (= pp. 65-166).

Volume II: [62^r] Act II tp, [62^v] blank, [63^r-79^v] *ACT II SCENE I* (= pp. 117-148), [80^v-92^r] *ACT II SCENE II* (= pp. 149-173), [92^v-125^v] *ACT II SCENE III* (= pp. 174-240).

Volume III: [126^r] Act III tp, [126^v] blank, [127^r-158^v] *ACT III SCENE I* (= pp. 241-304), [159^r-176^v] *ACT III SCENE II* (= pp. 305-340), [177^r-206^r] *ACT III SCENE III* (= pp. 341-399), [206^v-207^v] blank.

COLLATION: Volume I: [1-2] single leaves, [3-43] A-E^8, [44-47] F^4, [48-55] G^8, [56-61] H^6.

Volume II: [62], [63-119] A-G^8, [120-125] H^6.

Volume III: [126], [127-166] A-E^8, [167-176] F^{10}, [177-200] G-I^8, [201-206] J^6, [207].

FILM NUMBERS: B11 (frames 3-419).

A relatively clean score with few revisions and no conducting markings. The pencil annotations are not typical of Britten or Imogen Holst.[29]

---

16 Dec. 1952 Britten working on 3.ii.
Britten and Pears were at Harewood House after Christmas, so Imogen Holst's narrative is broken for a short period. When he saw her again on 13 January 1953 Act III was complete.
4 Feb. 1953 Britten was working on the *Second Dance*. CONCORD (2.i) in the aftermath of the 1953 east coast flood.
10 Feb. 1953 Britten working on fourth and fifth dances (2.i).
14 Feb. 1953 A play-through by Britten at Covent Garden.
[29] Work on the manuscript full score can be traced through Imogen Holst's diary entries.
27 Nov. 1952 Britten asked Imogen Holst if she would help by preparing the full score.
15 Feb. 1953 Work began on the full score, having been planned on the 13th.

This score was presented to the British Library by the composer's Executors and the Trustees of the Britten-Pears Library in 1980, on the occasion of the official opening of the Britten-Pears Library. See also (M)/H7-8.　　　　　　　　　　　　　　　　　　*GB-Lbl* Add. MS. 61815

For dyelines prepared from this manuscript, see F1 and (M)/F3, F5, F8-9.

H4　　　Stage orchestra score (paginated). Holograph and non-holograph ms.: black ink, pencil (Imogen Holst); with annotations and revisions: pencil, blue ballpoint (various unidentified hands). - [All Imogen Holst; r.h.:] <u>SCORE</u> // *GLORIANA* / *ACT II SCENE III* / *STAGE ORCHESTRA FOR DANCES.* [1953]. - [12] fol.: 24 staves, [maker:] J.E. & Co. ... / No. 8 / 24 linig, [span:] 29.7 cm. ; 33.8 x 27 cm.

ANALYSIS: [1^r] tp, [1^v-2^v] blank, [3^r-4^r] *ACT II SCENE III* / *1 PAVANE* (= pp. 1-3); [4^r-4^v] *2. CONVERSATION* (= pp. 3-4), [4^v-6^r] *3 GALLIARD* (= pp. 4-7), [6^v] *4. CONVERSATION AND THE QUEEN'S ENTRANCE* (= p. 8), [7^r-8^v] *5 LA VOLTA* (= pp. 9-12), [8^v-9^r] *6 CONVERSATION* (= pp. 12-13), [9^{r-v}] *7 MORRIS DANCE* (= pp. 13-14), [9^v] *8 RECITATIVE* (= pp. 14), [9^v] *9 THE QUEEN'S BURLESQUE* (= p. 14), [9^v-10^r] *QUARTET* (= pp. 14-15) [10^{r-v}] *11 MARCH* (= pp. 15-16), [11^r] *12 THE QUEEN'S ANNOUNCEMENT* (= p. 17), [11^{r-v}] *13 ENSEMBLE* (= pp. 17-18), [11^v-12^v] *14 CORANTO* (= pp. 18-20).

COLLATION: A^{12}

PROVENANCE: on loan from Boosey & Hawkes Music Publishers Limited.

In this manuscript Britten scores the short-score version found in H3 for five-part ensemble (the clefs of which are one treble, two tenor and two bass). The following instrumentation has been indicated in pencil (unidentified hand) at the beginning of the first system: vln + ob., vla 1 + cor anglais 1, vla 2 + cor anglais 2, vcl. 1 + bsn 1, vcl. 2 + bsn 2; this instrumentation seems to have been adopted in the preparation of the part set (P5). Some of the pencil annotations remove unnecessary vocal cues, and others appear to be printer's marks.　　　*GB-ALb* 2-9300508

For photocopies of this score, see F2.1-2.2.

For a dyeline copy used in the preparation of the Symphonic Suite, see (D)/H3.

For a dyeline of this score used in the production of the study score of the opera, see (M)/F7.

---

27 Feb. 1953　　Imogen Holst begins work on the preparation of full score pages of 2.iii.
1 Mar. 1953　　Imogen Holst working on preparation of 2.iii and 2.i. pages
2 Mar. 1953　　2.i pages not quite finished. Britten completed 2.iii at 12.20, and 'planned the orchestration' of 3.i so that Imogen Holst could begin work.
9 Mar. 1953　　3.ii completed and 3.iii begun.
13 Mar. 1953　　'Ben finished *Gloriana* at 3 o'clock this afternoon!!!'; some things remained to be 'filled in and tidied up', a task left to Imogen Holst.
29 Mar. 1953　　Imogen Holst finished her work on the full score.
8 Apr. 1953　　Peter Pears 'managed to collect Acts II & III', to deliver them to Aldeburgh (they had perhaps been sent to Boosey & Hawkes for duplication).
See also pp. 104-5 above.

Vocal scores

V1 Holograph and non-holograph draft arrangement (incomplete, various paginations). Holograph and non-holograph ms.: blue ink, black ink, pencil (Imogen Holst); with annotations: pencil, red ballpoint (Erwin Stein, Benjamin Britten). - [Untitled]. - [1953]. - [111] fol. : 12 staves, [span:] 30.3 cm. ; 36.2 x 27 cm. + 12 paste-overs [a-l].

ANALYSIS: $[1^r]$ tp, $[1^v]$ blank, $[2^r$-$27^r]$ Act I, sc. 1 (= pp. 1-51), $[28^r]$ tp, $[28^v]$ blank, $[29^r$-$47^r]$ Act I, sc. 2 (= pp. 1-37), $[47^v$-$48^v]$ blank, $[49^r$-$61^v]$ Act II, sc. 2 (= pp. 1-26), $[62]$ blank, $[63^r]$ tp, $[63^v]$ blank, $[64^r$-$88^r]$ Act II, sc. 3 (= pp. 1-48), $[88^v$-$90^v]$ blank, $[91^r$-$110^r]$ Act III, sc. 1, $[110^v$-$112^v]$ blank.

COLLATION: [1], [2-27] A-M^2 ([a-b] on $[2^v]$, [c] on $[3^v]$, [d] on $[4^v]$, [e] on $[5^r]$, [f] on $[6^r]$, [g] on $[8^r]$, [h] on $[24^r]$), [28], [29-38] N-R^2, [39-40] single sheets ([i] on $[40^r]$), [41-48] S-V^2 ([j] on $[43^r]$), [49-62] W-AC^2 ([k] on $[53^r]$), [63/90] wrapper, [64-88] AD-AP^2 ([l] on $[76^v]$), [91-110] AQ-AZ^2, [111], [112] BA^2.

CONTENTS: Act I, 2.ii, 2.iii, 3.i.

Most of this manuscript is in the hand of Imogen Holst. It is probably one of the earliest surviving documents to reflect Imogen Holst's role in Britten's working life. The evidence of the various annotations on the document suggests that she prepared this ink draft for Britten's comments (see, for example, fol. [74]) before making a completely new vocal score [V2] from which dyeline copies were then made for the cast.[30] The recopied version was presumably the source used for the published vocal score.   *GB-ALb* 2-9202585

[V2] [Manuscript fair copy. Imogen Holst. - [November 1952-1953]. - Not located.]

This copy[31] was dyelined to prepare the vocal material for the first performance (V3 below).

---

30 Work on the original vocal score can be traced through Imogen Holst's diary entries:

7 Nov. 1952 Imogen Holst completed 1.i and delivered it to Britten.

17 Nov. 1952 Imogen Holst 'went [home] to collect Act I Scene II': probably her draft, which she planned to show Britten.

20 Nov. 1952 Some of 1.ii was corrected by Britten.

26 Nov. 1952 Imogen Holst was probably working on 2.ii.

1 Dec. 1952 Imogen Holst collected 2.ii from Crag House, Britten's home.

2 Dec. 1952 Corrections to 2.ii discussed with Britten.

9 Dec. 1952 Final queries for Act I corrected.

11 Dec. 1952 Britten looked at some of 2.iii.

19 Dec. 1952 Britten corrected some of 3.i.

23 Dec. 1952 Britten decided to correct Imogen Holst's 'first copies' (this might refer to the fair copy, [V2]) over Christmas'.

Britten and Pears were at Harewood House after Christmas, so Imogen Holst's narrative is broken for a short period.

5 Feb. 1953 Imogen Holst collected 3.ii (it's not clear whether this was H1 or one of her manuscript copies of the vocal score).

8 Feb. 1953 Imogen Holst working on 3.ii.

23 Feb. 1953 Imogen Holst collected 2.i of the composition draft (H1) to be copied at home. Whether she prepared a preliminary draft of this scene, or worked straight into fair copy (i.e. [V2]) is not clear.

31 The progress of this second copy can be traced in the entries in Imogen Holst's diary:

28 Nov. 1952 Imogen Holst, Britten and Erwin Stein discussed the copying of *Gloriana* at a meeting in Aldeburgh.

V3.1   Interim copy (incomplete, paginated). Manuscript (dyeline) (Imogen Holst). -
        [Untitled]. - [1953]. - 4 vols (26, [ii]; 39 [i]; 30, [ii]; 39, [i] p.), thick, off-white
        card, wire spiral binding ; 36.2 - 36.7 cm.
        ANALYSIS: Volume I: [fo] [blue ballpoint:] *ACT II SCENE II* / *VOCAL SCORE*
        / [rubber-stamp:] *BOOSEY & HAWKES LTD.* / *HIRE LIBRARY* / * 295,
        *REGENT STREET., LONDON, W.1**, [fi] blank, 1-26 *ACT II SCENE II* [i-ii]
        blank ms. paper, [ri-ro] blank.
        Volume II: [fo] [pencil, Benjamin Britten:] *ACT III SC. 1* / *VOCAL SCORE*,
        [fi] blank, 1-39 *ACT III SCENE I*, [i] blank, [ri-ro] blank.
        Volume III: [fo] [blue ballpoint:] *Gloriana* / *ACT III SCENE II* , [fi] blank,
        1-30 *ACT III SCENE II*, [i-ii] blank, [ri-ro] blank.
        Volume IV: [fo] [blue ballpoint:] *Gloriana* / *ACT III SCENE III* , [fi] blank,
        1-39 *ACT III SCENE II*, [i] blank.
        CONTENTS: 2.ii, 3.i-3.iii only.
        Dyeline copy of [V2].   GB-ALb 2-9000040-9000043

V3.2   - Another copy (incomplete: role copy (Essex), various paginations). Manuscript
        (dyeline) (Imogen Holst, [unidentified]): with annotations, pencil, red
        ballpoint, blue ink ([unidentified]). - 248 pp., thick manilla card,
        2 interlinked wire spiral bindings ; 36.2 cm. + 4 paste-overs ([a-d]).
        ANALYSIS: [fo] [rubber stamp:] *BOOSEY & HAWKES LTD.* / *HIRE LIBRARY*
        ..., [fi] blank, 1-53 *ACT I SCENE I*, [54] blank, 55-93 *ACT I SCENE II*, [92]
        blank, [93-127] *ACT II SCENE I* (= pp. 1-35), [128] blank, [129-154] *ACT II
        SCENE II* (= pp. 1-26), [155-6] blank, [157-207] *ACT II SCENE III* (= pp. 1-
        51), [208] blank, [209-47] *ACT III SCENE I* (= pp. 1-39), [248] blank, [ri-ro]
        blank.
        CONTENTS: 1.i-1.ii, 2.i-2.iii, 3.i.
        Paste-overs appear on pp. 70 ([a-b]) and 71 (c-d]).
        Note on [fo] [l.h., red ballpoint:] *GLORIANA* / *ESSEX* / [rule] / [r.h.,
        blue pencil, encircled:] *O*.
        As implied by the note on the front cover, the part of Essex has been
        marked up for performance with extensive production notes.
        Some of the original sheets had been marked up for printing
        (presumably in preparation of the first edition) before they were
        dyelined: [104-106, 108-110, 112-127].   GB-Lbh Hire Library

V3.3   - Another copy (incomplete: role copy (Elizabeth), various paginations). With
        annotations and corrections, pencil, red ballpoint, blue ink (Constance
        Shacklock?). - 248 pp., thick manilla card, wire spiral binding ; 36.2 cm.
        ANALYSIS: [fo] [rubber stamp:] *BOOSEY & HAWKES LTD.* / *HIRE LIBRARY*
        ..., [fi] blank, 1-32 *ACT II SCENE I*, [33-83] *ACT II SCENE III* (= pp. 1-51),
        [84] blank, [85-123] *ACT III SCENE I* (= pp. 1-39), [124] blank, [125-63]
        ACT III SCENE III (= pp. 1-39), [164] blank, [ri-ro] blank.
        CONTENTS: 2.i, 2.iii, 3.i, 3.iii.

---

14 Dec. 1952   1.i ready to go to Boosey & Hawkes.
6 Feb. 1953   3.iii revised prior to dispatch to Boosey & Hawkes.
13 Feb. 1953   Neat copy of 3.ii given to Britten for correction.
23 Feb. 1953   See fn. 30 above.
On 26 and 30 April Imogen Holst and Britten worked on Acts II and III of the opera,
presumably tidying up the fair copy of the vocal score prior to dispatch to Boosey & Hawkes
(see fn. 33 below).

Notes on [fo]: [pencil:] *ELIZABETH* [blue ink:] *Constance Shacklock* / [l.h., pencil:] *Act II - Scene I* [r.h., blue ink:] *Property of Royal Opera House / Covent Garden* / [blue pencil, encircled:] *P*.
Marked up for performance, but with relatively few production notes.

GB-Lbh Hire Library

V3.4   - Another copy (Act I, paginated). With annotations, pencil, orange pencil, blue ink ([unidentified]). - *GLORIANA / ACT I.* - [92] pp., thick manilla card, wire spiral binding ; 35.2 cm.
ANALYSIS: [fo] [rubber stamp:] *BOOSEY & HAWKES LTD. / HIRE LIBRARY* ..., [fi] blank, 1-53 *ACT I SCENE I*, [54] blank, 55-91 *ACT I SCENE II*, [92] blank [ri-ro] blank.
Title from [fo]
This copy was probably used for the role of Mountjoy, but the part has not been extensively marked. *GB-Lbh* Hire Library

V3.5   - Another copy (Act III, various paginations). With annotations, pencil, blue ink ([unidentified]). - *GLORIANA / ACT III.* - [112] pp., thick manilla card, wire spiral binding ; 35.2 cm.
ANALYSIS: [fo] [rubber stamp:] *BOOSEY & HAWKES LTD. / HIRE LIBRARY* ..., [fi] blank, 1-39 *ACT III, SCENE I*, [40] blank, [41-70] *ACT III SCENE II* (= pp. 1-30), [71-72] blank, [73-111] *ACT III SCENE III* (= pp. 1-39), [112] blank.
Title from [fo].
There are a few annotations in the role of Cecil in 3.iii.

GB-Lbh Hire Library

V4   First edition, proofs (incomplete). - Printed from engraved plates. - *GLORIANA.* - [May-June 1953. - [S.l.] : [s.n.], [n.d.], c1953. Pl. no.: B.& H. 17376. - 100 pp., unbound in mottled blue folder ; 31.2 x 25.1 cm.
ANALYSIS: 1-47 *ACT I SCENE I*, 48-76 *SCENE II*, 77-98 *ACT II SCENE I*, 99-100 *SCENE II*.
Title from heading on p. 1. Note on front cover (blue felt-tip): 'GLORIANA / VOCAL SCORE / ACT I SCENE 1 & 2 / ACT II Scene 1 A & B / + SCENE 2.'
Copyright 1953 by Hawkes & Son (London), Ltd.
Imogen Holst was working on the proofs of the vocal score during the rehearsals for the première at the end of May and the beginning of June. Because of the urgency, the final proofs were seen by Erwin Stein and Imogen Holst, but not by Britten. The only copy so far located is this unmarked and incomplete set. *GB-ALb* 2-9300503

[V5]   [Pre-publication copies. - May 1953. - Not located]
According to the records of Boosey & Hawkes 20 copies of the vocal score were produced in May 1953 for Covent Garden. No further information is available, but it is possible that these were originated from the engraved plates rather than from [V2].

V6   Hire material. - *GLORIANA / An Opera in Three Acts / by / WILLIAM PLOMER / Music by / BENJAMIN BRITTEN / Opus 53 / Vocal Score by / Imogen Holst / BOOSEY & HAWKES, LTD., / London · Paris · Bonn · Capetown / Sydney · Toronto · New York.* - London : Boosey & Hawkes, Ltd., [1953]. Pl. no.: B.& H. 17376. - [i-viii], 229, [ix-xi] p., in thick red paper cover ; 35.5 cm.

ANALYSIS: [fo] blank, [fi] blank, [i] tp, [ii] copyright statement, [iii] dedication, [iv] blank, [v] list of characters, [vi], list of scenes, orchestration, [vii] list of original cast, [viii] blank, 1-47 *ACT I SCENE I*, 48-76 *SCENE II*, 77-98 *ACT II SCENE I*, 99-118 *SCENE II*, 119-156 *SCENE III*, 157-183 *ACT III SCENE I*, 184-203 *SCENE II*, 204-229 *SCENE III*, [ix-xi] blank, [ri-ro] blank.

PRINT CODE: none   ORDERED: 14.5.53   DELIVERED: 6.6.53
PRINT RUN: 100

Copyright 1953 by Hawkes & Son (London), Ltd.

Not the special edition of 100 copies or the additional ten copies (V7). One hundred of these 'Library copies' were produced, of which 41 survived until 1966.[32] Of the eleven which still survive at *GB-Lbh* one was signed by William McAlpine, and some of the others were held at Boosey & Hawkes's New York Hire Library at some time.

The hire copies were ordered by Boosey & Hawkes at the same time as the deluxe first edition, and were delivered five days earlier, on 6 June 1953; the British Library copy of V6 (*GB-Lbl* H.2472.p.) is date stamped (blue) '8 Jun 53'.

For a copy marked-up as the masters for the second edition, see V9.

V7.1   First edition. - *GLORIANA* / *An Opera in Three Acts* / *by* / *WILLIAM PLOMER* / *Music by* / *BENJAMIN BRITTEN* / *Opus 53* / *Vocal Score by* / *Imogen Holst* / *BOOSEY & HAWKES LTD.,* / *London · Paris · Bonn · Capetown* / *Sydney · Toronto · New York.* - London : Boosey & Hawkes, Ltd., c1953. Pl. no.: B.& H. 17376. - [i-viii], 229, [ix-xi] p., bound in parchment, with gold tooling on spine and front board ; 40 cm.

ANALYSIS: [fo] [gold tooling:] *Benjamin Britten*, [fi] blank, [3 end-papers], [i] tp, [ii] copyright statement, [iii] dedication, [iv] blank, [v] list of characters, [vi], list of scenes, orchestration, [vii] list of original cast, [viii] blank, 1-47 *ACT I SCENE I*, 48-76 *SCENE II*, 77-98 *ACT II SCENE I*, 99-118 *SCENE II*, 119-156 *SCENE III*, 157-183 *ACT III SCENE I*, 184-203 *SCENE II*, 204-229 *SCENE III*, [ix] blank, [x] colophon with signatures, [xi] blank, [3 end-papers], [ri-ro] blank.

PRINT CODE: none   ORDERED: 14.5.53   DELIVERED: 11.6.53
PRINT RUN: 110 copies

A special edition of 100 copies printed on hand-made paper and bound in real parchment, signed [blue ink:] 'Benjamin Britten', [purple ink:] 'William Plomer'. The Queen's copy arrived for Britten's signature on the morning of June 8, ahead of the rest of the order.

This first, limited, edition was hurriedly prepared[33] and contained a number of errors which were corrected in the second edition (V10), issued later the same year. In addition to the main print run, a further 10

---

[32] In a letter from Martin Hall to Rosamund Strode, dated 1 June 1966, it was suggested that these copies (provided with revision patches) be used for the 1966 production, an idea categorically rejected in favour of scrapping the lot.

[33] Imogen Holst was told of Boosey & Hawkes' plan to issue this edition on 19 April 1953.

copies were run off with the same binding.[34] The edition remained on sale until at least the end of 1965 (i.e. after the second edition had gone out of print).

V7.2   - Annotated copy.
Signed on title-page (black ballpoint): 'For Eva / with my love / Ben / 1968'.
PROVENANCE: Gift of Eva, Countess of Rosebery.
No. 76 of the edition. Given to Lady Rosebery by Britten in 1968 when he was a featured composer at the Edinburgh Festival (Lady Rosebery was one of the founders of the Festival and in 1968 was a member of the Edinburgh Festival Society Council). It subsequently formed part of Lady Rosebery's gift to the Britten-Pears Library.   GB-ALb 2-9104466

[V8]   [Second edition (preparatory copy). - [July 1953]. - Not located.]
This was probably an annotated copy of the above.[35]

V9   Second edition, master copy (marked-up copy of the hire edition, V6). Printed; with annotations, revisions: pencil, red ballpoint, red crayon. - *GLORIANA* / *An Opera in Three Acts* / *by* / *WILLIAM PLOMER* / *Music by* / *BENJAMIN BRITTEN* / *Opus 53* / *Vocal Score by* / *Imogen Holst* / *BOOSEY & HAWKES, LTD.,* / *London · Paris · Bonn · Capetown* / *Sydney · Toronto · New York.* - London : Boosey & Hawkes, Ltd., 1953. Pl. no.: B.& H. 17376. - [i-viii], 229, [ix-xi] p., thick red paper cover ; 35.6 cm. + 1 printed insert, [1] fol.; 28 cm.
ANALYSIS: [fo] [black felt-tip (Martin Hall):] *BENJAMIN BRITTEN* / [rule] / *GLORIANA* / *OP. 53* / *Original edition (June 1953)* / *marked for reprint Dec. 1953* / [rule] / *Note: this copy ...* [pencil, (John Andrewes):] *May 1966 Martin Hall* / [rule] / *Vocal Score,* [otherwise, as for V6].
The insert gives the revised ending to the Dance of Time and Concord (p. 88) and is a copy of the additional leaf (= pp. 28A/28B) printed for insertion in the choral score (CS2).   GB-ALb 2-9000039

V10.1   Second edition, first impression. - *GLORIANA* / *An Opera in Three Acts* / *by* / *WILLIAM PLOMER* / *Music by* / *BENJAMIN BRITTEN* / *Opus 53* / *Vocal Score by* / *Imogen Holst* / *BOOSEY & HAWKES, LTD.,* / *London · Paris · Bonn · Capetown* / *Sydney · Toronto · New York.* - London : Boosey & Hawkes, Ltd., 1954. Pl. no.: B.& H. 17376. - [i-viii], 230, [ix-x] p., thick paper cover ; 36 cm.
ANALYSIS: [fo] *GLORIANA* / *Benjamin Britten,* [fi] blank, [i] tp, [ii] copyright statement, [iii] dedication, [iv] blank, [v] list of characters, [vi], list of scenes, orchestration, [vii] list of original cast, [viii] blank, 1-47 *ACT I SCENE I,* 48-76 *SCENE II,* 77-99 *ACT II SCENE I,* 100-119 *SCENE II,* 120-157 *SCENE III,* 158-184 *ACT III SCENE I,* 185-204 *SCENE II Ballad*

---

[34]   Letter of Anthony Gishford to the Earl of Harewood dated 12 June 1953; Lord Harewood was to receive the first of these additional copies. The British Library's copyright copy (*GB-Lbl* K.5.d.8) is 'B' from this second group of copies.

[35]   Imogen Holst and Britten worked on the corrections and revisions (including the addition of metronome marks) on 28 July 1953. A 'corrected score' (probably a vocal score) was left with Erwin Stein on 30 July, following a visit by Imogen Holst and Britten, but work on the metronome marks continued on 11 and 12 August. During the first session Britten also 'wrote in an extra entry of the tune in canon in the last scene ("in some unhaunted [desert]" [3.iii.7, Fig. 169+2: the additional trombone entry]) where he 'felt it was too naked'.

Rondo, 205-230 *SCENE III*, [ix-x] blank, [ri] blank, [ro] advert (no. 600, dated 9/51).

PRINT CODE: 11.53 L. & B.   ORDERED: 29.10.53   DELIVERED: 21.12.53
PRINT RUN: 500.

Copyright 1953 by Hawkes & Song (London), Ltd.

Pages 88-89 were re-engraved to incorporate the longer version of the second Choral Dance and all subsequent pages re-numbered. The front cover was designed by John Piper (costume design for Elizabeth).

The few remaining copies were transferred to the Boosey & Hawkes Hire Library in 1957,[36] the plates melted on 20 February 1958, and the edition declared out-of-print in 1960.

V10.2   - An annotated copy (Peter Pears's copy). With annotations: pencil (Peter Pears, Benjamin Britten). - Bound in brown boards with gold tooling on spine.

Retains the original pictorial front cover.

Pencil initials on tp: 'PP'.   Used by Pears for the 1963 concert performance; the annotations by the composer list the cast.

GB-ALb 2-9200257

V10.3   - An annotated copy (Benjamin Britten's copy).   With annotations and corrections: pencil, grey ink (Benjamin Britten).

Black ink initials on front cover: 'BB'.

Includes a ms. errata list (dyeline) by Rosamund Strode, dated May 1966 which only partially corresponds to the corrections marked in the copy. None of the 1966 revisions appear in this copy.   *GB-ALb* 2-9200282

V10.4   - An annotated copy (Rosamund Strode's copy). With annotations, corrections and revisions: pencil, purple pencil, red pencil (Benjamin Britten, Rosamund Strode).

Signed and dated on tp, blue ballpoint: 'Rosamund Strode / 1964'.

This copy contains revisions for three subsequent works: the revised 1966 version of the opera ((M)) (including the revision patches), the *Gloriana* fanfare (1967) ((O)) and the Symphonic Suite (version with chorus) ((P)).

GB-ALrs

V10.5   - An annotated copy. With corrections, pencil (Imogen Holst).

Signed on tp, pencil: 'Imogen Holst'.

With copies of L16, (M)/V12.2 and (M)/V13.2, and also a sketch leaf for Imogen Holst's 70th birthday greeting for Peter Pears (which incorporated material from *Gloriana*).   *GB-ALhf*

V10.6   - Another copy.

Annotation on tp, pencil: 'Helen Watkins'.   *GB-Lbh* Hire Library

For Britten's file copy (containing most of the 1966 revisions) see (M)/V14.

V11.1   Second edition, second impression. Printed. - *GLORIANA | An Opera in Three Acts | by | WILLIAM PLOMER | Music by | BENJAMIN BRITTEN | Opus 53 | Vocal Score by | Imogen Holst | BOOSEY & HAWKES, LTD., | London · Paris · Bonn · Johannesburg | Sydney · Toronto · New York*. - London : Boosey & Hawkes, Ltd., 1966. Pl. no.: B.& H. 17376. - [i-viii], 230, [ix-x] p., thick paper cover, ; 35.5 cm.

ANALYSIS: [as for V10 except:] [ro] advert (no. 2, dated 8.65).

---

[36] The British Library copy (*GB-Lbl* H.2472.r.) is date-stamped '22 Apr 58'.

PRINT CODE: 6.66 L & B   ORDERED: 17.5.66   DELIVERED: 17.6.53
PRINT RUN: 250.
>Copyright 1953 by Hawkes & Son (London), Ltd.
>Front cover retains the design by John Piper.
>As the first impression of the second edition had been out-of-print since 1960 it was agreed in 1966 that a short run of its unrevised text should be printed, partly for use by Sadler's Wells for the new production, and also for sale to the public.[37]

V11.2   - An annotated copy. With annotations: pencil.   *GB-ALb* 2-9200289

Choral scores

CS1.1   Hire material, first state. - *GLORIANA* / [l.h.:] *Choral Score* [r.h.:] *BENJAMIN BRITTEN.* - London : Hawkes & Son (London) Ltd., [n.d.], c1953. Pl. no.: B.& H. 17319. - [1]-62, [i-ii] p., unbound ; 25.2 cm.
>ANALYSIS: [1]-16 *ACT I* / *SCENE I*, 17-39 *ACT II Scene I*, 40-43 *ACT II SCENE 3*, 44-49 *ACT III Scene I*, 50-57 *ACT III Scene II*, 59-62 *ACT III SCENE III*, [i] advert (no. 655, dated 2.52), [ii] advert (no. 643, dated 11.51).
>PRINT RUN: 200
>Title from heading on p. [1]; no wrapper: made up of four signatures.
>Probably printed in April 1953.[38]   *GB-ALb* 2-9300002

CS1.2   Hire material, off-printed sheets (2.i, 3.iii.7). Printed. - [Untitled]. - [S.l.], [s.n.], [n.d.]. Pl. no.: B & H 17319. - [6] fol.; unbound ; 26 cm.
>ANALYSIS: [1^r-2^r] *ACT II* / *Scene I* (= pp. 1-3 (pp. 17-19 in CS1.1)), [2^v] blank, [3^r-4^v] Act II sc. 1 (= pp. 1-4 (pp. 36-39 in CS1.1)), [5^r] blank, [5^v-6^r] 3.iii.7 (= pp. 2-3 (pp. 61-62 in CS1.1)), [6^v] blank.
>The function of these off-prints is unclear. The text is that CS1.1. However it may be significant that they contain all the music for full chorus in the two scenes concerned.   *GB-Lbh* Hire Library

CS2   Hire material, revision leaves (2.i). Printed. - *GLORIANA New end for DANCE OF TIME AND CONCORD* / *ACT 2 SCENE 1* / *Choral score Page 28.* - [S.l.], [s.n.], [n.d.]. Pl. no.: B & H 17319. - [1] fol. ; 25.1 cm.
>ANALYSIS: [1^{r-v}] music (= pp. 28A, 28B).
>Copies of this leaf (containing the extended ending of the third choral dance) were presumably prepared for insertion into copies of CS1.1. These two pages were simply inserted into all subsequent printings of the choral score without any repagination.   *GB-Lbh* Hire Library

CS3   Hire material, second (?) state. - *GLORIANA* / [l.h.:] *CHORAL SCORE* [r.h.:] *BENJAMIN BRITTEN.* - London : Hawkes & Son (London) Ltd., [n.d.], c1953. Pl. no.: B.& H. 17319. - [64] p. ; 26 cm.
>ANALYSIS: [1]-16 *ACT I* / *SCENE I*, 17-28, 28A, 28B, 29-39 *ACT II Scene I*, 40-43 *ACT II SCENE 3*, 44-49 *ACT III Scene I*, 50-57 *ACT III Scene II*, 59-62 *ACT III SCENE III.*
>Title from heading on p. 1.
>A single gathering. Contains the extended version of the third dance in 2.i.

---

[37]   The decisions were set out in a letter of 17 May 1966 from Rosamund Strode to Martin Hall of Boosey & Hawkes (see also (M)).
[38]   Information from Boosey & Hawkes.

Full scores

F1   Hire material (paginated). Holograph and non-holograph (dyeline) (copyist: Imogen Holst). - [Untitled]. - [1953]. - 3 vol. (pp. 1-116, 117-240, 241-399, [i]), bound ; 55.6 cm.

ANALYSIS: Volume I: 1-64 *Act I SCENE I,* 65-116 *ACT I SCENE II.*

Volume II: 117-148 *ACT II SCENE I,* 149-173 *ACT II SCENE II,* 174-240 *ACT II SCENE III.*

Volume III: 241-304, *ACT III SCENE I,* 305-340 *ACT III SCENE II,* 341-399 *ACT III SCENE III,* [i], blank.

Reproduced from the fair copy, H3.

The British Library copy (*GB-Lbl* K.11.a.10) is date-stamped (red) '24 May 1954'; it was purchased from Boosey & Hawkes although such copies were not offered for sale to the public.[39]

For two annotated copies incorporating changes made in 1966, see (M)/F3 and (M)/F5.

F2.1-2.2   Hire material, stage orchestra score (paginated). Holograph and non-holograph ms. (photocopy) (Imogen Holst). - [All Imogen Holst; r.h.] <u>SCORE</u> // *GLORIANA | ACT II SCENE III | STAGE ORCHESTRA FOR DANCES. -* 20 pp.

ANALYSIS: [as for H4].

Copied from H4; 2 copies.   *GB-Lbh* Hire Library

For a copy used in the preparation of the study score, see (M)/F7.

Orchestral parts

P1   Hire material, orchestral parts, first state (incomplete set). Ms. copies (some dyeline): black ink (various unidentified copyists); with annotations, corrections and revisions. - *GLORIANA * Britten.* - [1953?]. - 9 vols, bound in Boosey & Hawkes' Manilla Covers ; various sizes.

CONTENTS: vln 1 (desk 7), vln 2 (desk 6), vla (desk 5), vcl. x 2 (desk 4, unassigned), db x 2 (desks 3, 4), stage trumpet 3, stage tabor.

Title from the front cover of the vln 1 part. All are marked 'uncorrected' or 'not corrected' in red ink. All marked 'Copyright 1953 by Hawkes & Son (London) Ltd. B & H 17362'. All except the stage tabor part are dyelines. The set as a whole was probably a mixture of dyelines (mainly the strings and duplicate parts) and ms. copies.

These parts are probably the remains of the set used at the first performance. This was the only set prepared at the time, and was probably completed by 11 May, the date scheduled for the first reading through for the orchestra;[40] the set was revised prior to the performances in 1954, and some of the changes mentioned by Imogen Holst in her diary are entered in red ink in these parts.[41] Paste-overs to the openings of 3.iii.6 and 3.iii.7 give revisions not mentioned by Imogen Holst.

GB-Lbh Hire Library

---

[39] According to information kindly supplied by Boosey and Hawkes, three such full scores were produced in May 1953, though it is not clear whether this copy is one of the initial batch.

[40] Letter of Ernst Roth to Britten, 19.02.1953.

[41] See p. 105 above.

P2 Manuscript harp part (incomplete, paginated). Ms. copy: black ink; with annotations: pencil. - [Untitled]. - [1953?]. - [1] fol.: 12 staves, [span:] 25.2 cm. ; 30.5 x 24.1 cm.
    ANALYSIS: [1^r] (= p. 5), [1^v] (= p. 6).
    CONTENTS: fragment of 1.ii.
    > Has at foot of both pages: 'B.H. 17362'. This leaf did not form part of the original from which P3 was copied, though the copyist of P2 did also copy some pages in P3.   *GB-Lbh* Hire Library

P3 Manuscript harp part (paginated). Ms. copy (photocopy) (various unidentified copyists); with annotations: pencil. - *GLORIANA*. - [n.d.]. - [13] fol., sellotaped together ; 35.2 x 25 cm.
    ANALYSIS: [1^r-2^v] *ACT I* / *Scene 1* (= pp. 1-4), [3^r-7^r] *Act I* / *Scene 2* (= pp. 5-13), [7^v-11^r] *ACT II SCENE 1* (= pp. 14-21), [12^v] *Act II* / *Scene 2* / *Tacet* (= p. 22), [12^r] *Act II scene 3* / *Tacet* (= p. 23)
    > Title from heading on p. 1.
    > Probably a copy of the original harp part.   *GB-Lbh* Hire Library

P4.1 Manuscript revison patches (3.iii.6, 3.iii.7). Ms. copy: black ink; with annotations. - [Untitled]. - [1954?]. - [2] fol.: [A:] 10 staves, [span:] 24.6 cm. ; 30.4 x 23.8 cm.: [B:] 11 staves (cut down from a larger sheet) ; 25.8 x 24.6 cm. + 1 paste-over.
    ANALYSIS: [1^{r-v}] *1st Violin*, [2^{r-v}] *cellos*.
    > Blue pencil notes on the two leaves call for six and four copies respectively. The revisions correspond to those found in P1.   *GB-Lbh* Hire Library

P4.2 - Additional copies. Ms. copies (dyeline). - [6] fol. ; various sizes.
    > Four copies of the vln 1 patch, two of the vcl. patch. *GB-Lbh* Hire Library

P5 Hire material, parts for on-stage instruments. Ms. copies (some photocopies) (various unidentified copyists); with annotations: various implements. - [n.d.] - 11 vols, bound in green, card covers ; various sizes.
    CONTENTS: drums (off-stage and on-stage), hp, stage orchestra vln/ob., stage orchestra vla 1 & 2, stage orchestra vcl. 1 & 2 [incomplete], stage orchestra cor anglais 1 & 2, stage orchestra bsn 1 & 2, stage perc., tabor, trpt 1 in C, trpt 2 in C, trpt 3 in C.
    > With parts labelled 'fl. 1 and cornet' (= stage orchestra vln/ob) and a manuscript part for bsn 2.   *GB-Lbh* Hire Library

Miscellaneous

M1 Incomplete manuscript vocal part (Act I only, role for Essex, paginated). Ms. copy: blue ink; with annotations: pencil, red pencil. - *GLORIANA*. - [n.d.] - [6] fol.: 12 staves, [span:] 25.3 cm., [maker:] *R.C. 1* / [Galleon logo] / *Printed in England* ; 31.3 x 23.4 cm.
    ANALYSIS: 1-5 Act I sc. 1, 6 blank, 7-11 *ACT I* / *SCENE II*,[42] [12] blank.
    COLLATION: A^6.
    > Title from heading on p. 1.
    > Pencil annotation on p. 1: 'John Lanigan'.   *GB-Lbh* Hire Library

---

[42] The part begins in this scene with the First Lute Song.

M2   Notes on Elizabethan masques and progresses (holograph, foliated). Holograph: biue ink (Imogen Holst). - [Notes]. - [1952]. - 11 fol. ; 17.85 x 13.7 cm.
       With postcards of portraits of Queen Elizabeth I, the Earl of Essex, Sir Philip Sidney, Robert Cecil and Sir Walter Raleigh.   *GB-ALb* 2-9200293

M3   Working notes. - [Rosamund Strode's working notes I : mainly relating to the publication of various works]. - 1964-1984. - [unfoliated] ; 35.5 cm.
       Includes notes on *Gloriana*.   *GB-ALb* 2-9100345

M4   Working notes. - *B & H. & MISC.* [= Rosamund Strode's working notes]. - 1965-1975. - [unfoliated] ; 27 cm.
       Includes notes on *Gloriana*.   *GB-ALb* 2-9100347

Recordings

Rec1   Unpublished off-air recording. - 1953. - [Not examined].
         A recording of one of the two broadcasts of the original production (8 June and 2 July 1953).   Private collection

Rec2   Incomplete unpublished off-air recording. - 1953. - 4 sound tape reels (ca. 80 min.) : analogue, 7.5 ips, mono ; 1/4 in. tape. [Not examined].
         CONTENTS: lacking 3.ii and 3.iii.
         A recording of one of the two broadcasts of the original production (8 June and 2 July 1953).   *GB-Lbh*

[Rec3.1] [Unpublished off-air recording. - 1953. - [unknown medium] (ca. 130 min.) : analogue, mono. - Lost.]
         PERFORMERS: Peter Pears (Essex); Ronald Lewis (Cuffe); Geraint Evans (Mountjoy); Joan Cross (Elizabeth); Frederick Dalberg (Raleigh); Arnold Matters (Raleigh); Marian Nowakowski (Recorder of Norwich); Jennifer Vyvyan (Penelope); Monica Sinclair (Frances); Adèle Leigh (Lady-in-waiting); Covent Garden Opera Chorus and Orchestra; John Pritchard, conductor.
         DATE AND PLACE OF RECORDING: 53.07.02 at the Royal Opera House, Covent Garden, London.
         PROVENANCE: originally in the possession of Joan Cross.
         This is a recording of the second broadcast of *Gloriana* made by the BBC Third Programme on 2 July 1953 (the first broadcast was of the première on 8 June 1953). For unknown reasons 2.i is missing from Rec3.2, though whether it was present on Rec3.1 is not clear.

Rec3.2   - Another copy (incomplete). - 2 sound cassettes (ca. 130 min.) : analogue, mono.
         CONTENTS: 2.i missing.
         PROVENANCE: Copied from Rec3.1., 1984.   *GB-ALb* 3-9300014

Rec3.3   - Another copy. - [unknown medium] (ca. 130 min.) : analogue, mono. - [Not examined].   Private Collection

[Rec4]   [Unpublished recording. - 1953. - Sound discs. - Not located.]
         Imogen Holst's diary for 8 November 1953 indicates that she heard 'records of *Gloriana*' at a meeting of the Friends of the Aldeburgh Festival. These were presumably private discs recorded from one of the broadcasts of the work.

Rec5   Incomplete unpublished recording. - 1963. - 3 sound tape reels (ca. 100 min.) : analogue, 7.5 ips, mono ; 2 x 8.75 in., 1 x 7 in. - [Item not examined.]

PERFORMERS: Peter Pears (Essex); Raimond Herincx (Mountjoy), Sylvia Fisher (Elizabeth); Forbes Robinson (Raleigh); Thomas Hemsley (Cecil); Trevor Anthony (Recorder of Norwich, Ballad Singer); Jennifer Vyvyan (Penelope); Joan Edwards (Frances); Pauline Stevens (a housewife); Duncan Robertson (Master of Ceremonies, Spirit of the Masque); Michael Rippon (City Crier); Royal Military School of Music Trumpeters; Elizabethan Singers; London Philharmonic Choir; Polyphonia Symphony Orchestra; Bryan Fairfax, conductor.

DATE AND PLACE OF RECORDING: 68.11.22 at Royal Festival Hall, London.

CONTENTS: 3.i and 3.ii omitted from the recording.[43]

GB-Lnsa Tapes P 16 W; P 15 R; 450 W

---

[43]   The omission may be connected with the assassination of President Kennedy which occurred on the evening of the performance.

(B) Second Lute Song (voice and piano)

Arranger: Imogen Holst

Dedication: *For Peter Pears*

Scoring: voice and piano

Duration: 5 min.

Date: 1953?-1954?

First performance: see the notes below

Publication: London: Boosey & Hawkes, 1954

Notes

This song appears in 1.ii; the text was written by Robert Devereux (1566-1601), second Earl of Essex. Britten's song quotes a phrase from a madrigal by John Wilbye, a setting of a different poem which begins with a similar opening line - 'Happy, O happy he' - from Wilbye's *Second Set of Madrigals* (1609). At the entry of the voice the quotation marks in the accompaniment enclose the phrase from Wilbye.

The arrangement derives directly from the vocal score except for the introduction and piano coda which embody some slight recomposition of the corresponding music in the opera. It is not clear when this arrangement was first heard in public: three early performances have been traced,[44] but as Britten was the pianist it is possible that on these occasions he simply adapted a vocal score.

Sources

V1.1   First edition. - *Benjamin Britten / Gloriana / The Second Lute Song / of the / Earl of Essex / Voice and Piano / Price 2/6 net / (1954) / Boosey & Hawkes*. - [S.l.] : Boosey & Hawkes, 1954. Pl. no.: B. & H. 17556. - [1]-5, [i] p. ; 31 cm.
ANALYSIS: [1] tp, 2-5 music, [i] advert (no. 601, dated 9.51).
PRINT CODE: 5.54. E   ORDERED: 14.5.54   DELIVERED: 25.5.54
PRINT RUN: 500

    Copyright 1954 by Hawkes & Son (London), Ltd / Revised Edition Copyright 1954 by Hawkes & Son (London), Ltd.

    The British Library copy (*GB-Lbl* H.2472.O.(2)) is date-stamped (blue) '31 May 54'.

    The plates were melted on 9 July 1957 and the edition declared out-of-print on 19 October 1973.

---

[44] The song was included in the *Opera Concert* given at the 1953 Aldeburgh Festival, on 28 June (introduced by Lord Harewood, who has kindly supplied a copy of the typescript programme) and it may have been the excerpt from the opera included in *An operatic concert* given at the Queen's Hall, Barnstaple, on 12 July, as part of the Taw and Torridge Festival (the pianist was Britten, and the singers Joan Cross (sop.), Nancy Evans (mezzo), Rowland Jones (ten.) and Michael Langdon (bass); the event was again introduced by Lord Harewood). A fortnight later, on 26 July 1953, at the Guildhall of St. George, King's Lynn, the song was certainly heard at a concert during the King's Lynn Festival. Peter Pears was accompanied by the composer. The Lute Song was not listed in the Festival programme, but was reported as having been specifically requested for the recital: 'the request was not refused. And the song, magnificently sung by Mr. Pears, provided an impressive finale to a brilliant concert' (*Lynn News and Advertiser*, (28 July 1953), p. 3). Unfortunately, as Imogen Holst recorded in her diary entry for 27 July, the performers were not so pleased with the event.

V1.2   - An annotated copy (Peter Pears's copy). With annotations: black ink, pencil (Peter Pears?, Osian Ellis?).

         The piano part has been marked up for performance by a harp (see Rec1).

         Initialled on tp (pencil: Benjamin Britten): 'PP'.   *GB-ALb* 2-9300003

V1.3   - An annotated copy (Benjamin Britten's copy). With annotations: black ballpoint (Peter Pears?).

         Initialled on tp (pencil: Benjamin Britten): 'BB'.   *GB-ALb* 2-9300008

Recording

Rec1   Sound recording (arrangement for voice and harp). - *Second lute song from "Gloriana", op. 53 / Benjamin Britten.* - London : Decca Record Company Limited, 1976. - Catalogue no.: Decca SXL 6788; Matrix no.: ZAL-14451-1A. - 1 track on 1 sound disc (4:45 min.) : analogue, 33.3 rpm, stereo ; 12 in.

      PERFORMERS: Peter Pears, ten.; Osian Ellis, hp.

      DATE AND PLACE OF RECORDING: 76.02.19, 76.02.20 at Snape Maltings; producer: Michael Woolcock; engineer: Kenneth Wilkinson.

      In this version the harp plays the piano part from the piano-and-voice arrangement.

      Notes by Donald Mitchell.

(C)   Choral Dances from *Gloriana*

1.   Time (SATB)
2.   Concord (SATB)
3.   Time and Concord (SATB)
4.   Country Girls (SA)
5.   Rustics and Fishermen (TTBB)
6.   Final Dance of Homage (SATB)

Scoring: SATB

Duration: 8 min.

Date: 1953

First performance: not traced

Publication:
> English version: London : Boosey & Hawkes Ltd., 1954 (18 impressions);
> 1980 (second state: six impressions).
> Dutch version (score and parts): London: Boosey & Hawkes Ltd., 1957.

Notes
Apart from minor alterations to the duration of their final chords, the dances are taken unchanged from the opera.

Chorus scores

CS1.1   First edition, first state, first impression. - *Benjamin Britten | Choral Dances | from | Gloriana | for Mixed Voices | Price 3/- net | (1954) | Boosey & Hawkes.* - London : Boosey & Hawkes Ltd., 1954.   Pl. no.: B. & H. 17411. - 23, [i] p., paper wrapper, stitched ; 26.5 cm.

> ANALYSIS: [fo], [fi] blank, 1-5 *1. Time*, 6-8 *2. Concord*, 9-13 *3. Time and Concord*, 14-15 *4. Country Girls*, 16-19 *5. Rustics and Fishermen*, 20-23 *6. Final Dance of Homage*, [i] advert (No. 515, dated 10.48), [ri] advert (no. 517, dated 10.48), [ro] advert (no. 601, dated 9.51).

> PRINT CODE: 2.54 E.   ORDERED 23.1.54   DELIVERED: 5.2.54
> PRINT RUN: 2000

> Copyright: Hawkes & Son (London) Ltd.; sole selling agent: Boosey & Hawkes, Ltd.
> Title from front wrapper. Includes tonic sol-fa notation and rehearsal piano for nos 1-3, 5-6.
> The British Library copy (*GB-Lbl* E.1603.b.(8)) is date-stamped (blue) '11 Feb 54'. The plates were melted on 12 September 1957.

CS1.2   - An annotated copy (file copy). - 23, [i] p., blue manilla card wrapper, stitched ; 26.5 cm.

> A copy of the first edition with revisions, including a typescript note on the dances by Rosamund Strode and Donald Mitchell attached to the inside front cover; dated June 1979. See CS20 below.   *GB-ALb* 2-9200227

CS2 First edition, first state, second impression. *Benjamin Britten ... (1955)*. - 23, [i] p.,
     in paper cover, stapled ; 26.5 cm.
     ANALYSIS: [as CS1 except:] [i] advert (no. 718, dated 4.54), [ri] advert (no. 719,
          dated 4.54), [ro] advert (no. 601, dated 9.51).
     PRINT CODE: 9.55 E.   ORDERED: 16.9.55   DELIVERED: 4.10.55
     PRINT RUN: 2000.

     For a mixed set of CS1 and CS2 used by Imogen Holst and the Purcell Singers, see
     (G)/CS2.

CS3 Dutch edition. - *Benjamin Britten / Koor Dansen / uit Gloriana / voor / Gemengde
     Stemmen / Boosey & Hawkes*. - [London] : Boosey & Hawkes, 1957. Pl. no.:
     B. & H. 17687. - 24 pp. , no wrapper or cover ; 26 cm.
     ANALYSIS: [1] tp, 2-6 *1. De Tijd*, 7-9 *2. Eendracht*, 10-14 *3. De Tijd en Eendracht*,
     15-16 *4. Op het land*, 17-20 *5. Landman en Visser*, 21-24 *6. Ere dans*.
     PRINT CODE: 3.57.E
          Copyright 1954 by Hawkes & Son (London), Ltd.   Dutch version
          Copyright c 1957 by Hawkes & Son (London), Ltd. Sole selling agents:
          Boosey & Hawkes, Ltd., 295 Regent Street, London, W.1.
          Dutch text only (by E. J. Kooij).
          The British Library copy (*GB-Lbl* E.1603.b.(14)) is date-stamped (blue)
          '5 Apr 57'.

CS4 First edition, first state, third impression. - 1961. - [No copy located].
     ORDERED: 10.11.60   DELIVERED: 21.1.61
     PRINT RUN: 1000.

CS5 First edition, first state, fourth impression. - 1961. - [No copy located].
     ORDERED: 8.12.61   DELIVERED: 12.2.61
     PRINT RUN: 1500.

CS6 First edition, first state, fifth impression. - 1963. - [No copy located].
     ORDERED: 6.3.63   DELIVERED: 30.4.63
     PRINT RUN: 1000.

CS7 First edition, first state, sixth impression. - 1964. - [No copy located].
     ORDERED: 26.8.64   DELIVERED: 21.9.64
     PRINT RUN: 1000.

CS8 First edition, first state, seventh impression. - 1965. - [No copy located].
     ORDERED: 13.1.65   DELIVERED: 1.2.65
     PRINT RUN: 1500.

CS9 First edition, first state, eighth impression. - 1965. - [No copy located].
     ORDERED: 20.8.65   DELIVERED: 9.10.65
     PRINT RUN: 1500.

CS10 First edition, first state, ninth impression. - *Benjamin Britten / Choral Dances / from /
     Gloriana / for Mixed Voices / Boosey & Hawkes* / [rubber-stamped:] *CURRENT
     PRICE / 5/- NET / BOOSEY & HAWKES LTD*. - 23, [i] p., in white paper
     wrapper, stapled ; 26.5 cm.
     ANALYSIS: [as CS1 except:] [i] advert, [ri-ro] blank.
     PRINT CODE: 10.66 E.   ORDERED: 30.9.66   DELIVERED: 21.10.66
     PRINT RUN: 2000.

CS11   First edition, first state, tenth impression. - 1968. - [No copy located].
        ORDERED: 29.2.68   DELIVERED: 26.3.68
        PRINT RUN: 2000.

CS12   [First edition, first state, eleventh impression. - 1968. - [No copy located].
        ORDERED: 21.10.68   DELIVERED: 5.11.68
        PRINT RUN: 1500.

CS13   First edition, first state, twelfth impression. - 1969. - [No copy located].
        ORDERED: 6.12.68   DELIVERED: 8.1.69
        PRINT RUN: 2000.

CS14   First edition, first state, thirteenth impression. - 1970. - [No copy located].
        ORDERED: 6.12.68   DELIVERED: 8.1.69
        PRINT RUN: 2000.

CS15   First edition, first state, fourteenth impression. - 1972. - [No copy located].
        ORDERED: 4.7.72   DELIVERED: 14.10.72
        PRINT RUN: 1000.

CS16   First edition, first state, fifteenth impression. - 1974. - [No copy located].
        ORDERED: 24.8.73   DELIVERED: 13.2.74
        PRINT RUN: 1500.

CS17   First edition, first state, sixteenth impression. - 1975. - [No copy located].
        ORDERED: 26.2.75   DELIVERED: 17.6.75
        PRINT RUN: 1499.

CS18   First edition, first state, seventeenth impression. - 1977. - [No copy located].
        ORDERED: 17.2.77   DELIVERED: 6.4.77
        PRINT RUN: 1036.

CS19   First edition, first state, eighteenth impression. - 1977. - [No copy located].
        ORDERED: 12.5.77   DELIVERED: 8.6.77
        PRINT RUN: 2045.

CS20   First edition, second state, first impression. - *Benjamin Britten / CHORAL
        DANCES / from GLORIANA*. - [London] : Boosey & Hawkes, [n.d.], c1954.
        Pl. no.: B. & H. 17411. - 23 p. [i], stiff paper wrapper, stapled; 26 cm.
        ANALYSIS: [fo], [fi] note, [1]-23 as for first state, [i] advert (no. 14, dated
        2/77), [ri] blank, [ro] advert (no. 2, dated 8.65).
        PRINT CODE: BHMP 4/77 [!] ORDERED: 5.11.79   DELIVERED: 8.2.80
        PRINT RUN: 2028
        Copyright Hawkes & Son (London) Ltd. (p. [1]); sole selling agent:
        Boosey & Hawkes Music Publishers Ltd.
        Title from front wrapper. Includes tonic sol-fa notation, a rehearsal
        piano part for nos. 1-3, 5-6 and a brief note on the work on the inside
        front cover (see CS1.2 above).
        In the Britten-Pears Library copy (*GB-ALb* 2-9200315) the print code has
        been revised in pencil to '2/80'.

CS21   First edition, second state, second impression. - 1981. - [No copy located].
        ORDERED: 14.4.81   DELIVERED: 30.7.81
        PRINT RUN: 2096.

CS22 [First edition, second state, third impression. - 1985. - [No copy located].
ORDERED: 28.3.85   DELIVERED: ?.?.85
PRINT RUN: 1000.

CS23 First edition, second state, fourth impression. - 1987. - [No copy located].
ORDERED: 13.4.87   DELIVERED: ?.5.87
PRINT RUN: 1000.

CS24 First edition, second state, fifth impression. - 1989. - [No copy located].
ORDERED: 16.5.89   DELIVERED: ?.8.89
PRINT RUN: 1000.

CS25 First edition, second state, sixth impression. - 1991. - [No copy located].
ORDERED: 24.6.91   DELIVERED: ?.9.91
PRINT RUN: 1000.

Chorus parts

CP   *Koor Dansen / uit "Gloriana" /* [l.h.] *Engelse tekst / WILLIAM PLOMER / Nederlandse tekst / E.J. KOOIJ //* [r.h.] *BENJAMIN BRITTEN* - [London : Boosey & Hawkes, Ltd., 1957]. Pl. no. B. & H. 17688, 17688a. - 10 parts (Soprani/Alti; Tenori/Bassi: 3, [i] p., 1, [i] p., 3, [i] p., 3, [i] p., 3, [i], p.; 3, [i] p., 1, [i] p., 3, [i] p., 3, [i] p., 3, [i] p.) ; 26 cm.
PRINT CODE: none
Title from heading on p.2. of No. 1 in the Soprani/Alti part.
Copyright 1954 by Hawkes & Son (London), Ltd. Dutch version Copyright c 1957 by Hawkes & Son (London), Ltd. Sole selling agents: Boosey & Hawkes, Ltd., 295 Regent Street, London, W.1.
Dutch text (by E.J. Kooij) only.
The British Library copy (*GB-Lbl* E.1603.b.(14)) is date-stamped (blue) '5 Apr 57'.
Such parts were only issued for the Dutch-language version.

Recordings

Rec1 Sound recording. - ...*Choral dances from Gloriana / Britten.* - London : Editions de l'Oiseau-Lyre, 1961. - Catalogue no.: l'Oiseau-Lyre SOL 60037; matrix no.: ZTT-572-2D. - 1 track on 1 side of 1 sound disc (ca. 8 min.) : analogue, 33.3 rpm, stereo ; 12 in.
PERFORMERS: Chorus of the LSO; George Malcolm, conductor.
DATE AND PLACE OF RECORDING: 61.03.17 at Kingsway Hall, London.
Notes by Philip Radcliffe.

Rec2 Sound recording. - *Part songs by Benjamin Britten...Choral dances from Gloriana / Britten.* - London : Argo Record Company Limited, 1963. - Catalogue no.: Argo ZRG 5424; matrix no.: ZRG-2644-6G. - 1 track on 1 sound disc (ca. 8 min.) : analogue, 33.3 rpm, stereo ; 12 in.
PERFORMERS: Elizabethan Singers; Louis Halsey, conductor.
Notes by Eric Roseberry.

Rec3 Unpublished sound recording. - [*Gloriana*: Choral Dances]. - 1964. - 1 side of one sound disc (9:00 min.) : analogue , mono ; 12 in.
PERFORMERS: Elizabethan Singers; Louis Halsey, conductor.
DATE AND PLACE OF RECORDING: 64.08.11, at the Royal Albert Hall.
A recording by the BBC Transcription Services of a Promenade concert.
GB-Lnsa BBC TS LP 114608 [side no.]

(D) *Gloriana*: Symphonic Suite, op. 53a

1.   The Tournament
2.   The Lute Song
3.   The Courtly Dances
                    March
                    Coranto
                    Pavane
                    Morris Dance
                    Galliard
                    Lavolta
                    [March]
4.   Gloriana moritura

Scoring: picc., 2 fls, 2 obs, cor anglais, 2 cls, 2 bsns, double bsn, 4 hns, 3 tpts, 3 trbs, tuba, timpani, perc., hp, strings, ten. solo (no. 2 only: may be replaced by a solo oboe).

Duration: 26 min.

Date of composition: September-December 1953.

First performance: 23 September 1954, Town Hall, Birmingham. Peter Pears, City of Birmingham Symphony Orchestra, conducted by Rudolf Schwarz.

Publication: Unpublished; material available on hire from Boosey & Hawkes Music Publishers Ltd.

Notes

The Symphonic Suite was prepared in the autumn of 1953, but Britten was severely affected by bursitis in the right arm and, to rest it, he was obliged to write with his left hand for several weeks. The first reference to this work in Imogen Holst's diary is on 5 September. It was discussed again on 20 October and by the 3 November she was beginning work on the Courtly Dances, the first movement to be finalized. It appears that work on the suite was not resumed until late November, after revisions to the score of the opera had been completed.

Imogen Holst made all the principal adjustments in the full score of the suite, using dyelined pages from the opera score as a basis with additional newly-copied pages where necessary (F1): it was undoubtedly this score which she completed on 14 December 1953.

The Courtly Dances (2.iii) required the most rescoring, since the band playing them in the opera consists of a small group of instruments on stage in a gallery. Britten also re-ordered the sequence of dances (in the opera they appear thus: Pavane, Galliard, Lavolta, Morris Dance, March, Coranto) which in the suite are played in the sequence: March, Coranto, Pavane, Morris Dance, Galliard, Lavolta, with the March repeated at the end. In the second movement the solo voice part of Essex's Second Lute Song ('Happy were he') may be taken by a solo oboe.

Both the second and third movements may be performed separately; the printed copies of the full score have the following typeset note pasted onto the inside of the front wrapper:

> It is the composer's recommendation that when this suite is to be performed in full, the following cuts should be made in the third movement, "The Courtly Dances": (i) From 8 bars before figure 4 to figure 4. (ii) The repeated sections 16 bars before figure 5 to 16 bars

after figure 5 to be played without repeats. (iii) The 3 bars before figure 16 to be played without repeat. These cuts should not be made when this movement is played separately.

Sources

Holographs	H1-H4
Full scores	F1-F2.2
Orchestral parts	P1-P2.3
Recording	Rec1

Holographs

H1   Sketch (3. Courtly Dances). Holograph: pencil. - [Untitled]. - [September-November 1953]. - [2] fol. : 20 staves, [span:] 33.45 cm. ; 36.6 x 27.1 cm.
ANALYSIS: [1ʳ] music and notes, [1ᵛ-2ʳ] blank, [2ᵛ] unidentified sketch.
COLLATION: [1-2] A².
FILM NUMBERS: A4 (frames 457-8).
Notes outlining the organization and scoring of the Courtly Dances.
GB-ALb 2-9202583

H2   Draft (2. Lute Song, incomplete full score, paginated). Holograph: pencil. - *Lute song*. - [1953]. - [2] fol. : 20 staves, [span:] 33.45 cm. ; 36.6 x 27.1 cm.
ANALYSIS: [1ʳ] music, [1ᵛ-2ᵛ] blank.
COLLATION: [1-2] A².
FILM NUMBERS: A4 (frame 424).
Kept in additional wrapper with H4; pencil note on wrapper (Rosamund Strode): 'written with difficulty by BB left-handed, his right arm being affected by bursitis at the time, which was the end of 1953.' This draft contains just the opening and the end of the movement - all that is needed to extract the music from the opera. *GB-ALb* 2-9202582

H3   Preparatory copy (3. Courtly Dances, full score, paginated). Holograph and non-holograph ms. (dyeline) (copyist: Imogen Holst); with annotations (Benjamin Britten, Rosamund Strode). - *SCORE / GLORIANA / ACT II SCENE III / STAGE ORCHESTRA FOR DANCES*. - [n.d.]. - [12] fol. ; 37 cm.
ANALYSIS: [1ʳ] tp, [1ᵛ-2ᵛ] blank, [3ʳ-4ʳ] *3 GALLIARD*, [6ᵛ] *4. CONVERSATION AND THE QUEEN'S ENTRANCE*, [7ʳ-8ᵛ] *5 LA VOLTA*, [8ᵛ-9ᵛ] *6 CONVERSATION*, [9ʳ-ᵛ] *7 MORRIS DANCE*, [9ᵛ] *8 RECITATIVE / 9 THE QUEEN'S BURLESQUE*, [9ᵛ-10ʳ] *10 QUARTET*, [10ʳ-ᵛ] *11 MARCH*, [11ʳ] *12 THE QUEEN'S ANNOUNCEMENT*, [11ʳ-11ᵛ] *13 ENSEMBLE*, [11ᵛ-12ᵛ] *14 CORANTO*.
FILM NUMBERS: A4 (frames 459-479).
A dyeline of the stage orchestra score for 2.iii ((A)/H4); note by Rosamund Strode: 'this copy was used as a "notebook" by BB in conjunction with the pencilled score [H4]....'[45] *GB-ALb* 2-9200287

---

[45] Britten played through 'the suite' (probably only the courtly dances) to Imogen Holst on 6 September 1953. There seems to have been a plan for a piano solo version to be arranged by Imogen Holst, but this did not materialize.

H4   Draft full score (3. Courtly dances, paginated). Holograph and non-holograph ms.: black ink, pencil (Benjamin Britten, Imogen Holst). - [Untitled]. - [September-October 1953]. - [16] fol. : 27 staves,[46] [span:] 37.7 cm. ; 44.5 x 29.2 cm.

       ANALYSIS: [1^r-16^v] music.

       COLLATION: [1-16] A-B^4.

       FILM NUMBERS: A4 (frames 425-456).

         Kept with H2 in additional wrapper (for text of note on [fo] see above).

         Prepared in conjunction with H3.[47]   *GB-ALb* 2-9202581

Full scores

F1   Interim full score (production copy, signed). Holograph and non-holograph ms. (single-sided dyeline), ms.: black ink (Imogen Holst); with annotations, corrections and revisions: various implements (Benjamin Britten, [unidentified]). - [Holograph (pencil):] *SYMPHONIC SUITE* / *"GLORIANA"* / *op. 53A* / *I The Tournament* / *II The Lute Song* / *III The Courtly Dances* / *IV Gloriana Moritura* / [rule] / *Benjamin Britten*. - [November-14 December 1953]. - [35] fol., bound in dark green cloth, gold tooling on spine ; various sizes : 34 staves, [span:] 45.2 cm., [maker:] GSCHIRMER/IMPERIAL BRAND/No. 14-34 Staves ; various sizes + 40 paste-overs [[a]-[an]].[48]

       ANALYSIS: [1^r] tp, [1^v] blank, [2^r-11^v] *The Tournament*, [12^r-14^v] *The Lute Song* ([13^v] blank), [15^r-25^v] *The Courtly Dances*, [26^r-35^v] *Gloriana moritura*.

       COLLATION:[49] [1] (unruled sheet), [2-8] (dyeline; [a-b] on [5^r]), [9-10] (type A), [11] (dyeline; [c-g] on 11^r, [h-j] on 11^v), [12^r] (type A), [12^v-13^r] (dyeline; [k-n] on 12^v, [o-p] on 13^r], [13^v] (type A;), [14] (dyeline; [q-s] on 14^r, [t-v] on 14^v), [15-26^r] (type A; [w] on [17^v], [x] on [18^r], [y] on [18^v]), [26^v-27^r] (dyeline), [27^v] (type A), [28-29] (dyeline; [aa-ab] on [28^v]), [30^r] (type A), [30^v] (dyeline; [ac-ad]), [31^r] (type A), [31^v] (dyeline), [32^r] (type A), [32^v-34^v] (dyeline; [ae-af] on [33^r], [ag-ai] on [33^v], [aj-am] on [34^v], [35] (type A; [an] on [34^v]).

       FILM NUMBER: A4 (frames 510-581).

         Pencil annotation [2^v]: 'Copyright 1954 by Hawkes & Son (London) Ltd.'

         Made up from dyelined pages from (A)/H3 of the opera, with paste-overs and inserted leaves copied by Imogen Holst. Copying began on 3 November 1953, Imogen Holst working on the Courtly Dances; she was probably ruling up fol. [15-25]. The idea of using dyelines when producing the copy was first discussed by Imogen Holst and the composer on 18 November. At this date the exact constitution of the Suite was still not finalized. Imogen Holst was given the 'dance suite score' to copy on 22 November, and her work on other movements was

---

[46] This unusual ruling is laid out for full scores, with the bottom five staves (for the strings) separated from the rest by a slightly larger gap; Imogen Holst seems not to have noticed this and used some sheets upside-down.

[47] Imogen Holst appears to have done the preparatory work on this score on 6 September 1953. On 25 October 1953 Britten was writing 'his score with his left hand' — presumably this full score.

[48] Blank paste-overs, or those simply replacing rehearsal numbers are not included in the document description.

[49] The binding is such that the original fascicle structure cannot be reconstructed.

under way on 7 December, when she began by 'correcting mistakes in the photographed pages'. The score has been lightly marked for printing.

GB-ALb 2-9200219

F2.1   Hire material. - *Benjamin Britten / Symphonic Suite / GLORIANA / I The Tournament / II The Lute Song / III The Courtly Dances / IV Gloriana Moritura / Full score / Hawkes & Son (London) Ltd. / Sole Selling Agents: BOOSEY & HAWKES Ltd. / London · Paris · Bonn · Capetown · Sydney · Toronto · New York.* - London : Hawkes & Son (London) Ltd., 1954. Pl. no.: B. & H. 17546. - [ii], [1]-100, [iii-iv] p., yellow thick paper cover ; 31 cm.

ANALYSIS: [fo] *Benjamin Britten / Symphonic Suite GLORIANA / Full score / Boosey & Hawkes*, [fi] blank with note pasted on, [i] tp, [ii] instrumentation, [1]-30 *I THE TOURNAMENT*, 31-42 *II THE LUTE SONG*, 43-79 *III THE COURTLY DANCES*, 80-100 *IV GLORIANA MORITURA*, [iii] advert (no. 531, dated 8/49), [iv] advert (no. 537, dated 8.49), [ri] blank, [ro] advert (no. 600, dated 9.51).

PRINT CODE: 10.54.E   ORDERED: 3.11.54

PRINT RUN: 255

Most copies bear a typeset note pasted onto [fi] giving details of cuts to be made in the third movement in performances of the complete suite.[50]

F2.2   - Annotated copy (file copy). Printed; with annotations and corrections: pencil (Rosamund Strode). - Bound in blue boards with gold tooling on spine and front board.

GB-ALb 2-9200228

For Britten's copy, received in 1954, and used as a conducting score, see (P)/F1.

Parts

[P1]   [Manuscript parts. - [1954]. - Not located.]
The originals from which the hire set P2 was produced.

P2.1-2.3 Hire material. Printed from ms. copies (various copyists). - *SYMPHONIC SUITE / GLORIANA / [r.h.] / Benjamin Britten / Op. 53a.* - [1954?]. - London: Hawkes & Son, (London) Ltd. Pl. no.: B. & H. 17532. - 31 vols ; 31.3 cm.

CONTENTS: fl. 1, fl. 2 and picc., picc. and fl. 3, ob. 1, ob. 2, cor anglais, cl. 1 in B flat, cl. 2 in B flat, bass cl., bsn 1, bsn 2, dbsn, hn 1 in F, hn 2 in F, hn 3 in F, hn 4 in F, trpt 1 in C, trpt 2 in C, trpt 3 in C, trb. 1, trb. 2, trb. 3, tuba, timpani, perc., hp, vln 1, vln 2, vla, vcl, db.

Title from heading on p. [1] of vln 1 part.

GB-Lbh houses three sets; the third contains a manuscript timpani part for the Coranto in the Courtly Dances.   GB-Lbh Hire Library

Recording

Rec1   Unpublished sound recording - *A Concert of contemporary British music* [...Symphonic suite from Gloriana / Britten]. - [Unpublished broadcast]. - Matrix no.: 12-FPD-100127. - 1 side of 1 sound disc (ca. 30 min.) : analogue, 33.3 rpm, mono ; 12 in.

DATE AND PLACE OF RECORDING: not known.

PERFORMERS: Philharmonia Orchestra; John Pritchard, conductor.

Disc made by the BBC Transcription Service.   GB-ALb 3-9203359

---

50   For a complete transcription, see pp. 130-131 above.

(E) March from the Courtly Dances, arranged for orchestra

Arranger: Imogen Holst

Scoring: not known

Duration: ca. 1 min.

Date: 1953?-1954?

First performance: 27 February 1954, Ipswich

Publication: unpublished

Notes:

Imogen Holst scored the March for the Suffolk Rural Music School's Adult Founders' Day concert in Ipswich, on 27 February 1954.[51] No sources for this arrangement have been located, but it may have been completed some time before the performance, to allow for adequate rehearsal time.

---

[51] 'Suffolk', *Making Music*, 25 (Summer 1954), 16.

(F) Morris Dance arranged for two descant recorders

Arranger: Imogen Holst

Scoring: 2 descant recorders

Duration: 1 min.

Date of arrangement: 1955?

First performance: not traced

Publication: London: Boosey & Hawkes, 1957

Notes

The series *Music for Recorders* was edited, nominally, by Imogen Holst and Benjamin Britten, though in fact most of the arrangements and the editorial work was undertaken by Imogen Holst. Nevertheless there can be no doubt that Britten would have approved Morris Dance and other items within the series. It is not clear when the arrangement was actually made, but the assignment of copyright is dated 12 December 1955 (*GB-ALhf*). The dance appears in the opera as 2.iii.7.

Sources

P1   First edition. - *MUSIC FOR RECORDERS* | *Morris dance from "Gloriana"* | [r.h.:]
      BENJAMIN BRITTEN ... | *Sole Selling Agents: Boosey & Hawkes, Ltd., 295
      Regent Street, London.W.1* | *Paris · Bonn · Capetown · Sydney · Toronto · Buenos
      Aires · New York.* - London : Boosey & Hawkes, Ltd., c1957. Pl. no.:
      B.& H. 18231b. Ed. no.: RP 14. - 3, [i] p. ; 27 cm.
      ANALYSIS: 1-3 [music], [i] advert (no. 758, dated 3.55).
          Title from front wrapper.
          Copyright c 1957 by Hawkes & Son (London), Ltd.
          Each item could be bought separately, or the group (nos. 13-18 in the
          series) purchased in thick paper wrappers ([fo] *MUSIC FOR
          RECORDERS* | *Edited by Benjamin Britten and Imogen Holst* | *RECORDER
          PIECES* | *From the 12th to the 20th Century* | *Price 1/- net each, or complete in
          folder 4/-d. net* | *(1956)* | *BOOSEY and HAWKES*).

(G) Choral Dances from *Gloriana* (version with tenor solo)

[Introduction]
1. Time (SATB)
2. Concord (SATB)
3. Time and Concord (SATB)
4. Country Girls (SA)
5. Rustics and Fishermen (TTBB)
6. Final Dance of Homage (SATB)

Arranger: Imogen Holst

Scoring: tenor solo, SATB

Duration: ca. 9 min.

Date of arrangement: 1955?-1956

First performance: 15 April 1956, Victoria & Albert Museum. Purcell Singers with Peter Pears, conducted by Imogen Holst.

Publication: unpublished

Notes

Prepared by Imogen Holst for Peter Pears, for concerts of unaccompanied music which he gave with the Purcell Singers in the later 1950s. The Choral Dances from *Gloriana* made a good final item in a programme; most of the solo tenor line derives from role of Spirit of the Masque, whose solos connect the dances in the opera, and accompanies the chorus in the final dance.

There is some evidence that this adaptation was prepared in stages: first, with the tenor solo only in no. 6 (CS1 below); then with all the linking recitatives (which simply omit the accompaniment and all vocal parts other than that of the Spirit of the Masque) with a brief introduction for solo tenor (from 'And now we summon') (see CS2); and finally with a more extended form of introduction using solo tenor and chorus (from Cuffe's 'The masque begins'). However the arrangement's evolution may have been more complex: see the notes to P1 below.

Sources

Chorus scores

CS1   Interim copy (marked-up copy of (C)/CS2). Printed; with revisions: pencil (Imogen Holst). - 23, [i] p., white paper wrapper ; 26.5 cm. + 8 paste-overs ([a-h]).

        ANALYSIS: as (C) CS2 except: 20-23 6. *Final Dance of Homage* ([a-b] on 20, [c-d] on 21, [e-f] on 22, [g-h] on 23).

        Wrapper annotated by Imogen Holst (pencil): 'Tenor Solo in No. 6 / Holst'.

        Solo tenor part added in No. 6 only ; the connecting solos are omitted.
                                           GB-ALb 2-9200225

CS2   Set of performance material (marked-up copies of (C)/CS1 and (C)/CS2). Printed; with annotations: pencil (Imogen Holst, unidentified hands). - 23, [i] p., white paper wrapper, stitched ; 27 cm.

           ANALYSIS: [description of no. 14[52] in the set:] [fo] title, [fi] various notes: pencil, black ink (Imogen Holst), including: *These dances are linked by Peter Pears singing unaccompanied recitatives. The cues are given in pencil before each number, 1-5 1. Time* ([a] on p. 1), *6-8 2. Concord* ([b] on p. 6), *9-13 3. Time and Concord* ([c] on p. 9), *14-15 4. Country Girls* ([d] on p. 14), *16-19 5. Rustics and Fishermen* ([e] on p. 16), *20-23 6. Final Dance of Homage* ([f] on p. 20), [the rest as (C)/CS1].

           22 copies, probably used by the Purcell Singers. Covers initialled (pencil): 'IH'. With 6 paste-overs [a-f] on copy no. 14, written out by Imogen Holst to give the tenor solos between dances as cues. In no. 6 the solo tenor part is notated (an octave higher than sounding) in the soprano stave: pencil (Imogen Holst).

           A set made up from copies of the first two impressions of the first edition of the Choral Dances, and revised for performances of the version with tenor solo: all copies have pencil indications (either verbal or musical) of the solo tenor introduction and connecting recitatives; some are in the hand of Imogen Holst.   *GB-ALb* 2-9206072

CS3.1   Manuscript copy (introduction only). Manuscript: black ink, blue ballpoint, pencil (Imogen Holst). - *INTRODUCTION TO GLORIANA DANCES* / [pencil, r.h.] *BRITTEN*. - [1956?]. - [1] fol. : 16 staves, [span:] 29.1 cm., [maker:] [galleon logo] / A.L. No 10 / Printed in England ; 35.5 x 26.3 cm.

           ANALYSIS: [1[r]] music, [1[v]] blank.

           Contains an extended introduction which opens with the solo tenor singing 'The masque begins' (sung by Cuffe in the opera) only; the incipit of the solo tenor's connecting recitative 'And now we summon' follows, and this in turn presumably led into the first dance as in the opera.

           GB-ALb 2-9200247

CS3.2   - Further copies. Ms. (dyeline) (copyist: Imogen Holst). - [1956?]. - [1] fol. ; 36 cm.

           ANALYSIS: [1[r]] music, [1[v]] blank.

           2 copies; pencil initials 'IH' on both.   *GB-ALb* 2-9100013

CS3.3   - Further copies. Ms. (dyeline) (copyist: Imogen Holst). - [1956?]. - [1] fol. ; 37 cm.

           22 copies; probably used with CS2 for performances by the Purcell Singers.

           All copies initialled (pencil): 'IH'.   *GB-ALb* 2-9206071

Part

P1   Manuscript solo part. Ms. copy: black ink, pencil (Imogen Holst, Peter Pears, Rosamund Strode); with annotations and revisions: black felt-tip (Peter Pears). - *Dances from the Norwich Scene in Gloriana*. - [1956?]. - [3] fol. : 16 staves, [span:] 23.4 cm. ; 27.3 x 18.3 cm.

           ANALYSIS: [1[r]-3[r]] music, [3[v]] Machaut: *Douce dame jolie, pour Dieu*.

           COLLATION: [1-2] A[2], [3] (copied by Rosamund Strode [3[r]] and Peter Pears [3[v]]).

---

[52] Probably prepared for a BBC sound producer.

CONTENTS: includes the melody and about half of the text of Guillaume de Machaut's virelai *Douce dame jolie, pour Dieu* copied by Peter Pears (pencil) [3ᵛ].[53]

FILM NUMBER: A19 (frames 267-276).

It seems likely that fol. [3ʳ] was copied first, for use in the earliest form of the adaptation, with the tenor solo appearing only in no. 6. The rest of the part was probably copied out later, but the content of the introduction is odd. It is musically continuous from Cuffe's 'The masque begins', and includes the chorus tenor line where there is no solo part. Moreover the original layer of copying corresponds metrically to the text of the opera, but it has been revised to correspond to the modified version adopted by Imogen Holst in CS3.1-3.3.

The Machaut virelai appeared at least twice in concerts by the Purcell Singers and Peter Pears which also included performances of the Choral Dances.[54]   *GB-ALb* 2-9202580

---

[53] Although this virelai has been annotated in Peter Pears's printed copy of the complete edition (*GB-ALb* 9104497: *Guillaume de Machaut: Musikalische Werke*, ed. F. Ludwig (Leipzig: VEB Breitkopf & Härtel, 1954), vol. 1, p. 71), textual discrepancies suggest this was not the source from which he copied this *aide-mémoire*.

[54] On 23 May 1955 (a BBC radio broadcast repeated on 11 October 1955) and on 10 September 1955 at Rainthorpe Hall (a performance attended by the composer).

(H) Courtly Dances, arranged for small orchestra

1. March
2. Coranto
3. Pavane
4. Morris Dance
5. Galliard
6. Lavolta

Scoring: fl., ob., cl., bsn, hn, trb., guitar, harpsichord, perc., strings

Duration: ca. 9.5 min.

Date of arrangement: 1957

First performance: 23 June 1957, Jubilee Hall, Aldeburgh. Members of the Aldeburgh
Festival Orchestra, conductor: Charles Mackerras.

Publication: unpublished

Notes

This arrangement was made specially for a concert in the 1957 Aldeburgh Festival:
the scoring of the arrangement was determined by the forces needed for the rest of the
programme (which included Henze's *Apollo et Hyazinthus*, and the Guitar Concerto by
Villa-Lobos). The material was produced by cannibalizing a printed score and parts of
the Symphonic Suite.

Although prepared for a specific occasion, this version was heard at least once more
during the composer's lifetime, conducted by Imogen Holst at a concert, with the English
Chamber Orchestra, at the Royal Festival Hall, on 10 January 1968.

Sources

Holograph

H1   Draft full score (paginated). Holograph: pencil. - *Courtly Dances* / [rule]. - [1957]. -
[14] fol. : 24 staves, [span:] 31.95 cm. ; 36 x 26.6 cm.
ANALYSIS: [1^r-14^v] music.
COLLATION: [1-14] A-G^2.
FILM NUMBERS: A4 (frames 480-509).
Pencil note on additional wrapper (Rosamund Strode): 'specially re-
scored for performance at The Aldeburgh Festival on 23rd June 1957
(NOT Bream Consort!)' - see (I) below.   *GB-ALb* 2-9202584

Full score

F1   Manuscript copy (paginated). Printed, ms. copy: pencil, (Imogen Holst); with
annotations: pencil (Imogen Holst). - [Printed, pasted on:] *Benjamin Britten* /
GLORIANA / *The Courtly Dances* / [pencil, Imogen Holst:] *Aldeburgh version*. -
[1957]. - [21] fol. : 24 staves, [span:] 29.1 cm., [maker:] [galleon logo] / AL /
No. 18 ; 35.6 x 25.8 cm. + 65 paste-overs [a-cm].
ANALYSIS: [1^r] tp, [1^v] blank, [2^r-4^r] *March* (= pp. 1-5), [4^r-7^r] *Coranto* (= pp. 5-
11), [7^r-10^r] *Pavane* (= pp. 11-17), [10^r-11^v] *Morris Dance* (= pp. 17-20), [11^v-
14^r] *Galliard* (= p. 20-25), [14^v-19^v] *Lavolta* (= pp. 26-36), [20^r-21^v] blank.

COLLATION: [1-4] single sheets, [5-6] A², [7-9] single sheets, [10-17] B⁸, [18-21] C⁴.
Made up of paste-overs cut from a score of the Symphonic Suite ((D)/F2) with the rest in the hand of Imogen Holst.   *GB-ALb* 2-9200272

Parts

P1   Manuscript parts (paginated). Ms. copies: black ink, red ink (Imogen Holst, [unidentified]); with annotations and corrections: pencil, blue ballpoint (Imogen Holst, James Blades, [unidentified]). - *THE COURTLY DANCES FROM GLORIANA / BRITTEN.* - [1957?]. - 15 vols ([39] fol.) : [A:] 12 staves, [span:] 25.55 cm., [maker:] R.C. 1 / [galleon logo] ; 30.5 x 22.9 cm. : [B:] 12 staves, [span:] 25.5 cm., [maker:] R.C. 1 / [galleon logo] / Printed in England ; 31.2 x 24.2 cm.
CONTENTS: fl., ob., cl., bsn, hn, trb., guitar, harpsichord, perc., vln 1 x 2, vln 2, vla, vcl., db.
Title from front wrapper of vln 1.
Imogen Holst copied the vln, vla and vcl. parts on paper A; the rest are copied on paper B in another hand. With P2 these formed a complete set of parts associated with the score, F1.   *GB-ALb* 2-9200274

P2   Printed parts. Printed; with annotations, deletions and revisions: pencil (Imogen Holst). - *SYMPHONIC SUITE / GLORIANA / [r.h.:] BENJAMIN BRITTEN / Op. 53a.* - London : Hawkes & Son (London) Ltd., [n.d.], c1954. Pl. no.: B. & H. 17532. - 4 vols (12, 11, 12, 11 pp.) ; 31.3 cm.
CONTENTS: vln 1 (x 2), vln 2 (x 2), vla, vcl.
Title from heading on p. 1 of vln 1.
An incomplete set of printed string parts for the Symphonic Suite ((D)/P2), revised for the 1957 arrangement for small orchestra of the Courtly Dances. Together with P1 these formed a complete set of parts associated with the score F1.   *GB-ALb* 2-9200273

Recording

Rec1   Unpublished recording. - [1957]. - *Aldeburgh Festival of Music and the Arts.* - 1 side on 1 sound disc (9:27 min.) : analogue, 33.3 rpm, mono, 12 in. - [Item not examined].
PERFORMERS: Members of the Aldeburgh Festival Orchestra; conductor: Charles Mackerras.
DATE AND PLACE OF RECORDING: 57.06.23, at the Jubilee Hall, Aldeburgh.
Part of a complete recording of the Aldeburgh Festival Concert by the BBC Transcription Service.   *GB-Lnsa* BBC TS LP 94281 [side no.]

(I) Courtly Dances, arranged for lute and ensemble

1. March
2. Corante
3. Pavan
4. Morris Dance
5. Galliard
6. La Volta
7. March

Arranger: Julian Bream

Scoring: Fl. (doubling picc., alto fl.), vln, bass viols, tabor, lute.

Date of arrangement: 1962?

First performance: 18 June 1962, the Workmen's Club, Thorpeness. The Julian Bream
    Consort (Olive Zorian, Joy Hall, David Sandeman, Desmond Dupré, and Robert
    Spencer) directed by Julian Bream.

Publication: unpublished

Notes
No manuscript or printed sources for this arrangement have been located.

Recording

Rec1   Sound recording. - *Julian Bream...The courtly dances from "Gloriana"* / *Britten ; set by*
    Julian Bream. - [New York] : Radio Corporation of America, 1965. - Catalogue
    no.: RCA Victor Red Seal SB-6635; matrix no.: PRRS-6808-2G. - 1 track on
    1 sound disc : analogue, 33.3 rpm, stereo ; 12 in.
    PERFORMERS: Julian Bream, lute; Olive Zorian, vln; David Sandeman, fl.; Joy
        Hall, bass viol; Desmond Dupré, bass viol; Robert Spencer, tabor.
    Pencil note on record sleeve (Rosamund Strode): 'p1965 UK'.
    Released 6.64, USA.
    Product of the Decca Record Company Ltd., London, made from a
    master recording of R.C.A., N.Y.
    Notes by Gene Lees.

(J) Second Lute Song, arranged for voice and guitar

Arranger: Julian Bream

Scoring: voice and guitar

Duration: 5 min.

Date of arrangement: 1962?-1963?

First performance: not traced

Publication: unpublished

Notes

   Julian Bream first performed at Aldeburgh in the 1952 Festival and from 1954 gave joint recitals with Peter Pears. This partnership, for which Britten composed the *Songs from the Chinese* in 1959, was to last for twenty years, and offered Pears an opportunity to explore a repertoire which did not appear in his recitals with Britten. Bream would accompany sixteenth- and seventeenth-century songs on lute, transferring to guitar for the twentieth-century items. This transcription was certainly prepared for such a concert.

Sources

Arrangements

P1   Manuscript guitar part.   Manuscript: blue ballpoint (Julian Bream); with annotation: blue ballpoint (Peter Pears). - *GLORIANA*. - [n.d.]. - [2] fol. : 10 staves, [span:] 27.3 cm., [maker:] [logo] Papier Carpentier No. 110, Système Siestrop, déposé ; 33.7 x 25.2 cm.
ANALYSIS: [1^r] tp, [1^v-2^r] music, [2^v] unidentified music on two staves.
COLLATION: [1-2] A^2.
FILM NUMBERS: A19 (frames 277-281).
      The text is in the hand of Peter Pears.   *GB-ALb* 2-9202579

Recordings

Rec1   Sound recording. - *Music for voice and guitar...The second lute song from Gloriana / Britten*. - [S.l.] : Radio Corporation of America, c1965. - Catalogue no.: RCA Victor Red Seal LSC-2718; matrix no.: PRRS-6840–1S. - 1 track on 1 side of 1 sound disc (ca. 5 min.) : analogue, 33.3 rpm, stereo ; 12 in.
PERFORMERS: Peter Pears, ten.; Julian Bream, guitar.
PLACE OF RECORDING: Adam Library at Kenwood House, London.
      Notes by Marcia Drennen

Rec2   Unpublished sound recording. - *Julian Bream / Peter Pears*. - 1976. - 1 sound tape reel (ca. 5 min.) : analogue, 15 ips, 2 track, mono.
PERFORMERS: Peter Pears, ten.; Julian Bream, guitar.
DATE AND PLACE OF RECORDING: 76.09.25 at Snape Maltings.
      Recorded live at a public concert.
      On deposit from the Aldeburgh Foundation.   *GB-ALb* 3-9102522

(K) Five Courtly Dances from *Gloriana*, arranged for school orchestra

1.   March
2.   Coranto
3.   Pavane
4.   Morris Dance
5.   Lavolta
[6.   Reprise of the March]

Arranger: David Stone

Scoring: fl., ob., 2 cls in B flat, bsn, 2 hns, 2 trpts in B flat, trb., timpani, perc. (cymbals, tambourine, side drum, tenor drum, bass drum), piano, strings; the following optional parts are supplied but do not appear in the score: 2 desc. recs, treb. rec., E flat cl., B flat bass cl., E flat alto sax., B flat ten. sax., vln III.[55]

Date of arrangement: 1963

First performance: untraced

Publication: Full score, piano conductor and parts: London: Boosey & Hawkes, 1965

Notes

This arrangement was suggested by Donald Mitchell;[56] recalling his period as consultant at Boosey and Hawkes, Donald Mitchell wrote: '[Britten] was particularly anxious for me to explore ... the whole educational area and in particular the creation of new works for young musicians to perform. We all know how close to Britten's heart that particular musical dimension was. I thought it would be a great idea to kick off with something by Britten himself. *Gloriana* was much in my mind because I was involved in 1963 with the revival of the work at the Festival Hall .... There was certainly no hope of Britten writing an original work but it seemed to me a distinct possibility that the dances could be effectively arranged - I think David Stone did a very good job here - and would turn out to be a success, which I am delighted to see ... has proved to be the case.'[57]

David Stone was for many years the orchestral/schools music adviser to Boosey & Hawkes. One of his projects was the editorship and arrangement of many of the *Hawkes School Series*, and he too had been struck by the suitability of the Dances for inclusion in the series. Mr Stone recalls: 'I think I most probably made the arrangement in the summer of 1963, but ... I have no written records apart from the contract dated 21/11/63.'[58]

A copy of the Five Courtly Dances was sent to Britten for approval on 3 September 1963.[59] The Galliard was omitted as it would 'make the collection too long, and also would be ineffectual if performed by inferior forces.'[60] Britten's response was positive but was perhaps unduly modest about his experience of writing for children:

---

55   A surrogate viola part.
56   Letter from Donald Mitchell to Britten, 5 October 1963.
57   Letter to Paul Banks, 16 February 1993.
58   Letter to Paul Banks, 4 March 1993.
59   Letter from Geoffrey Russell-Smith (Manager, Education Department at Boosey & Hawkes) to Britten.
60   From the letter by Russell-Smith cited above.

I fear this is something rather outside my experience, and if David Stone is an authority on what is need[ed], I certainly give my approval to this publication. I quite approve of the idea of leaving out the Galliard. I have made one or two tiny suggestions, particularly on pages 30-31; if there is a bright boy, it would be a pity not to include some of the trombone glissandos which are in my score.[61]

David Stone also recalls 'a brief note from the composer about some small amendments to the trombone requirements (see Lavolta fig. 10). I also think there was some discussion about the desirability or not of putting dynamic markings in the recorder parts: Britten I think considered it best to omit them, being of the opinion that seeing f would just result in children tending to play sharp.'

Sources

Scores

Manuscript	F1
Printed	F2-F12

Parts   P1-P25

Scores

[F1]   [Manuscript arrangement. - 1963. - Not located.]
> This source would have been retained by Boosey & Hawkes and it, or more probably a copy of it, was sent to Britten for his comments in September 1963.

F2   First edition. - *BENJAMIN BRITTEN* / *FIVE COURTLY DANCES* / *FROM* / *GLORIANA* / *Arranged by* / *DAVID STONE* / *ORCHESTRAL SCORE* / *BOOSEY & HAWKES.* - London : Boosey & Hawkes, [1965], c1964. Pl. no.: B. & H. 19200. Ed. no.: H.S.S. 95. - 40 p., orange thin card wrapper ; 31.3 cm. - (Hawkes School Series ; No. 95).
> ANALYSIS: [fo] *H.S.S. No. 95* / [next six lines boxed:] *BENJAMIN BRITTEN* / *FIVE COURTLY DANCES* / *FROM* / *GLORIANA* / *Arranged by* / *DAVID STONE* / *ORCHESTRAL SCORE* / *BOOSEY & HAWKES*, [fi] blank, 1-4 *March*, 5-11 *Coranto*, 12-18 *Pavane*, 19-26 *Morris Dance*, 27-40 *Lavolta*, [ri] blank, [ro] advert (no. 8c, dated 9.64).
> PRINT CODE: 12.64.E.   ORDERED: 5.11.64   DELIVERED: 12.1.65
> PRINT RUN: 1150
> Title from front cover.

F3   First edition, second impression. - 1966. - [No copy located].
> ORDERED: 26.5.66   DELIVERED: 24.6.66
> PRINT RUN: 250

F4   First edition, third impression. - 1968. - [No copy located].
> ORDERED: 6.3.68   DELIVERED: 2.4.68
> PRINT RUN: 250

F5   First edition, fourth impression. - 1968. - [No copy located].
> ORDERED: 6.11.68   DELIVERED: 27.11.68
> PRINT RUN: 250

---

[61] Letter from Britten to John Andrewes, 17th September 1963, sent with the copy of the score.

F6   First edition, fifth impression. - 1969. - [No copy located].
           ORDERED: 6.10.69   DELIVERED: 12.12.69
           PRINT RUN: 500

F7   First edition, sixth impression. - 1974. - [No copy located].
           ORDERED: 8.11.73   DELIVERED: ?.1.74
           PRINT RUN: 500

F8   First edition, seventh impression. - 1978. - [No copy located].
           ORDERED: 5.1.78   DELIVERED: 6.3.78
           PRINT RUN: 150

F9   First edition, eighth impression. - 1979. - [No copy located].
           ORDERED: 13.2.79   DELIVERED: 30.5.79
           PRINT RUN: 200

F10   First edition, ninth impression. - 1982. - [No copy located].
           ORDERED: 1.3.82   DELIVERED: 5.10.82
           PRINT RUN: 270

F11   First edition, tenth impression. - 1984. - [No copy located].
           ORDERED: 21.6.84   DELIVERED: ?.8.84
           PRINT RUN: 100

F12   First edition, eleventh impression. - 1987. - [No copy located].
           ORDERED: 8.12.86   DELIVERED: ?.1.87
           PRINT RUN: 500

Parts

P1   First   edition. - [all within box:] *HAWKES' SCHOOL SERIES /
           SCHULORCHESTER-AUSGABE / [double rule] / BENJAMIN BRITTEN /
           FIVE COURTLY DANCES / FROM / GLORIANA / Arranged by / DAVID
           STONE / [logo] / H.S.S. No. 95 / BOOSEY & HAWKES.* - London : Boosey &
           Hawkes, [1965], c1964. Pl. no.: B. & H. 19200. Ed. no.: H.S.S. no. 95. -
           28 instr. parts, in grey-green, thick paper wrapper ; 31.3 cm.
           ANALYSIS: Wrapper: [fo] title as above, [fi] blank, [ri] blank, [ro] advert
           (no. 8c, dated 9.64).
           ORDERED: 5.11.64   DELIVERED: 12.1.65
           PRINT RUN: 1250 (sets), 2000 (piano conductor), 10,000 (extra strings)[62]
               Parts: fl., desc. recs 1, 2, treb. rec., ob., cls 1, 2, E flat cl., bass cl., alto sax.,
               ten. sax., bsn, 2 hns, 2 trpts, 1 trb., timpani, cymbal, tambourine, side
               drum, tenor drum, bass drum, vln 1, 2, 3, vla, vcl., db., piano conductor.
               Title from front of wrapper.

P2   First edition, second impression. - 1967. - [No copy located].
           ORDERED: 9.5.67   DELIVERED: 18.5.67
           PRINT RUN: 2250 (strings), 750 (wind)

P3   First edition, third impression. - 1968. - [No copy located].
           ORDERED: 28.2.68   DELIVERED: 16.5.68
           PRINT RUN: 1500 (strings)

---

[62] Unless otherwise indicated, here, as elsewhere in the following entries for this arrangement, the figures probably refer to individual parts, not string (or wind) sets.

P4   First edition, fourth impression. - 1968. - [No copy located].
        ORDERED: 18.6.68   DELIVERED: 6.8.68
        PRINT RUN: 1750 (strings), 1300 (wind)

P5   First edition, fifth impression. - 1968. - [No copy located].
        ORDERED: 6.11.68   DELIVERED: 2.12.68
        PRINT RUN: 250 (piano conductor), 6000 (strings), 4150 (wind)

P6   First edition, sixth impression. - 1968. - [No copy located].
        ORDERED: 5.12.68   DELIVERED: 13.12.68
        PRINT RUN: 250 (perc.)

P7   First edition, seventh impression. - 1969. - [No copy located].
        ORDERED: 8.10.69   DELIVERED: 8.12.69
        PRINT RUN: 1850 (strings), 2500 (wind)

P8   First edition, eighth impression. - 1971. - [No copy located].
        ORDERED: 6.4.71   DELIVERED: 3.6.71
        PRINT RUN: 350 (covers), 250 (piano conductor), 3000 (strings), 3800 (wind)

P9   First edition, ninth impression. - 1973. - [No copy located].
        ORDERED: 10.3.73   DELIVERED: 10.5.73
        PRINT RUN: 250 (piano conductor), 3750 (strings), 1250 (wind)

P10   First edition, tenth impression. - 1974. - [No copy located].
        ORDERED: 8.11.73   DELIVERED: 15.1.74
        PRINT RUN: 2750 (strings), 2750 (wind)

P11   First edition, eleventh impression. - 1977. - [No copy located].
        ORDERED: 12.1.77   DELIVERED: ?.1.77
        PRINT RUN: 1200 (strings), 450 (wind)

P12   First edition, twelfth impression. - 1978. - [No copy located].
        ORDERED: 5.1.78   DELIVERED: 4.4.78
        PRINT RUN: 700 (strings), 800 (wind)

P13   First edition, thirteenth impression. - 1979. - [No copy located].
        ORDERED: 13.2.79   DELIVERED: 3.8.79
        PRINT RUN: 1500 (strings), 1200 (wind)

P14   First edition, fourteenth impression. - 1980. - [No copy located].
        ORDERED: 6.11.79   DELIVERED: 4.6.80
        PRINT RUN: 250 (covers), 3000 (strings), 1800 (wind)

P15   First edition, fifteenth impression. - 1982. - [No copy located].
        ORDERED: 1.3.82   DELIVERED: 26.10.82
        PRINT RUN: 100 (covers), 1300 (strings), 2850 (wind)

P16   First edition, sixteenth impression. - 1983. - [No copy located].
        ORDERED: 23.5.83   DELIVERED: ?.9.83
        PRINT RUN: 200 (piano conductor), 150 (strings sets), 50 (wind sets)

P17   First edition, seventeenth impression. - 1985. - [No copy located].
        ORDERED: 31.8.84   DELIVERED: ?.2.85
        PRINT RUN: 104 (string sets), 150 (wind sets)

P18   First edition, eighteenth impression. - 1985. - [No copy located].
        ORDERED: 30.9.83   DELIVERED: ?.11.85
        PRINT RUN: 200 (piano conductor)

P19 First edition, nineteenth impression. - 1986. - [No copy located].
   ORDERED: 3.2.86   DELIVERED: ?.4.86
   PRINT RUN: 164 (string sets)

P20 First edition, twentieth impression. - 1986. - [No copy located].
   ORDERED: 22.9.86   DELIVERED: ?.10.86
   PRINT RUN: 150 (wind sets)

P21 First edition, twenty-first impression. - 1987. - [No copy located].
   ORDERED: 31.7.87   DELIVERED: ?.9.87
   PRINT RUN: 150 (string sets)

P22 First edition, twenty-second impression. - 1988. - [No copy located].
   ORDERED: 1.8.88   DELIVERED: ?.9.88
   PRINT RUN: 20 (piano conductor), 150 (wind sets)

P23 First edition, twenty-third impression. - 1989. - [No copy located].
   ORDERED: 19.9.89   DELIVERED: ?.11.89
   PRINT RUN: 150 (string sets)

P24 First edition, twenty-fourth impression. - 1989. - [No copy located].
   ORDERED: 10.10.89   DELIVERED: ?.11.89
   PRINT RUN: 150 (piano conductor)

P25 First edition, twenty-fifth impression. - 1991. - [No copy located].
   ORDERED: 19.2.91   DELIVERED: ?.4.91
   PRINT RUN: 150 (string sets), 150 (wind sets)

(L)   Courtly Dances, arranged for chamber ensemble

1.   March
2.   Coranto
3.   Pavane
4.   Morris Dance
5.   Galliard
6.   Lavolta
[7.   Reprise of the March]

Arranger: John Dingle

Scoring: fl., spinet, vln, vla, vcl. and tabor.

Duration: 10:30 min.

Date: 1965?

First performance: 29 September 1965, Rainbow Hall, Cheapside, Reading as part of the Evening Post Festival. The Delian Ensemble (Barbara White, fl; Simon Johnson, spinet; Evelyn Budden, vln; Peter Denny, vla; Fritz Lustig, vcl.) directed by John Dingle.

Publication: unpublished

Notes

The arranger wrote from Tilehurst, Berkshire, requesting permission for the adaptation in July 1965; the composer's agreement, scribbled on the letter in blue ballpoint was a simple 'I don't mind'. Boosey & Hawkes also agreed, on condition that the arrangement was for the sole use of the Delian Ensemble for local performance.

Sources

Score

F1   Manuscript full score. Manuscript: pencil (John Dingle). - [1965?]. - [Item not examined].   Private Collection

Parts

P1   Manuscript parts. - [1965?]. - [Item not examined.]   Private Collection

Recording

Rec1.1 Unpublished recording. - [1965]. - [Item not examined].
        PERFORMERS: Delian Ensemble, John Dingle, director.
        DATE AND PLACE OF RECORDING: 65.09.29, at Rainbow Hall, Cheapside, Reading.
        A recording of the first performance.   Private Collection

Rec1.2 Another copy. - 1 track on 1 side of 1 sound cassette (10:30 min.): analogue, mono.   *GB-ALb* 3-9301002

(M) Revised version (1966)

Cast and instrumentation: Queen Elizabeth the First (sop.), Robert Devereux, Earl of Essex (ten.), Frances, Countess of Essex (mezzo), Charles Blount, Lord Mountjoy (bar.), Penelope, (Lady Rich) sister to Essex (sop.), Sir Robert Cecil, Secretary of the Council (bar.),[63] Sir Walter Raleigh, Captain of the Guard (bass),[63] Henry Cuffe, a satellite of Essex (bar.), a Lady-in-Waiting (sop.), a blind Ballad-Singer (bass), the Recorder of Norwich (bass), a Housewife (mezzo), the Spirit of the Masque (ten.), the Master of Ceremonies (ten.), the City Crier (bar.). Chorus: Citizens, Maids of Honour, Ladies and Gentlemen of the Household, Courtiers, Masquers, Old Men, Men and Boys of Essex's following, Councillors. Dancers: Time, Concord, Country Girls, Rustics, Fishermen, Morris Dancer. Actors: Pages, Ballad-Singer's runner, Phantom of the Queen.

3 fls (II, III doubling picc.), 2 obs, english horn, 2 cls, bass cl., 2 bsns, dbsn, 4 hns, 3 tpts, 3 trbs, tuba, timpani, perc., hp, strings. Instruments on the stage: 1.i, trumpets (multiples of three); 2.iii, orchestra for dances: five strings and/or five woodwind, pipe (flute), tabor (small side drum without snares); 3.ii, gittern, drum (on stage), side drums (off stage); 3.iii, cymbals, side drum, bass drum, wind machine;[64] on stage: hp.

Date of revisions: 1966

First performance: 21 October 1966, Sadler's Wells Opera. Queen Elizabeth I: Sylvia Fisher; Earl of Essex: John Wakefield; Lady Essex: Shirley Chapman; Lord Mountjoy: Donald McIntyre; Penelope, Lady Rich: Jennifer Vyvyan; Sir Robert Cecil: John Cameron; Sir Walter Raleigh: Don Garrard; Henry Cuffe: David Bowman; Lady-in-Waiting: Wendy Baldwin; a blind Ballad-Singer: Eric Stannard; the Recorder of Norwich: Charles Draper; a Housewife: Ailene Fischer; the Spirit of the Masque: David Morton-Gray; the Master of Ceremonies: Neville Griffiths; the City Crier: Leigh Maurice; Time: Terry John Bates; Concord: Caroline Douglas; Morris Dancer: Norman Milne.

Setting: Alix Stone and Colin Graham; costumes: Alix Stone; producer: Colin Graham; choreographer: Peter Darrell; lighting: Charles Bristow; chorus master: Hazel Vivienne; conductor: Mario Bernardi.

Publication:

Libretto: London: Boosey & Hawkes Ltd., 1980

Vocal score: London: Boosey & Hawkes Ltd., 1968 (third edition); 1981 (fourth edition)

Study score: London: Boosey & Hawkes Music Publishers Ltd., 1990

Full score: unpublished; available, on hire only, from Boosey & Hawkes Music Publishers Ltd.

Instrumental parts: unpublished; available, on hire only, from Boosey & Hawkes Music Publishers Ltd.

Notes

After the last performances of the first production in 1954, *Gloriana* was not heard again in Britain until 1963, when Bryan Fairfax conducted a concert performance at the

---

[63] Bears a footnote reference in the list of characters on p. [v] of the vocal score: 'Pronunciation Note: Throughout the Opera RALEIGH should be *RAWLEIGH* / CECIL should be *CICIL*'.

[64] See fn. 17.

Royal Festival Hall to mark Britten's fiftieth birthday.[65] The composer was consulted about various aspects of the performance, and having re-heard the opera he decided to make revisions, though it was not until 1966 that serious work on the changes began.

The revisions chiefly concerned three passages: the Queen's Soliloquy and Prayer (1.ii.5) and the entrance of Cecil (3.iii.8) — which were both shortened — and the Epilogue. The history of the revisions to the latter has been recounted by Colin Graham:

> Ben was dissatisfied with the Epilogue: he didn't want any new characters to appear that we hadn't already seen and he wanted the dialogue to be as short and pithy as possible. Accordingly I prepared what was to become the present version for his approval. He passed it on to William Plomer and we all sat outside the library for tea one sunny day in 1966[66] and confirmed it.
>
> The only further alteration subsequently concerned Elizabeth meeting her own ghost: this was also an unsatisfactory moment. When we first did the new production at Sadler's Wells we had a double enter to confront the Queen, wearing a face mask of Sylvia Fisher. This was not convincing and I persuaded Ben that she should confront her self within herself in the form of a kind of heart Tremor which made her stagger against the throne into which she then climbed with difficulty. This is how we did it, with Ben's blessing, for every one of the many performances and revivals thereafter.[67]

Britten's dissatisfaction with the Epilogue was obviously of long standing, as the ghostly procession had been modified in the 1954 performances of the work.[68] Work on the musical changes in 1.ii.5 and 3.iii.8 was probably begun in May 1966 and were completed in July, after the Aldeburgh Festival.

At the time the second edition of the vocal score was out of print (though the deluxe first edition was still available), so it was agreed that a short run of its unrevised text should be printed, partly for rehearsals of the new production, and also for sale to the public ((A)/V10); revision patches were prepared by Rosamund Strode, to be pasted into the copies supplied to Sadler's Wells ((M)/V12-13).

Sources

Librettos	L15-L24
First edition, second impression	L20
Second edition	L24
Holographs	H5-H8
Vocal score	V12-V17
Third edition	V16
Fourth edition	V17

---

65 Donald Mitchell, who was involved in this revival, recalls that 'it was a rather reluctant and uncertain composer who finally agreed to this event, while warning me that my head would be on the block if it proved not to be a success!' (Letter to Paul Banks, 16 February 1993.)

66 Colin Graham remembered 1965, but Britten's correspondence with Plomer indicates that the revisions were probably not discussed until the following year. The Red House Visitors' Book shows that Graham and Plomer visited the composer during 2-4 June 1966.

67 Fax to Paul Banks, 15 March 1993. The elimination of the ghost of Elizabeth I is not reflected in either the third or fourth editions of the vocal score, or the study score.

68 The early revisions were probably discussed with Basil Coleman during his visit to Aldeburgh on 13 December 1954 (see above, p. 105).

Choral score   CS4
Full scores   F3-F13
   Study score   F11
Orchestral parts   P6-P8
Production material   Pr1-Pr2
Recordings   Rec6-Rec8

Librettos

L15 Revisions, list 1. Typescript; with annotations and corrections: blue ballpoint. -
    GLORIANA : TEXTUAL ALTERATIONS 1966. - June 1966. - [2] fol. ; 25.5 cm.
    ANALYSIS: [1^r] text, [1^v] blank, [2^r] text, [2^v] blank.
    Prepared by Colin Graham.
    Heading on 1^r (blue ballpoint): '<u>BB</u>' [deleted in pencil].
                    GB-ALb 2-9000044

L16 Revisions, list 2. Typescript (carbon copy). - *GLORIANA* / *TEXTUAL*
    ALTERATIONS, June 1966. - 6 June 1966. - [1] fol. ; 33.1 cm.
    ANALYSIS: [1^r] text, [1^v] blank.
    A new version of L15 retyped by Rosamund Strode.[69] Three photocopies
    of this list also survive at Aldeburgh (*GB-ALb* 2-9200202). *GB-ALb*.[70]

L17 Interim copy (file copy, marked-up copy of the first edition, (A)/L13). Printed;
    with annotations, corrections and revisions: red ballpoint, blue ballpoint,
    pencil (Rosamund Strode). - [ca. 1966]. - [1]-62, [ii] p., original red thick
    paper wrapper, with extra outer wrapper of yellow card, stitched ; 20.5 cm.
    The revisions bring the text into line with the 1966 version. With a
    typescript insert ([1] fol.) containing a revised version of 'Quick music is
    best'.   GB-ALb 2-9200220

L18 Interim copy (marked-up copy of the first edition, (A)/L13). Printed; with
    annotations, corrections and revisions: black ink, blue ballpoint, pencil
    (Rosamund Strode). - [ca. 1966]. - [1]-62, [ii] p., original red thick paper
    wrapper ; 20.5 cm.
    Rosamund Strode's annotated copy of the first edition, (A)/L13. The
    revisions bring the text into line with the 1966 version. The black ink
    annotation on p. [4] gives the cast list for the third performance (13 June
    1953).   GB-ALrs

L19 Interim copy (marked up copy of the first edition, (A)/L13). Printed; with
    annotations, corrections and revisions. - [ca. 1966]. - [Not examined].
    Photocopies of the revised pages are held at *GB-ALb*.
    Bears note: 'NB. THIS COPY CONTAINS THE TEXTUAL / REVISIONS
    MADE IN JUNE 1966. / see pages: 2, 6, 8, 9, 10, 28, 33, 59, 60, 61.' Further
    annotation on [2], beneath original copyright statement: 'Revised Edition
    c Copyright / 1966 by Hawkes & Son (London) / Ltd.
    Some of the annotations could be in the hand of William Plomer. A
    revised version of the libretto was not published until 1980 (see L24).
                  GB-Lbh Hire Library

---

[69] Letter from Rosamund Strode to Martin Hall (Boosey & Hawkes), dated 6 June 1966.
[70] Kept with correspondence in the *Gloriana* file at *GB-ALb*.

L20   First edition, second impression. - *GLORIANA / OPERA IN THREE ACTS / The music by / BENJAMIN BRITTEN / The libretto by / WILLIAM PLOMER / Boosey & Hawkes / Music Publishers Limited / London · Paris · Bonn · Johannesburg · Sydney · Toronto · New York.* - London : Boosey & Hawkes Ltd., 1973. - 62, [ii] p., red stiff paper cover ; 20.5 cm.
ANALYSIS: [as for L14.1 except:] [i-ii] blank, [ri-ro] blank.
PRINT CODE: M.P. 7.73   DELIVERED: 30.08.73
PRINT RUN: 1000.

Through an oversight the original version of the libretto was reprinted in 1973, seven years after the revised version had been performed for the first time. For a marked up copy see also L21.

L21   Second edition, master copy (marked-up copy of L20). Printed; with annotations and revisions: red ballpoint, blue ballpoint, pencil (Rosamund Strode, [unidentified]). - November 1978. - [1]-62, [ii] p., red thick paper wrapper; 20.5 cm. + 2 inserts.

Annotation on [fo]: blue ballpoint (Rosamund Strode): 'CORRECTED NOV. 1978 / RS'.

The inserts are 2 fol. of single-sided typescript (carbon copy) stapled onto p. 59; the first is headed (blue ballpoint, Rosamund Strode): 'GLORIANA End, revised version / libretto page 59'.

GB-Lbh Production Department

L22.1   Second edition, test pages (incomplete, unmarked).   Printed (single-sided photocopy). - *GLORIANA.* - [1979?]. - [2] fol. ; 33.3 cm.
ANALYSIS: [printing on *rectos* only] [1^r] *CHARACTERS* (= p. 5), [2^r] *ACT II / Scene 1* (= p. 25).

These pages probably represent an early stage in the production of the proofs; p. 5 does not correspond to iii in L23.1, but p. 25 does correspond to p. 13 in the latter source.   *GB-Lbh* Production Department

L22.2   - An annotated copy (incomplete).   Printed (single-sided photocopy); with annotations and corrections: black ballpoint, red ballpoint ([unidentified]). - June 1979.

The same pages as in L22.1.

Annotation at r.h. foot of [1^r] (red ballpoint): 'Passed 29.6.79 / John Purchase informed / by telephone'.   *GB-Lbh* Production Department

L23.1   Second edition, first proofs.   Printed (single-sided photocopy); with annotations and corrections: red ballpoint, blue ballpoint, pencil (John Andrewes, Rosamund Strode, [unidentified]). - *GLORIANA / OPERA IN THREE ACTS / The libretto by / WILLIAM PLOMER / Music by / BENJAMIN BRITTEN / Op. 53 / Boosey & Hawkes / Music Publishers Limited / London · Paris · Bonn · Johannesburg · Sydney · Toronto · New York.* - [1979?[71]]. - [23] fol., unbound ; 27.2 x 39.6 cm. + 1 insert.
ANALYSIS: [printing on *rectos* only] [1] tp, [2] copyright note, list of characters (= pp. [ii], iii), [3] list of characters, *ACT I / Scene 1* (= pp. iv, 1), [4-6] Act I scene 1 (= pp. 2-7), [6-9] *Scene 2* (= pp. 7-12), [9-11] *Act II / Scene 1*

---

[71]   L21, L22.1 and L22.2 are housed in a Boosey's Library Bag marked 'GLORIANA / June 1979 / Libretto'.

(= pp. 13-16), [11-13[72]] *Scene 2* (= pp. 17-19), [13-16] *Scene 3* (= pp. 19-24); [16-19] *ACT III* / *Scene 1* (= pp. 25-30), [19-21] *Scene 2* (= pp. 30-34); [21-23] *Scene 3* (= pp. 34-39).

Most leaves carry two pages of text. The insert bears on its *recto* a manuscript (pencil) copy of the dedication; the *verso* is blank. John Andrewes corrected and marked up this copy before sending it to Rosamund Strode, who revised the proofs in blue ballpoint. Her corrections were then incorporated into the publisher's set (L23.2).

Annotation on tp (red ballpoint, boxed): 'PROOF FOR R.S.'.

GB-Lbh Production Department

L23.2   - Another copy. With annotations and corrections: various implements (probably John Andrewes). - [1979?]. - [44] fol., stapled ; 27.2 cm. + 1 insert and one stapled-on collette.

ANALYSIS: [1[r]] [blue ballpoint:] *1* [encircled] / *"GLORIANA"* / *MASTER FIRST PROOF.*, [1[v]] blank, [2[r]] tp, [2[v]-3[r]] blank, [3[v]] copyright statement and collette, [4[r]] list of characters (= p. iii), [4[v]-5[r]] blank, [5[v]] list of characters (= p. iv), [6[r]] ACT I / SCENE 1 (= p. 1), [6[v]-7[r]] blank [pattern of alternating pairs of printed and blank pages continues to:] [44[v]] blank. COLLATION: A-V[2].

Annotation on tp (red ballpoint, boxed:) 'MASTER 1st PROOF'. The insert bears on its *recto* a manuscript (pencil) copy of the dedication; the *verso* is blank. The corrections in V22.1 have been transferred to this copy.

GB-Lbh Production Department

L23.3   - Another copy (incomplete, unmarked). - [3] fol.

Pp. ii-1. 2 sets.   *GB-Lbh* Production Department

L24   Second edition. - GLORIANA / OPERA IN THREE ACTS / The libretto by / WILLIAM PLOMER / The music by / BENJAMIN BRITTEN / Op. 53 / New corrected edition / 1980 / Boosey & Hawkes / Music Publishers Limited / London · Paris · Bonn · Johannesburg · Sydney · Toronto · New York. - London: Boosey & Hawkes, 1980. - [vi], 39, [vii-ix] pp., green card wrapper ; 25.9 cm.

ANALYSIS: [fo] [in double border] *Gloriana* / *Opera in Three Acts* / BENJAMIN BRITTEN / OP. 53 / *The Libretto by William Plomer* / *New corrected edition* 1980 / BOOSEY & HAWKES, [fi] blank, [i] tp, ii copyright statement, iii dedication, iv-v list of characters, [vi] blank, 1-7 *ACT I* / *Scene 1*, 7-12 *Scene 2*, 13-16 *ACT II* / *Scene 1*, 17-19 *Scene 2*, 19-24 *Scene 3*, 25-30 *ACT III* / *Scene 1*, 30-34 *Scene 2*, 34-39 *Scene 3*, [vii-ix] blank, [ri] blank, [ro] advert (no. 2, dated 8.65).

PRINT CODE: none   ORDERED: 8.7.80   DELIVERED: 1.8.80
PRINT RUN: 2087

A reset text in a format larger than that of the first edition.

---

[72] Fol. [12] is an earlier version of fol. [13], with no commencement of 2.iii printed at the foot of p. 19.

Holograph manuscripts

H5   Revisions, draft (vocal score). Holograph: pencil. - [Untitled]. - [May?-June 1966].
      - [2] fol. : 16 staves, [span:] 31.6 cm. ; 38.1 x 28 cm.
      ANALYSIS: [1^r-2^r] drafts, [2^v] blank.
      COLLATION: [1-2] A^2.
      CONTENTS: revisions to 1.ii.8 (V10, p. 72ff) and 3.i.5 (V10, p. 177).
      FILM NUMBER: A3 (frames 227-229).
      Britten revised three passages of music in 1966: two contractions were
      made to the Queen's 'Soliloquy and Aria'; a contraction was also made to
      'The entrance of Cecil' in Act III. For dates, see the note to H6.
      GB-ALb 2-9202576

H6   Revisions, fair copy (vocal score). Holograph: pencil; with annotation: pencil
      (Rosamund Strode). - [Untitled]. - [May?-June 1966]. - [2] fol. : 16 staves,
      [span:] 31.6 cm. ; 38.1 x 28 cm.
      ANALYSIS: [1^r-2^r] revisions, [2^v] blank.
      COLLATION: [1-2] A^2.
      CONTENTS: revisions to 1.ii.8 (V10, p. 72ff) and 3.i.5 (V10, p. 177).
      FILM NUMBER: A3 (frames 230-232).
      The Act I revisions were ready by 24 May 1966 (when Rosamund Strode
      sent her copies to Boosey & Hawkes), but the Act III revision was
      probably undertaken between that date and 3 June.   *GB-ALb* 2-9202577

H7   Revisions (Act I, full score).   Holograph: pencil; with annotations, pencil
      (Rosamund Strode). - [Pencil (Rosamund Strode):]   *INSERT A | Act I
      Revisions (1966)*. - [July 1966]. - [4] fol. : 30 staves, [maker:] PASSANTINO /
      BRANDS // NUMBER 30 / 30 Stave Narrow, [span:] 40.8 cm.; 48.3 x
      31.6 cm.
      ANALYSIS: [1^r] tp, [1^v] blank, [2^r-4^v] music.
      COLLATION: [1-4] A^4.
      FILM NUMBER: B11 (frames 123-128).
      Presented, together with (A)/H3 to the British Library by the composer's
      Executors and the Trustees of the Britten-Pears Library in 1980, on the
      occasion of the official opening of the Britten-Pears Library.
      Work on the full score revisions was delayed until after the 1966
      Aldeburgh Festival.[73]   *GB-Lbl* Add. MS. 61814

H8   Revisions (Act III, full score).   Holograph: pencil; with annotations, pencil
      (Rosamund Strode). - [Top r.h. corner, pencil (Rosamund Strode):] *Act III
      Revisions / 1966* // [pencil (Benjamin Britten:] *Insert B*. - [July 1966]. - [2] fol. :
      30 staves, [maker:] PASSANTINO / BRANDS // NUMBER 30 / 30 Stave
      Narrow, [span:] 40.8 cm.; 48.3 x 31.6 cm.
      ANALYSIS: [1^r] tp, [1^v-2^r] music, [2^v] blank.
      COLLATION: [1-2] A^2.
      FILM NUMBER: B11 (frames 417-419).
      Presented, together with (A)/H3 to the British Library by the composer's
      Executors and the Trustees of the Britten-Pears Library in 1980, on the
      occasion of the official opening of the Britten-Pears Library.
      Work on the full score revisions was delayed until after the 1966
      Aldeburgh Festival.   *GB-Lbl* Add. MS. 61814

---

[73] Letter from Rosamund Strode to Martin Hall, dated 3 June 1966.

Vocal scores

[V12.1]   [Revision patches (1.ii.8, dated). Ms. copy (Rosamund Strode). - May 1966. - Not located.[74]]

CONTENTS: revisions to 1.ii.8 (V10, p. 72ff).

Transparencies of revision patches to be pasted onto copies of the second edition of the vocal score. When in May 1966 it was decided to reprint the second edition of the original version, it was also agreed that revision patches would be produced for inclusion in the Sadler's Wells set. The first three patches were sent to Boosey & Hawkes for dyelining on 24 May 1966. A further revision sheet was produced in June; see V13. On 24 July Rosamund Strode telephoned a correction to one of the patches to Boosey & Hawkes.

V12.2   - Additional copies.   Ms. copy (single-sided dyeline) (Rosamund Strode). - *Benjamin Britten* / <u>*GLORIANA*</u> / *Vocal score Revisions and Corrections - May 1966.* - [2] fol. ; 35.7 cm.

ANALYSIS: 1^r music, [1^v] blank, [2^r] music, [2^v] blank.

Sheets produced from V12.1, to be pasted onto copies of the second edition of the vocal score (original version). 100 copies of each were produced and 6 of each sheet sent to Aldeburgh on 1 June.

2 copies.   GB-ALb 2-9200203

[V13.1]   [Revision patch (3.i.5, dated). Ms. copy (Rosamund Strode). - 3.vi 1966. - Not located.]

CONTENTS: revision to 3.i.5 (V10, p. 177).

Transparency of the additional revision patch to be pasted onto copies of the second edition of the vocal score (original version). An addition to the revision sheets produced in May 1966; it was sent to Boosey & Hawkes on 3 June 1966 and received by 6 June.

V13.2   - Another copy. Ms. copy (printed) (Rosamund Strode). - <u>*GLORIANA*</u> / *SHEET 3*. - [1] fol. ; 18.4 x 22.9 cm.

ANALYSIS: [1^r] music, [1^v] blank.

Revision patch, produced from V13.1 to be pasted onto copies of the second edition of the vocal score (original version).

2 copies.   GB-ALb 2-9200204

V14   Interim copy (file copy, marked-up second edition, signed).   Printed; with annotations, revisions and corrections: pencil, blue ballpoint (Benjamin Britten, Rosamund Strode). - [i-viii], 230, [ix-x] p., bound, blue cloth, retaining original wrapper ; 36 cm. + 4 paste-overs [a-d].

ANALYSIS: [as for (A)/V10].

Signed (blue ballpoint) on tp: 'Benjamin Britten'.

The ms. paste-overs (Rosamund Strode) are on pp. 72, 73, 74 and 178; there are no revisions to the text in the final scene, though otherwise the musical revisions of the 1966 version have been incorporated.

GB-ALb 2-9200283

---

[74] The staves were hand-ruled to obtain appropriate spacings between them.

V15   Third edition, preparatory copy (marked-up copy of (A)/V10). Printed; with
       annotations and corrections: various implements (various hands). -
       *GLORIANA | An Opera in Three Acts | by | WILLIAM PLOMER | Music by |
       BENJAMIN BRITTEN | Opus 53 | Vocal Score by | Imogen Holst |* [black ink:]
       <u>*Revised Edition 1967*</u> [last digit corrected in pencil to '8'] .... - 1966-68. - Pl. no.:
       B. & H. 17376. - [i-viii], 230, [ix-x] p., thick paper cover ; 35.5 cm.
           Includes some dyeline paste-overs copied by Rosamund Strode.[75]
           Typescript note on front cover *verso*: 'This master-copy Vocal Score
           contains musical and textual emendations made by Benjamin Britten and
           Colin Graham .... The actual copy is of one of the 1st reprinted edition ...
           made in November 1953 .... London, 17 June 1966'.
           Blue ballpoint note on tp (Leopold Spinner): 'photoproofs (music
           pp 1-230) corrections ~~checked in photoproofs~~ / 12.1.68'.
           See also (A)/V10.4.   *GB-ALb* 2-9200092

V16   Third edition. - *GLORIANA | An Opera in Three Acts | by | WILLIAM PLOMER |
       Music by | BENJAMIN BRITTEN | Opus 53 | Vocal Score by | Imogen Holst |
       Revised Edition 1968 | BOOSEY & HAWKES, LTD., | London · Paris · Bonn ·
       Johannesburg | Sydney · Toronto · New York.* - London : Boosey & Hawkes,
       Ltd., 1968. Pl. no.: B.& H. 17376. - [i-viii], 230, [ix-x] p., thick paper covers ;
       35.5 cm.
       ANALYSIS: [as for (A)/V10 except:] [ro] advert (no. 2, dated 8.65).
       PRINT CODE: 2.68 L & B   ORDERED: 24.1.68   DELIVERED: 13.3.68
       PRINT RUN: 253
           Copyright by Hawkes & Son (London), Ltd.
           Retains the front cover design by John Piper. Page 72 was revised
           extensively and pp. 73-74, 178-9 and 226-227 re-originated for this
           edition.

V17.1   Fourth edition. - *GLORIANA | An Opera in Three Acts | by | WILLIAM PLOMER |
       Music by | BENJAMIN BRITTEN | Opus 53 | Vocal Score by | Imogen Holst |
       Revised Edition 1981 | BOOSEY & HAWKES, LTD., | London · Paris · Bonn ·
       Johannesburg | Sydney · Toronto · New York.* - Revised Edition. - London :
       Boosey & Hawkes, Ltd., 1981. Pl. no.: B. & H. 17376. - [i-viii], 230, [ix-x] p.,
       thick paper cover ; 31 cm.
       ANALYSIS: [as for V16].
       PRINT CODE: none   ORDERED: 11.5.81   DELIVERED: 3.11.81
       PRINT RUN: 773
           Copyright 1953 by Hawkes & Son (London) Ltd.
           The cover retains the John Piper design; the overall dimensions are
           slightly reduced, and rehearsal numbers replace rehearsal letters.

V17.2   - An annotated copy. Printed; with annotations and corrections: pencil.
           This copy was used during the preparation of F9, particularly as a source
           for the text. The annotations show the casting-off of the full score; the
           corrections pick up residual errors in the music and the text.
                                                       GB-Lbh Production Department

---

[75] This score was sent to Rosamund Strode for revision ca. 17 May 1966, and returned to Boosey &
      Hawkes on or before 24 May 1966.

Choral score

CS4.1 Hire material, third state. - *BENJAMIN BRITTEN | GLORIANA | CHORAL SCORE* / [rubber-stamped:] *BOOSEY & HAWKES | MUSIC PUBLISHERS LTD. | 295 REGENT STREET | LONDON W.1. |* [printed:] *BOOSEY & HAWKES* - London : Boosey & Hawkes Music Publishers Ltd., 1971. Pl. no.: B.& H. 17319. - pp. [1]-28, 28A, 28B, 29-62, thin grey card wrapper ; 25.1 cm.
ANALYSIS: [fo] title, [fi] blank, [1]-16 *ACT I | SCENE I,* 17-39 *ACT II | Scene I,* 40-43 *ACT II | SCENE 3,* 44-49 *ACT III Scene I,* 50-57 *ACT III Scene II,* 58-62 *ACT III | SCENE III,* [ri-ro] blank.
PRINT CODE: none   DELIVERED: ?.5.71
PRINT RUN: 250
Copyright 1953 by Hawkes & Son (London) Ltd.
Title from front cover. Pp. 1-16 were re-set for this edition in December 1970.

CS4.2 - An annotated copy. Printed; with annotations: pencil (Benjamin Britten).
GB-ALb 2-9200223

Full scores

F3 - Hire material (marked-up copy of (A)/F1). Dyeline, with annotations, corrections, revisions: various implements (Benjamin Britten, ?Reginald Goodall, Rosamund Strode, [unidentified]). - [Untitled]. [1953-1966]. - 3 vols (pp. 1-116, 117-240, 241-399), bound in dark green cloth boards with gold tooling on the spine ; 55.6 cm. + 3 paste-overs [a-c].
See also (M)/F5.
The paste-overs appear on pp. 136 ([a-b]) and 189 ([c]).
This copy of the dyeline interim score was apparently used by the conductor Reginald Goodall in 1953 and 1954. Britten's revisions are fairly extensive but not substantial: they consist mostly of the rescoring of passages and were probably made after hearing the work in rehearsal and performance, in early November 1953. The passages changed in 1966 are deleted and notes indicate their replacement by new pages (which are not present in this score).   GB-ALb 2-9200221

F4.1 [Revision patches and list (dated). Ms. copy (Rosamund Strode). - July 1966. - 30 staves, [maker:] PASSANTINO / BRANDS // NUMBER 30 / 30 Stave Narrow. - Not located.]
A list of revisions, together with recopied pages.[76]

F4.2 - Additional copies.[77] Ms. copy (single-sided dyeline) (Rosamund Strode). - *GLORIANA* - *Benjamin Britten |* Alterations *to Full Score, July 1966.* - [8] fol. ; 46.8 cm.   GB-ALb 2-9200205

F5 - Hire material (marked-up copy of (A)/F1). Dyeline; with annotations, corrections, revisions: various implements (Colin Graham, various unidentified hands). - *GLORIANA | * | Britten.* - [1953-1984]. - 3 vols (pp. 1-116, 117-240, 241-399), bound in black cloth boards ; 55.6 cm. + 3 paste-overs [a-c].
Title from label on [fo] (vol. I). The binding is similar to that of (A)/F1 before the latter was rebound in 1992.

---

[76] Sent to Boosey & Hawkes on 27 July.
[77] This set was sent to Aldeburgh on 19 August 1966.

157

Pp. 105-6, 108-110, 289-90 are replaced by full page revision patches copied by Rosamund Strode (F4.2; further partial patches from that set appear on pp. 112-3, 116).

Red ballpoint note (unidentified hand) on p. 117: 'COR[.] 15/IV / 53 / incomplete!!'. Pencil note (Colin Graham) at the foot of p. 385: 'PUBLISHER - Please note that dialogue alterations marked CG / are those made by the composer when he revised the work in / 1966 and should be adhered to / Colin Graham / 1984'. *GB-Lbh* Hire Library

F6.1   Revision pages. Ms. copy (dyeline) (Rosamund Strode, Imogen Holst, Benjamin Britten). - *8. Soliloquy and Prayer*. - [?1966]. - [6] fol. ; 50.8 cm.

ANALYSIS: [1-6] *8. Soliloquy and Prayer* (= pp. 105-116).

COLLATION: A⁶ ([1^{r-v}] Rosamund Strode, [2^r] Imogen Holst and Benjamin Britten, revised Rosamund Strode, [2^v-3^v] Rosamund Strode, [4^r-5^r] Imogen Holst and Benjamin Britten, revised Rosamund Strode, [6^r] Imogen Holst and Benjamin Britten, [6^v] Imogen Holst and Benjamin Britten, revised Rosamund Strode.

Title from heading on [1^r].

A single gathering made up from newly copied pages (F4.2) and dyeline pages from (A)/H3 which have been revised. *GB-Lbh* Hire Library

F6.2   - Annotated copy. Ms. copy (dyeline) (Rosamund Strode, Imogen Holst, Benjamin Britten); with annotations.

Annotation on [1^r]: [black felt-tip:] *BRITTEN . GLORIANA* / [blue ballpoint:] *Soliloquy and Prayer*. *GB-Lbh* Hire Library

F7   Master copy, stage orchestra score (a marked-up copy of (A)/F2). Holograph and non-holograph ms. (dyeline); with annotations and corrections: pencil and felt-tip, black ballpoint, (Colin Matthews, [unidentified]). - [All Imogen Holst; r.h.:] *SCORE // GLORIANA / ACT II SCENE III / STAGE ORCHESTRA FOR DANCES*. - [1970-1978?]. - 20 pp.

ANALYSIS: [as for (A)/F2].

Kept (together with a photocopy of the edited text) with F8 and used in the production of the second master copy of the full score, F9.

GB-Lbh Production Department

F8   First master score (marked-up copy of (A)/F1). Holograph and non-holograph (dyeline) (copyists: Imogen Holst, Rosamund Strode); with annotations and corrections: various implements (Colin Matthews, Rosamund Strode). - *GLORIANA / An Opera in Three Acts / by / WILLIAM PLOMER / Music by / BENJAMIN BRITTEN / Opus 53 / Full Score / Revised 1966 / BOOSEY & HAWKES, LTD., / London · Paris · Bonn · Johannesburg / Sydney · Toronto · New York*. - 1970-1978. - [i-x], [1]-399, [xi-xiii] p., bound in boards ; 54.4 cm. + 55 paste-overs.

ANALYSIS: [fo] [red felt-tip:] *MASTER COPY / edited by Colin Matthews / includes unbound copy / of Stage Band Score (p. 182) / BRITTEN /* [black:] *"GLORIANA"* [red:] *OPERA IN 3 ACTS /* [black:] *FULL SCORE /* [black parentheses, red text:] *(REVISED 1966) /* [hire label], [fi] blank, [i] [red ballpoint:] *Fsc. from Alan Bousted with corrections / (checked with BB's score @ Aldeburgh) June 1972./* [blue pencil (Rosamund Strode):] *October 1970 / Blue amendments taken from the full score at The Red House, Aldeburgh. (This is the score once used by Reginald Goodall.) / Rosamund Strode /* [red felt-tip (Colin Matthews):] *Revised 1974-8 by Colin Matthews / (in consultation with*

B.B. & R.S.), [ii] blank, [iii] tp, [iv] copyright statement, [v] dedication (= p. iii), [vi] blank (= p. iv), [vii] list of characters (= p. v), [viii] scenes, orchestration (= p. vi), [ix] list of original cast (= p. vii), [x] blank, [collation as (A)/F1 to:] [xi-xiii] blank, [ri-ro] blank.

Prelims derived from the (second edition[?] of the) vocal score; pp. 105-116 and 289-90 are copies of the revisions leaves prepared or revised by Rosamund Strode (F4).

Paste-overs appear on pp. 16, 36, 38, 41-2, 44, 47, 60-1, 65, 70, 72, 75, 80, 85, 89, 117, 129, 132, 142, 149, 154, 157, 161, 174, 178, 183-4, 188, 194, 198, 201, 209, 217 (x 2), 224, 241, 255, 260, 282, 292, 297, 305, 341, 351, 354, 362, 367, 372, 382, 385, 387, 390, 398.

Kept with:

a) single-sided photocopies of selected pages from the score, each made up from two sheets sellotaped together ([13] fol., ca. 45 x 26.8 cm. = pp. 1, 61-64, 392-399);

b) *Gloriana* / *Instructions,* a style sheet for the score ([1] fol.);

c) manuscript notes on the score: black ballpoint ([unidentified]). [1] fol. ; 29.8 x 20.9 cm. Headed 'M/C Fsc & Vsc. GLORIANA edited by Colin Matthews. Rcd. 2/3/79';

d) a dyeline and photocopy of the holograph stage orchestra score, F7.

This score was one of three sources used in the preparation of the second master copy (F9). *GB-Lbh* Production Department

F9   Second master score (marked-up copy of (A)/F1)). Holograph and non-holograph (dyeline) (copyists: Imogen Holst, Rosamund Strode); with annotations, corrections and revisions: various implements ([unidentified]). - *GLORIANA....* - [n.d.]. - 399, [iii] p. , unbound ; 50 x 37.5 cm. + numerous paste-overs.

ANALYSIS: as for F8 except, [i-iii] blank.

Title from paste-over at head of p. 1.

Pp. 105-116 and 289-90 are copies of the revisions leaves prepared or revised by Rosamund Strode (F4). This is the master score from which the master sheets (F10) were copied; it was prepared using three sources: the first master score (F8), a marked-up vocal score which was used chiefly for the text (V17.2), and an edited dyeline of the stage orchestra score (F7). *GB-Lbh* Production Department

F10   Transfer sheets. Single-sided dry transfer sheets. *HPS 1118 / GLORIANA / An Opera in Three Acts / by / WILLIAM PLOMER / Music by / BENJAMIN BRITTEN / Opus 53 / BOOSEY & HAWKES / MUSIC PUBLISHERS LIMITED / London · New York · Bonn · Gothenburg / Sydney · Tokyo · Toronto.* - [n.d.] - vi, 366 fol., unbound ; 53.2 x 36 cm. + 6 duplicates of the prelims.

ANALYSIS: (music/text on *rectos* only) [i] tp, [ii] copyright statement, [iii] dedication, [iv] list of characters, [v] list of original cast, [vi] list of scenes, duration of acts, [vii] orchestration, [1]-69 *ACT I SCENE 1,* 70-116 *SCENE 2,* 117-149 *ACT II SCENE 1,* 150-174 *SCENE 2,* 175-232 *SCENE 3,* 233-292 *ACT III SCENE 1,* 293-319 *SCENE 2,* 320-366 *SCENE 3.*

With the paste-ups of the prelims (6 fol.).

The sheets from which the study score (F11) was printed.

GB-Lbh Production Department

F11   First edition (study score). - *HPS 1118 | GLORIANA | An Opera in Three Acts | by | WILLIAM PLOMER | Music by | BENJAMIN BRITTEN | Opus 53 | BOOSEY & HAWKES | MUSIC PUBLISHERS LIMITED | London · New York · Bonn · Gothenburg | Sydney · Tokyo · Toronto*. - London : Boosey & Hawkes Music Publishers Limited, 1990. Ed. no.: HPS 1118. - [i-viii], 366, [ix-x] p., publisher's binding, blue cloth with gold tooling on spine and embossed initials on front board ; 27.5 cm.

ANALYSIS: [i] tp, [ii] copyright statement, [iii] dedication, [iv] list of characters, [v] list of original cast, [vi] blank, [vii] list of scenes, duration of acts, [viii] orchestration, [1]-69 *ACT I SCENE 1*, 70-116 *SCENE 2*, 117-149 *ACT II SCENE 1*, 150-174 *SCENE 2*, 175-232 *SCENE 3*, 233-292 *ACT III SCENE 1*, 293-319 *SCENE 2*, 320-366 *SCENE 3*, [ix-x] blank.

PRINT CODE: none   ORDERED: 15.12.89   DELIVERED: 6.1.90
PRINT RUN: 500.

Copyright 1953 by Hawkes & Son (London) Ltd. Full score copyright 1977 by Hawkes & Son (London) Ltd.

This, the first published full score, was supervised by John Arthur of Boosey & Hawkes, who undertook this mammoth task as he retired from the firm where he had been in charge of the copying for many years.

F12   Hire material (full score). - *HPS 1118 | GLORIANA | An Opera in Three Acts | by | WILLIAM PLOMER | Music by | BENJAMIN BRITTEN | Opus 53 | BOOSEY & HAWKES | MUSIC PUBLISHERS LIMITED | London · New York · Bonn · Gothenburg | Sydney · Tokyo · Toronto*. - London : Boosey & Hawkes Music Publishers Limited, [n.d.]. - 3 vols ([i-vi], 1-116; 117-232; 233-366 pp.), orange thick paper covers, ring bound ; 35.5 cm.

ANALYSIS: Volume I: [fo] *GLORIANA | BENJAMIN BRITTEN* | [label:] *BOOSEY & HAWKES*, [fi] blank, [i] tp, [ii] dedication, [iii] list of characters, [iv] list of original cast, [v] list of scenes, [vi] orchestration, [1]-69 *ACT I SCENE 1*, 70-116 *SCENE 2*, [ri-ro] blank.

Volume II: [fo] *GLORIANA | BENJAMIN BRITTEN* | [label:] *BOOSEY & HAWKES*, [fi] blank, 117-149 *ACT II SCENE 1*, 150-174 *SCENE 2*, 175-232 *SCENE 3*, [ri-ro] blank.

Volume III: [fo] *GLORIANA | BENJAMIN BRITTEN* | [label:] *BOOSEY & HAWKES*, [fi] blank, 233-292 *ACT III SCENE 1*, 293-319 *SCENE 2*, 320-366 *SCENE 3*, [ri-ro] blank.

An enlarged photocopy of F11. Copy marked 'Set 100' on [fo].

GB-Lbh Hire Library

F13   Hire material (full score). - *HPS 1118 | GLORIANA | An Opera in Three Acts | by | WILLIAM PLOMER | Music by | BENJAMIN BRITTEN | Opus 53 | BOOSEY & HAWKES | MUSIC PUBLISHERS LIMITED | London · New York · Bonn · Gothenburg | Sydney · Tokyo · Toronto*. - London : Boosey & Hawkes Music Publishers Limited, [n.d.]. - 3 vols ([i-viii], 1-116; 117-232; 233-366 pp.), white card covers, ring bound ; 53.8 cm.

ANALYSIS: Volume I: [fo] [label:] ... *BRITTEN | GLORIANA | ACT I*, [fi] blank, [i] tp, [ii] blank, [iii] dedication, [iv] list of characters, [v] list of original cast, [vi] list of scenes, [vii] orchestration [viii] blank, [rest as F12].

Volume II: [fo] [label:] ... *BRITTEN | GLORIANA | ACT II*, [rest as F12].

Volume III: [fo] [label:] ... *BRITTEN | GLORIANA | ACT III*, [rest as F12].

An enlarged photocopy of F11 but in larger format than F12.

GB-Lbh Hire Library

Orchestral Parts

P6   Hire material, second state (incomplete set). Ms. copies (dyeline) (various copyists); with annotations and corrections: various implements. - [l.h.: rubber stamp:] *1st VIOLIN // INSTRUMENT* / [red felt-tip:] *BRITTEN* / [black felt-tip:] *"GLORIANA"* [red:] *OPERA* / [black, red parentheses:] *(REVISED 1966 VERSION)* / *BOOSEY & HAWKES* / *MUSIC PUBLISHERS LTD.* / *HIRE LIBRARY* / [hire label]. - [1966]. - 33 vols, bound in thick green card covers ; various sizes.

     CONTENTS: vln 1 (x 8), vln 2 (x 8), vla (x 7), vcl. (x 5), db. (x 5).

     Title from front cover of vln 1 part.

     Note on all parts: 'Copyright 1953 by Hawkes & Son (London) Ltd. B.H. 17362'.

     The part set prepared for the first production ((A)/P1) was simply revised by Boosey & Hawkes in August 1966, in preparation for orchestral rehearsals which began in September 1966.[78] The revisions found in P1 and those of 1966 have been entered into the masters before dyelining.   *GB-Lbh* Hire Library

P7   Hire material, third state (incomplete set). Ms. copies (photocopies) (various copyists). - *Boosey & Hawkes Music Publishers Limited ... Benjamin Britten* / *GLORIANA* / *(viola)* .... - [after 1981?]. - 32 vols, blue card, ring bound ; 31 cm.

     CONTENTS: fl. 1, fl. 2, fl. 3 & picc., ob. 1, ob. 2, cor anglais, cl. 1 in B flat, cl. 2 in B flat, bass cl., bsn 1, bsn 2, dbsn, hn 1 in F, hn 2 in F, hn 3 in F, hn 4 in F, trpt 1 in C, trpt 2 in C, trpt 3 in C, trb. 1, trb. 2, trb. 3, tuba, timpani, perc., hp, celesta, vln 1, vln 2, vla, vcl, db.

     Title from label on front cover of vla part.

     Note on all parts: 'Copyright 1953 by Hawkes & Son (London) Ltd. B.H. 17362'.

     Unlike all earlier sets, this has rehearsal numbers in place of rehearsal letters. Associated parts for on-stage instruments not present.

                 GB-Lbh Hire Library

P8   Hire material, parts for on-stage instruments (incomplete). Ms. copies (photocopies). - [Untitled]. - [n.d.]. - 2 vols.

     CONTENTS: vln/ob., tabor.

     Recopied versions of these two parts.   *GB-Lbh* Hire Library

Production material

Pr1   First production, revised version, producer's copy (a marked-up copy of (A)/V10). Printed; with annotations and corrections: various implements (Rosamund Strode, Colin Graham). - [i-viii], 230, [ix-x] p., [115] fol. interleaved, bound ; 36 cm. + 4 paste-overs and various additional leaves stapled or sellotaped in, or loose.

     PROVENANCE: on loan from Colin Graham.

     Colin Graham's copy for the first production of the revised version: blue ballpoint initials on front wrapper: 'CG'. Some of the changes to the

---

[78]   See letter from Martin Hall to Rosamund Strode, dated 1 June 1966.

libretto are marked with initials 'WP' (William Plomer), and annotations to the music with 'BB' (Benjamin Britten) indicated their authorization.[79] The paste-overs are dyelined revision patches prepared by Rosamund Strode (see V12, V13). *GB-ALb* 9200311

Pr2   First production, revised version, revivals (marked-up copies of (A)/V10). - 37 copies.

Most of the material used by Sadler's Wells Opera and later English National Opera, has been returned to Boosey & Hawkes. This remaining set consists of 3 interleaved production scores ('no. 7' once used by Colin Graham) and 34 vocal scores used by singers and music staff. *GB-Leno*

Recordings

Rec6   Unpublished off-air recording. - 1968. - 2 sound tape reels (138:20 min.) : analogue, 7.5 ips, stereo ; 7 in., 0.25 in. tape.

PERFORMERS: David Hillman (Essex); Tom McDonnell (Cuffe); Gerwyn Morgan (Mountjoy); Sylvia Fisher (Elizabeth); Don Garrard (Raleigh); Derek Hammond-Stroud (Cecil); Charles Draper (Recorder of Norwich), Milla Andrew (Penelope); Shirley Chapman (Frances); Sadler's Wells Opera Chorus and Orchestra; Mario Bernardi, conductor.

DATE AND PLACE OF RECORDING: 68.06.12 or 68.06.13 at Snape Maltings.

PROVENANCE: Ex coll. Dwayne Phillips.

Recorded during the Aldeburgh Festival, 1968; includes announcement at end of opera (1:20 min.). *GB-ALb* 3-9300004

Rec7.1 Unpublished off-air recording. - 1973. - 2 sound tape reels (144:45 min.) : analogue, 7.5 ips, stereo ; 7 in., 0.25 in. tape.

PERFORMERS: John Kitchiner (Cuffe); David Hillman (Essex); Terence Sharpe (Mountjoy); Ava June (Elizabeth); Don Garrard (Raleigh); Derek Hammond-Stroud (Cecil); Harry Coghill (Recorder of Norwich); Jennifer Vyvyan (Penelope); Maureen Morelle (Frances); Sadler's Wells Opera Chorus and Orchestra; Charles Mackerras, conductor.

DATE AND PLACE OF RECORDING: 73.09.02 at the Albert Hall, London.

PROVENANCE: Ex coll. Dwayne Phillips.

Recorded during the Henry Wood Promenade Concerts, 1973
GB-ALb 3-9300005

Rec7.2 - Another copy. - [1973]. - 1 sound cassette (180:00 min.) : analogue, mono.

With recording of William Plomer speaking about *Gloriana*.
GB-ALb 3-9300006

Rec8   Unpublished sound recording. - [*Gloriana*]. - 1973. - [Item not examined].

DATE AND PLACE OF RECORDING: 73.09.02.

A complete tape recording of the Sadler's Wells Opera production.
GB-Lbbc BBC SA Tape 60395

---

[79] The authorization was given during 'a session sitting in the sun on the patio outside the [Britten-Pears] library' (fax from Colin Graham, dated 23 November 1992); the date of the session was probably 2-4 June 1966 (see p. 150).

(N) Choral Dances from *Gloriana* (version for tenor solo, harp and chorus)

[Introduction]
1. Time (SATB)
2. Concord (SATB)
3. Time and Concord (SATB)
4. Country Girls (SA)
5. Rustics and Fishermen (TTBB)
6. Final Dance of Homage (SATB)

Scoring: tenor solo, harp, mixed chorus.

Duration: 11 min.

Date of composition: 1967

First performance: 1 March 1967, Queen Elizabeth Hall. Peter Pears, ten.; Osian Ellis, hp; Ambrosian Singers; Benjamin Britten, conductor.

Publication: London : Boosey & Hawkes Music Publishers Limited, 1982 (3 impressions).

Notes

Apart from a new work composed and conducted by Sir Arthur Bliss, Britten conducted all the items in the first two concerts to take place at the new Queen Elizabeth Hall early in 1967. As a royal tribute (HM The Queen was present on 1 March, the official opening day) another version of the Choral Dances with tenor soloist was prepared. This time the chorus sang, as in the opera, the 'Melt earth to sea' eight-bar section at the start, to the accompaniment of solo harp. The links, which in the opera connect the dances, are retained in this version, though adapted in some cases to removed parts for characters other than that of the Spirit of the Masque, whose words and music are given to the solo tenor. The harp accompanies the introduction and linking passages — a relatively modest revision of the harp part from the opera — and the final dance, for which Britten composed an accompaniment (see F2.4 below).

Sources
Holograph

H1   Composition draft. Holograph: pencil. - *Gloriana Dances / Version for Tenor Solo Harp & Chorus*. - [1967]. - [4] fol. : 16 staves, [span:] 31.6 cm. ; 38 x 28 cm.
ANALYSIS: [1^r-3^v] music, [4] blank.
COLLATION: [1-4] A-B^2.
FILM NUMBER: A3 (frames 234-242).
> The manuscript contains only those passages which differ from the version in the vocal score of the complete opera: Britten wrote out as much as was necessary, referring the copyist (Rosamund Strode) to the published vocal score for the remaining details.   *GB-ALb* 2-9202578

Scores

[F1]   [Hire material. Printed (photocopied from vocal score), ms.: ink (Rosamund
        Strode). - [1967]. - Not located.]
        Pasted-up from sections of the vocal score (including all the relevant
        chorus parts) and newly copied material. This material was held by
        Boosey & Hawkes until at least 1972.[80]

F2.1   Hire material. Printed (dyeline), ms. (dyeline) (Rosamund Strode); with
        correction: pencil (Rosamund Strode). - *BRITTEN / GLORIANA / CHORAL
        DANCES / BOOSEY & HAWKES / MUSIC PUBLISHERS LTD / HIRE
        LIBRARY*. - [S.l.] : Boosey & Hawkes Music Publishers Ltd., Hire Library,
        [1967?], c1953. - [1]-15, [i] p., pink card wrapper, stitched ; 33.1 cm.
        ANALYSIS: [fo] title, [fi-1] blank, 2-3 Introduction, 4-6 *First Dance. TIME.*, 6-7
        Second Dance. CONCORD., 7-9 *Third Dance. TIME and CONCORD*, 10-11
        Fourth Dance. COUNTRY GIRLS., 12-13 *Fifth Dance. RUSTICS and
        FISHERMEN.*, 13-15 *Sixth Dance. Final Dance of Homage.*, [i] blank, [ri-ro]
        blank.
        Title from front wrapper.
        Copyright 1953 by Hawkes & Son (London), Ltd.
        Produced from F1. All the pink wrappers for this and the following
        items were cut down by and the sheets pamphlet-stitched into them by
        Rosamund Strode. In this state there is no harp part for the final dance.
                                                                    GB-ALb 2-9200271

F2.2   - An annotated copy. With annotations: pencil.
        Pencil note on p. 1 (Rosamund Strode): '(Uncorrected) Oct 77'.
                                                                    GB-ALb 2-9200270

F2.3   - An annotated copy. With revision and annotations: black ballpoint, pencil
        (Peter Pears?).
        Initialled on front wrapper (pencil: Rosamund Strode): 'PP's'.
                                                                    GB-ALb 2-9300009

F2.4   - A revised copy. With annotations and revisions: pencil (Rosamund Strode,
        Benjamin Britten). - [i], [1]-15, [ii] p., pink card wrapper, stitched ; 33.1 cm.
        Title from front cover. Front wrapper signed (pencil): 'Benjamin Britten'.
        The holograph revisions on pp. 13-15 add the harp accompaniment to the
        final dance. Pencil note on p. 1 (Rosamund Strode): '[rule] / NB Full
        Harp part not / shown between pages 14 [*recte* 13] & 15 / - just
        indications of it - see separate / ms insertion in OE's part. [rule] / [arrow
        to last line] now with OE: RS has a xerox copy.' (See F2.5 and F2.6.)
        Used by Britten as a conducting score on 1 and 2 March 1967.
                                                                    GB-ALb 2-9200258

F2.5   - A revised copy. With annotations: pencil, blue pencil (Rosamund Strode). -
        [1]-15, [i] p., pink card wrapper, stitched ; 33.1 cm. + harp part to Sixth
        Dance, ms. copy (Rosamund Strode) (2 fol. : 12 staves, [span:] 25.6 cm.,
        [maker:] R.C. 1 / [galleon logo] ; 30.6 x 22.7 cm.).
        PROVENANCE: Ex coll. Osian Ellis.
        Title from front cover.

---

[80] Boosey & Hawkes Inter-departmental communication from John Andrewes to Miss R.
Ampenoff dated 21 April 1972.

Copyright 1953 by Hawkes & Son (London), Ltd.
This is the part referred to in annotations on F2.4 and F2.6.

GB-ALb 2-9300504

F2.6 - A revised copy. With annotations: pencil (Rosamund Strode). - [1]-15, [i] p.,
pink card wrapper, stitched ; 33.1 cm. + 2 paste-overs.
Title from front cover.
Paste-overs (photocopies of the ms. leaves added to F1.6) on pp. 14, 15
give the harp accompaniment to the final dance. Red pencil note on p. 1
(Rosamund Strode): 'NB Osian Ellis now has his own part (the one he
used originally from this set) to keep. Sept. 1977'. (See F2.4 and F2.5.)

GB-ALb 2-9200094

F3.1 First edition, first impression. - *Benjamin Britten | CHORAL DANCES | from
'Gloriana' | Version for Tenor, Harp, and Chorus | Words by William Plomer |
Vocal Score | Boosey & Hawkes | Music Publishers Limited | London · Paris · Bonn
· Johannesburg · Sydney · Toronto · New York.* - London : Boosey & Hawkes
Music Publishers Limited, 1982. Pl. no.: B. & H. 20560. - [ii], 18 p., thick grey
paper wrapper, stapled ; 31 cm.
Analysis: [fo] *Benjamin Britten | CHORAL DANCES | from 'Gloriana' |
Version for Tenor, Harp, and Chorus | Vocal Score | BOOSEY & HAWKES*,
[fi] blank, [i], tp, [ii], note, [1]-18 music, [ri] blank, [ro] advert (no. 2,
dated 8.65).
Print code: none   Ordered: 25.1.82   Delivered: 10.2.82
Print run: 500.

F3.2 First edition, second impression. - 1984. - [No copy located].
Ordered: 1.10.84
Print run: 500.

F3.3 First edition, third impression.[81] - 1991. - [No copy located].
Ordered: 16.10.91   Delivered: 31.1.92
Print run: 500.

Recording

Rec1 Unpublished sound recording. - [Gloriana - Choral Dances]. - [1967]. - 1 side of
one sound disc (11:12 min.) : analogue, mono. - [Item not examined.]
Performers: Peter Pears, ten.; Osian Ellis, hp; Ambrosian Singers; Benjamin
Britten, conductor.
Date and place of recording: 67.03.01, at the Queen Elizabeth Hall,
London.
The première: part of a complete recording of the inaugural concert of
the Queen Elizabeth Hall by the BBC Transcription Service.

GB-Lnsa BBC TS LP 120725 [side number]

---

[81] A deleted entry on the Boosey & Hawkes card refers to an order for 500 copies, placed on
16.8.90, with 'Jan.' indicated as the date of delivery.

(O) *Gloriana* Fanfare

Scoring: trumpets in multiples of three.

Duration: 0:28 min.

Date of arrangement: 1967

First performance: 2 June 1967, Aldeburgh and Snape Maltings Concert Hall.[82] Herald Trumpeters of the Royal Artillery Band, Woolwich.

Publication: unpublished.

Notes

This fanfare, derived from the fanfares in 1.i, was prepared by Rosamund Strode, working under the composer's supervision. It was first heard at the opening ceremonies of the 1967 Aldeburgh Festival, which also incorporated the opening of the Concert Hall, Snape Maltings by HM the Queen. There are two endings: the second, longer ending was played inside the concert hall itself.[83] The fanfare was heard again in 1970 (see the notes to (P)), when the performers were the Trumpeters of the Royal Military School of Music, Kneller Hall.

The notion of extracting these fanfares for a ceremonial occasion was first mooted many years earlier. In an irate letter to David Webster dated 1 June 1953, Britten outlined the history of the discussions about the music to preceded *Gloriana* on the opening night (a fanfare and an arrangement of the National Anthem): he was refusing to become involved at such a late date. In doing so he referred to a much earlier suggestion (probably from the composer himself), that the fanfares in *Gloriana* be used, a plan which would have provided a fascinating and unmistakable link between the present and the operatically-evoked past.

Sources

Score

F1   Interim score. Manuscripts (chemical photocopy) (Rosamund Strode); with annotations: pencil (Rosamund Strode). - *GLORIANA* / [l.h.] *Trumpet Fanfare from Act I* / [r.h.] *Benjamin Britten, Op. 53.* - [1967]. - [1] fol. ; 32.9 cm.
     ANALYSIS: [1ᵛ] music, [1ᵛ] blank.

     Copyright 1953 by Boosey & Hawkes Ltd, London.

     A short score showing the three trumpet parts only. This was prepared by Rosamund Strode under the supervision of the composer from a marked-up copy of the vocal score of the opera (second edition, first impression, (A)/V10.4).

     With a second, un-annotated copy.   *GB-ALb* 2-9200093

---

[82] Although not certain, it is probable that the *Gloriana* fanfare used at Snape was also the fanfare played as HM the Queen reached the steps of the Moot Hall, Aldeburgh, earlier the same day.

[83] A quite different fanfare was prepared from the on-stage trumpet parts for a gala at the London Coliseum on 28 May 1981. The arranger was probably Denis Eagen, music librarian of English National Opera, and the surviving material (copies of score and parts) are kept at *GB-Leno*; photocopies of this material are also held at *GB-ALb* (2-9200312).

Recordings

Rec1   Unpublished test pressing - *Maltings I*...[Fanfare and speech]. - London : Decca, 1972. - Matrix no.: EXP-BS-602-1W. - 1 track on 1 side of 1 sound disc (0:28 min.) : analogue, 33.3 rpm, stereo ; 12 in.
PERFORMERS: Herald Trumpeters of the Royal Artillery Band, Woolwich.
DATE AND PLACE OF RECORDING: 67.06.02 at Snape Maltings.

    The fanfare shares a track with a speech by Benjamin Britten. The first performance, recorded by Decca at the opening concert of the Snape Maltings Concert Hall on 2 June 1967; later published (without the speech) as part of the anthology: *25 Years at the Aldeburgh Festival* (Rec2 below).

    Two copies.   *GB-ALb* 3-9203291

Rec2   Sound recording - *25 years at the Aldeburgh Festival...Gloriana - Fanfare / Britten*. - London : Decca Record Company Limited, 1972. - Catalogue no.: Decca 5BB 120; matrix no.: EAL-11327-3W. - 1 track on 1 side of 2 sound discs (0:28 min.) : analogue, 33.3 rpm, stereo ; 12 in.
PERFORMERS: Herald Trumpeters of the Royal Artillery Band, Woolwich.
DATE AND PLACE OF RECORDING: 67.06.02 at Snape Maltings, as part of the Aldeburgh Festival, 1967.

    Notes by Peter Pears and Anthony Gishford.

(P)   *Gloriana*: Symphonic Suite (version with chorus)

1.   The Tournament
2.   The Lute Song
3.   Courtly Dances[84]
4.   Apotheosis

Scoring: Picc., 2 fls, 2 obs, cor anglais, 2 cls, 2 bsns, dbsn, 4 hns, 3 trpts, 3 trbs, tuba, timpani, perc., hp, strings, ten. solo, chorus.

Duration: 16:30 min.

Date of arrangement: 1970

First performance: 5 June 1970, The Maltings, Snape. Peter Pears, ten.; the Aldeburgh Festival Singers; the English Chamber Orchestra; conducted by Benjamin Britten.

Publication: unpublished.

Notes

Britten made this arrangement for a concert on 5 June 1970, when HM The Queen came a second time to Snape Maltings Concert Hall, which she had opened only three years earlier; on this occasion she attended the first concert to take place in the rebuilt hall, destroyed by fire on the first night of the 1969 Aldeburgh Festival. As in 1969 ceremonial military trumpeters played the three-part fanfare written for the entry of Gloriana ((O)) as the Queen arrived in the concert hall, and in 1970 the final item in the concert was 'Three scenes from *Gloriana*' - or three movements from the Symphonic Suite ((D)) (omitting the Courtly Dances) in a new guise.

In the first ('The Tournament') a chorus was included, singing its commentary on the bout between Essex and Mountjoy from 1.i; the 'Lute Song' was again sung by Peter Pears. The last movement was retitled 'Apotheosis' for this concert (under the circumstances a good deal more appropriate and tactful than the published heading 'Gloriana moritura') and the final 'Green leaves are we' was sung by the chorus, as at the close of the opera.

The chorus and piano-conductor parts prepared for the performance (CS1.2, P1) seem to indicate that originally all four movements of the suite were to be performed (with the chorus tacet in the Courtly Dances). The shorter, three-movement version was more suitable for the concert on 5 June 1970.

Sources

Score

F1   Full score (marked-up copy of (D)/F2, signed). Printed; with annotations, corrections and revisions: blue ink, blue pencil, pencil (Benjamin Britten, Rosamund Strode, unidentified hand).

> Signed in ink on tp: 'Benjamin Britten / 1954'. This indicates that the copy was one of the initial batch supplied to the composer on publication of the Suite. This score, used at the première of (P) as the conducting score, has the chorus text added in blue ink, and with Britten's revisions in pencil; it is the only primary source. It was clearly used by Britten on another occasion for a performance (perhaps in Germany) of the version without chorus.   *GB-ALb* 2-9200281

---

84   Not included in the only performance: see the notes.

Choral scores

CS1   Intermediate copy (marked-up copy of (A)/CS3). Printed; with annotations: pencil (Rosamund Strode). - pp. [1]-28, 28A, 28B, 29-62, marbled green thick paper wrapper, stapled ; 25.1 cm.

        ANALYSIS: [fo] [black ink:] *GLORIANA / by / Benjamin Britten / (CHORAL SCORE) /* [rubber-stamped:] *BOOSEY & HAWKES / MUSIC PUBLISHERS LTD. / HIRE LIBRARY,* [fo] blank, [otherwise as for (A)/CS3].

        Pencil note on p. 1: 'Used ~~to make up~~ [replaced with:] in preparation of the / <u>Choral</u> version of the SUITE, performed at The Maltings / in June 1970 / (RS)'. The other source for the choral parts of the suite was the marked-up vocal score (second edition, first impression) prepared by Rosamund Strode (see (A)/V10.4).   *GB-ALb* 2-9200226

CS2.1   Hire material. Ms. (dyeline) (Rosamund Strode); with annotations: pencil (Rosamund Strode). - [r.h.] *CHORUS SCORE // Benjamin Britten / GLORIANA / Symphonic Suite / (Version with Chorus).* - London : Boosey & Hawkes Music Publishers Limited, [1970]. - [1]-11, [i] p., thick marbled green paper wrapper ; 35.6 cm.

        ANALYSIS: [fo] *CHORAL SCORE // GLORIANA / BRITTEN / SYMPHONIC SUITE / VERSION WITH CHORUS //* [rubber-stamped:] *BOOSEY & HAWKES MUSIC PUBLISHERS LTD. / HIRE LIBRARY / 295, REGENT STREET / LONDON W.1.,* [fi] blank, [1] tp, [2]-11 music, [i] blank, [ri-ro] blank.

        Copyright 1953 by Hawkes & Son (London), Ltd.
        Initialled 'RS' on front wrapper.   *GB-ALb* 2-9100011

CS2.2   - Another copy (Benjamin Britten's copy).
        Initialled (Rosamund Strode) 'BB' on front wrapper.   *GB-ALb* 2-9100011

Parts

P1.1   Hire material, piano-conductor score (Benjamin Britten's copy). Printed, manuscript (dyeline) (copyist: Rosamund Strode). - [r.h.] *PIANO CONDUCTOR SCORE / for Chorus rehearsals // Benjamin Britten / GLORIANA / Symphonic Suite / (Version with Chorus) /* [sticker]. - London : Boosey & Hawkes Music Publishers Limited, [1970]. - [1]-11, [i] p., thick marbled green paper wrapper ; 35.6 cm.

        ANALYSIS: [fo] [l.h., black felt-tip:] *PIANO CONDUCTOR / SCORE + CHORUS //* [rubber-stamped:] *GLORIANA / BRITTEN / SYMPHONIC SUITE / VERSION WITH CHORUS /* [rubber-stamped:] *BOOSEY & HAWKES MUSIC PUBLISHERS LTD. / HIRE LIBRARY / 295, REGENT STREET / LONDON W.1.,* [fi] blank, [1] tp, [2]-11 music, [i] blank, [ri-ro] blank.

        Copyright 1953 by Hawkes & Son (London), Ltd.
        Initialled (Rosamund Strode) 'BB' on front wrapper.   *GB-ALb* 2-9100012

P1.2   - Another copy.
        Initialled (Rosamund Strode) 'RS' on front wrapper.   *GB-ALb* 2-9100012

(Q) Courtly Dances, arranged for ensemble

1.   March
2.   Corante
3.   Pavan
4.   Morris Dance
5.   Galliard
6.   La Volta

Arranger: Bernard Pierrot

Scoring: rec. (sopranino or treb.), treble viol, bass viol, lute, pandora, darbouka.[85]

Date: 1970?

First performance: untraced

Publication: unpublished

Notes

This arrangement was prepared by Bernard Pierrot for performance by *Les Menestriers*, an early music ensemble. Britten's permission was sought in a letter dated 11 January 1971 and on 5 August he replied, making a number of suggestions for improvements. At the same time he returned the score with some annotations of his own (F1). A revised score was sent to Britten on 2 October 1971. No copy of the arrangement has been located at the Britten-Pears Library.

The arrangement was prepared from the score of the Symphonic Suite (in view of this it is likely that despite any indication in F1 of a repeat of the March at the end, such a return was planned), and with a knowledge of the earlier arrangement by Julian Bream (I).

The possibility of performances and a recording were mentioned in the correspondence between composer and arranger, but as yet it is not clear whether the arrangement was heard in public; no recording was made.

Sources

F1   Manuscript full score. Manuscript: black ink, blue ball-point (Bernard Pierrot); with annotations and corrections: pencil (Benjamin Britten). - [Untitled]. - [1970-71?]. - [6] fol. : 14 staves, [span:] 22.5 cm. ; 27.3 x 35.2 cm.
       ANALYSIS: [1^r] *March*, [1^v-2^r] *CORANTO*, [2^v-3^r] *PAVANE*, [3^v] *Morris Dance*, [4^{r-v}] *GALLIARD*, [5^r-6^r] *LA VOLTA*, [6^v] blank.
       COLLATION: A^6

Private Collection

---

85 The darabukka is a single-headed goblet drum from the Islamic Middle-East and North Africa.

7

Gloriana: A Bibliography

ANTONIA MALLOY

This bibliography is a list of writings about *Gloriana*, not a bibliography of works cited in this volume or consulted in its preparation. Any publications cited which do not fall within the criteria for inclusion in the bibliography, are listed under the author's name in the index.

I am indebted to the staff of the Royal Opera House Archive for their assistance in locating a large number of articles (many of which are not listed in other sources), and for permission to use the two volumes of relevant press cuttings preserved there.

1. GENERAL

'This Month's Personality: David Webster.' *Music and Musicians* 2/12 (August 1954): 7.
'Peter Pears.' *Music and Musicians* 12/3 (November 1963): 11.
Benjamin Britten: a Complete Catalogue of his Published Works. London: Boosey & Hawkes and Faber Music, 1973.
Alexander, Peter F. *William Plomer.* Oxford: Oxford University Press, 1990.
Blyth, Alan. 'Influence and Example'. *Gramophone* 68/808 (September 1990), 475.
—— *Remembering Britten.* London: Hutchinson, 1981.
Britten, Benjamin. 'On Writing English Opera.' *Opera* 12/1 (January 1961): 7–8.
—— 'Freeman of Lowestoft'. *Tempo* 21 (Autumn 1951): 3–5.
Carpenter, Humphrey. *Benjamin Britten: A Biography.* London: Faber and Faber, 1992.
Coleman, Basil. 'Producing the Operas.' *London Magazine.* 3/7 (October 1963): 104–108.
Cross, Joan. 'The Bad Old Days'. In *Tribute to Benjamin Britten on his Fiftieth Birthday,* edited by Anthony Gishford, 175–84. London: Faber and Faber, 1963.
—— 'Recollections of a Dowager Lady Billows'. In *Aldeburgh Anthology,* ed. Ronald Blythe, 124–5. Faber: London, 1972.
Evans, Peter. '*Gloriana.*' In *The Music of Benjamin Britten,* 188–202. 2nd ed. London: J.M Dent & Sons, 1989.
—— 'Britten's celebration of musical Englishness'. In the sleeve notes to DECCA 440 213–2 2HO2.
Haltrecht, Montague. *The Quiet Showman: A Biography of David Webster.* London: Collins, 1975.
Hardy, Channell. 'Joan Cross.' *Opera* 1/1 (February 1950): 22–8.
Harewood, George. 'Benjamin Britten.' In *The Tongs and the Bones: The Memoirs of Lord Harewood,* 129–49. London: Weidenfeld and Nicolson, 1981.
—— 'Joan Cross – A Birthday Celebration'. *Opera* 41/9 (September 1990): 1032–9.
Headington, Christopher. *Peter Pears: A Biography.* London: Faber and Faber, 1992.

Herbert, David, ed. *The Operas of Benjamin Britten.* 2nd ed. London, The Herbert Press, 1989.

Holst, Imogen. 'Working for Benjamin Britten.' *MT* 118/1695 (February 1977): 202–206.

Howard, Patricia. '*Gloriana.*' In *The Operas of Benjamin Britten*, 101–124. London: Barrie and Rockliff, 1969.

John, Nicholas, ed. *Peter Grimes / Gloriana.* English National Opera Guides Series, no. 24. London: John Calder, 1983.

Kennedy, Michael. '*Gloriana.*' In *Britten*, 202–205. Rev. ed. The Dent Master Musicians. London: J.M. Dent, 1993.

Klein, John W. '*Gloriana*: eine Krönungs-Oper.' In *Musik der Zeit*, ed. Heinrich Lindlar, vol. 11, 22–26. Bonn: Verlag Boosey & Hawkes GmbH, 1955.

Lucas, John. *Reggie: The Life of Reginald Goodall.* London: Julia Macrea Books, 1993.

McDonald, Ellen. 'Women in Benjamin Britten's Operas.' *Opera Quarterly* 4/3 (Autumn 1986): 83–101.

Martin, George. 'Benjamin Britten: 25 Years of Opera.' *Yale Review* 60/1 (October 1970): 24–44.

Mitchell, Donald. 'Fit for a Queen? The Reception of *Gloriana*'. In the sleeve notes to DECCA 440 213–2 2HO2.

Mitchell, Donald, and Keller, Hans, eds. *Benjamin Britten: A Commentary on his Works from a Group of Specialists.* London: Rockliff, 1952.

Mitchell, Donald, and Reed, Philip, eds. *Letters from a Life: the Selected Letters and Diaries of Benjamin Britten 1913–1976.* Vols 1–2. London: Faber and Faber, 1991.

—— 'The creation of *Gloriana*: excerpts from Britten's correspondence, 1952–3'. In the sleeve notes to DECCA 440 213–2 2HO2.

Palmer, Christopher, ed. *The Britten Companion.* London: Faber and Faber, 1984.

Percival, John. *Theatre in My Blood: A Biography of John Cranko.* London: The Herbert Press, 1983.

Piper, Myfanwy. 'Portrait of a Choreographer.' *Tempo* 32 (Summer 1954): 14–23.

Plomer, William. 'Let's Crab an Opera.' *London Magazine* 3/7 (October 1964): 101–4.

Plomer, William. *The Autobiography of William Plomer.* London: Jonathan Cape, 1975.

Raynor, Henry. 'The Battle of Britten.' *Musical Opinion* 76/910 (July 1953): 593–7.

Rosenthal, Harold. *Two Centuries of Opera at Covent Garden.* London: Putnam, 1958.

Tracey, Edmund. 'Benjamin Britten Talks to Edmund Tracey.' *Sadler's Wells Magazine* 4 (Autumn 1966): 5–7.

White, Eric Walter. '*Gloriana.*' In *Benjamin Britten: His Life and Operas*, 190–201. 2nd ed. London: Faber and Faber, 1983.

Whittall, Arnold. 'Britten: From 'Canticle II' to 'Winter Words' (1952–3).' In *The Music of Britten and Tippett: Studies in Themes and Techniques*, 144–52. 2nd ed. Cambridge: Cambridge University Press, 1990.

2. GENESIS

(a) Literary and Historical Background

Holroyd, Michael. 'Elizabeth and Strachey.' In *Lytton Strachey: A Critical Biography.* Vol. 2, 578–616. London: Heinemann, 1967.

Neale, J. E. *Queen Elizabeth I.* 1934. Reprint of revised ed. London: Pelican, 1971.

Porter, Andrew. 'Gloriana and Lytton Strachey.' *Opera* 4/8 (August 1953): 464–467.

Strachey. Lytton. *Elizabeth and Essex: A Tragic History.* 1928. Reprint. London: Penguin, 1971.

(b) Social and Aesthetic Background

'Coronation Opera.' *Star.* 29 December 1952.

'Gala – Command.' *Yorkshire Observer.* 23 January 1953.

Barnard, T. 'Art's Restless Era' [Letter]. *Daily Telegraph.* 16 June 1953.

Bell, Michael. 'Eccentric Music' [Letter]. *Daily Telegraph.* 15 June 1953.

Bennet, Archibald. 'Music and the Spirit of the Age' [Letter]. *Musical Opinion* 76/912 (September 1953): 709

Cartier, Jean. 'State Control' [Letter]. *Musical Opinion* 76/908 (May 1953): 463.

Hare, G. Kenneth. 'Art and Its Age' [Letter]. *Daily Telegraph.* 20 June 1953.

Hewison, Robert. *In Anger: Culture in the Cold War 1945–60.* London: Weidenfeld and Nicolson, 1981.

Leslie, Ian. 'Eccentric Music' [Letter]. *Daily Telegraph.* 15 June 1953.

Rawlinson, Lynette. 'Art's Restless Era' [Letter]. *Daily Telegraph.* 16 June 1953.

Raynor, Henry. 'Arts Council of Great Britain.' In *Grove 6.* ed. Stanley Sadie. Vol. 1, p. 646. London: Macmillan, 1980.

Rosenthal, Irving. 'State Control' [Letter]. *Musical Opinion* 76/908 (May 1953): 463.

Siderfin, Rev. John K. 'Ugliness in Art' [Letter]. *Daily Telegraph.* 18 June 1953.

Sutcliffe, D. 'Music and the Spirit of the Age' [Letter]. *Musical Opinion* 76/912 (September 1953): 709.

Waller, R. 'Art and Its Age' [Letter]. *Daily Telegraph.* 20 June 1953.

Wood, Sinjon [pseud.]. 'The Menace of State Control' [Letter]. *Musical Opinion* 76/906 (March 1953): 343–345.

(c) Preparing the First Production

Alexander, Peter F. 'The Process of Composition of the Libretto of Britten's "Gloriana".' *ML* 67/2 (April 1986): 147–158.

Coleman, Basil. 'Problems and Solutions in the Production of *Gloriana*.' *Tempo* 28 (Summer 1953): 14–16.

—— 'Inszenierungsvorschläge zu "Gloriana".' In *Musik der Zeit*, ed. Heinrich Lindlar, vol. 11. Bonn: Verlag Boosey & Hawkes GmbH, 1955, 26–30.

Muller, Robert. '*Gloriana* is Born.' *Picture Post* 59/11 (13 June 1953): 67.

Plomer, William. 'Writing *Gloriana* with Benjamin Britten.' *Radio Times.* 5 June 1953.

—— 'The *Gloriana* Libretto.' *Sadler's Wells Magazine* 4 (Autumn 1966): 8–9.

—— 'Notes on the Libretto of *Gloriana*.' *Tempo* 28 (Summer 1953): 5–7.

3. THE FIRST PRODUCTION (1953–54)

(a) Previews[1]

'Coronation Opera.' *Liverpool Daily Post.* 28 May 1952.

'Coronation Opera.' *Evening News.* 29 May 1952.

' "Elizabeth and Essex" – Mr. Britten's Plans.' *Manchester Guardian.* 30 May 1952.

'Coronation Opera.' *Rhodesian Herald.* 31 May 1952.

[Untitled]. *Ottago Daily Times.* 19 June 1952.

'Britten's New Opera.' *Evening Standard.* 7 July 1952.

---

[1] All unsigned articles are arranged in chronological order.

[Untitled]. *Stage*. 2 October 1952.

'Britten Names His Coronation Opera.' *Courier and Advertiser*. 18 October 1952.

'Opera for the Queen.' *Manchester Daily Dispatch*. 17 January 1953.

'Cranko Creates Ballet for *Gloriana*.' *Bulawayo Chronicle*. 20 March 1953.

'Will Porters Whistle?.' *News Chronicle*. 20 March 1953.

'Gala Opera – Then and Now.' *Daily Telegraph*. 21 March 1953.

'6,000 Apply for Coronation Gala Opera.' *Daily Telegraph*. 1 April 1953.

'Britten's *Gloriana*.' *Stage*. 2 April 1953.

'Britten Hopes New Opera His Best.' *Evening Star*. 15 April 1953.

'Mr. Britten Discusses *Gloriana*.' *Lowestoft Journal*. 17 April 1953.

'*Elizabeth and Essex*: Britten Discusses *Gloriana*.' *Stage*. 23 April 1953.

[Untitled]. *Sphere*. 25 April 1953.

'Britten Music at Private Party.' *Daily Telegraph*. 19 May 1953.

'Composer's Holiday.' *Star*. 20 May 1953.

'Coronation Opera Completed.' *International Music News* 45/3 (May–June 1953): 10

'*Gloriana*: A Synopsis.' *Tempo*. 28 (Summer 1953): 8–13.

Baxter, Beverley. 'Mr. Britten Has a Problem in Romance.' *Sunday Express*. 1 June 1952.

Benson, Preston. 'The Coronation Opera.' *Star*. 29 May 1952.

Cross, Arthur. 'Give Us a Tune, Mr. B.!' [Letter]. *News Chronicle*. 18 April 1953.

Gishford, Anthony. 'Britten's Opera for the Coronation is "An Offering for the Queen".' *Music and Musicians*. 1/10 (June 1953): 6.

Goddard, Scott. 'New Opera in Time for the Coronation.' *News Chronicle*. 14 March 1953.

Noville, Constance. 'The Queen to Hear *Gloriana* First?.' *Huddersfield Daily Examiner*. 24 April 1953.

Sagittarius [pseud.]. 'Elizabethans.' *New Statesman and Nation*. 43/1109 (7 June 1952): 665.

Stein, Erwin. '*Gloriana*.' *Listener* 49/1266 (4 June 1953): 949.

Thomas, James. 'Mr. Britten Talks About His *Gloriana*.' *News Chronicle*. 15 April 1953.

Williams, Stephen. 'Opera from Covent Garden and Glyndebourne.' *Radio Times*. 5 June 1953.

(b) **Responses**[1]

'The Queen Goes to See New Britten Opera.' *Daily Telegraph*. 9 June 1953.

'Gala Night.' *Evening News*. 9 June 1953.

'Prince Philip Does a Lot of Reading at Opera.' *Evening Standard*. 9 June 1953.

'Queen at Coronation Opera.' *Glasgow Herald*. 9 June 1953.

'*Gloriana* Was Memorable.' *Liverpool Daily Post*. 9 June 1953.

'Greatest First Night of All.' *News Chronicle*. 9 June 1953.

'The Queen's Praise.' *Star*. 9 June 1953.

'Royal Opera House *Gloriana*.' *The Times*. 9 June 1953.

'A Splendid Occasion.' *Truth* 153/4003 (9 June 1953): 705.

'Mr. Piper's Weather.' *Manchester Guardian*. 10 June 1953.

'Second Visit to Opera House.' *News Chronicle*. 10 June 1953.

'Tiara-boom Di-a!.' *News Chronicle*. 10 June 1953.

'Benjamin Britten's Coronation Opera.' *The Times Weekly Review*. 11 June 1953.

'[. . .]Repeat *Gloriana*.' *Yorkshire Evening Post*. 11 June 1953.

---

1 All unsigned articles are arranged in chronological order.

'Bow for Britten.' *Daily Express*. 12 June 1953.

'Warm Applause for Britten.' *Yorkshire Observer*. 13 June 1953.

'*Gloriana* (Covent Garden).' *Empire News*. 14 June 1953.

'Playtime.' *Reynolds News*. 14 June 1953.

'Bill for *Gloriana*.' *Evening Standard*. 15 June 1953.

'Covent Garden *Gloriana*.' *Stage*. 18 June 1953.

'Is Mr. Britten Slipping? *Gloriana* Reveals Need for Strong Libretto.' *Stage*. 18 June 1953.

'*Gloriana*.' *The Times Educational Supplement*. 19 June 1953.

'Royal Opera House *Gloriana*.' *The Times*. 1 July 1953.

'Glory or *Gloriana*?.' *Music and Musicians* 1/11 (July 1953): 5.

'Sic Transit *Gloriana*?.' *Musical Opinion* 76/910 (July 1953): 581–582.

'*Gloriana*: A Great Event in English Music.' *National and English Review* (July 1953): 34–36.

'*Gloriana*: A Synopsis.' *Tempo* 28 (Summer 1953): 8–13.

'Notes of the Day.' *Monthly Musical Record* 83/949 (September 1953): 169–172.

'*Gloriana* de Benjamin Britten.' *Revista Musical Chilena* 9/44 (January 1954): 102–103.

Anderson, W. R. 'Round About Radio.' *MT* 94/1326 (August 1953): 359–60.

Austin, N. F. 'Excellent' [Letter]. *Daily Express*. 22 June 1953.

Barker, Frank Granville. '*Gloriana*: The Coronation Opera.' *Opera News* 18/1 (19 October 1953): 10–11.

Bayliss, Stanley. 'It Has Some Charm, but It's Not Great.' *Daily Mail*. 9 June 1953.

—— 'Not a Great Britten.' *Daily Mail*. 10 June 1953.

Baxter, Beverley. 'Covent Garden's Strangest Night: Mr. Britten Puts a Chill on the Merrie England Mood.' *Evening Standard*. 9 June 1953.

Benson, Preston. '*Gloriana* Has Real Majesty.' *Star*. 9 June 1953.

Billamy, Fred. ' "It's a Wonderful Work", Queen Tells Britten.' *Manchester Daily Dispatch*. 9 June 1953.

Blom, Eric. '*Gloriana*.' *Sunday Observer*. 14 June 1953.

Bonnyman, J. '*Gloriana*' [Letter]. *Music and Musicians* 1/12 (August 1953): 23.

Bradbury, Ernest '*Gloriana* Has Its First Performance.' *Yorkshire Post*. 9 June 1953.

—— '*Gloriana*: Later Impressions.' *Yorkshire Post*. 13 June 1953.

—— 'Opera in London.' *MT* 94/1326 (August 1953): 372.

Brahms, Caryl. '*Gloriana*' [Letter]. *The Times*. 19 June 1953.

Bristow, Sir Robert. 'Eccentric Music' [Letter]. *Daily Telegraph*. 15 June 1953.

Butcher, Margaret H. '*Gloriana*'s Voice' [Letter]. *Radio Times*. 19 June 1953.

A.V.C. [A. V. Cotton.]. 'Opera: *Gloriana*.' *Music Review* 14/3 (August 1953): 228–230.

M.C. '*Gloriana*.' *Daily Telegraph*. 1 July 1953.

R.C. [Richard Capell.]. 'Opera and Concerts.' *Monthly Musical Record* 83/948 (July–August 1953): 157.

Capell, Richard. '*Gloriana* at Covent Garden.' *Daily Telegraph*. 9 June 1953.

—— 'Reflections on *Gloriana*.' *Daily Telegraph*. 13 June 1953.

Carner, Mosco. '*Gloriana*.' *Time and Tide* 34/25 (20 June 1953): 818.

Cooper, Martin. '*Gloriana* and Benjamin Britten.' *Score* 8 (September 1953): 61.

—— '*Gloriana*.' *Spectator*. 12 June 1953.

—— 'Britten at Bay.' *Spectator*. 19 June 1953.

Cotton, A. V. '*Gloriana*.' *Music Review* 14/3 (August 1953): 228–30.

Cross, Joan. 'Singers on Safari.' *Tempo* 30 (Winter 1953–4): 27–30.

Diapason [Hendrik Sprutyenburg, pseud.]. 'Britten's Coronation Opera Acclaimed.' *East Anglian Daily Times*. 9 June 1953.

Goddard, Scott. '*Gloriana* (Cont.).' *News Chronicle*. 12 June 1953.

—— 'London Letter.' *Chesterian* 28/176 (October 1953): 53–6.

Goodwin, Noel. 'Music.' *Truth* (19 June 1953): 751.

C.G.H. 'Britten's *Gloriana* Needed to Be Seen as Well as Heard. *Croydon Advertiser*. 19 June 1953.

Harrison, Sidney. 'Homage to Queens.' *John O'London's Weekly* 62/1511 (26 June 1953): 573.

Heinitz, Thomas. 'The Other Side (Imported Recordings).' *Saturday Review* 36/30 (25 July 1953): 58.

Hope-Wallace, Philip. '*Gloriana*: Royal Opera Gala at Covent Garden.' *Manchester Guardian Weekly*. 11 June 1953.

—— 'L'Art Officiel and *Gloriana* (Not to Mention TV Monoply).' *Time and Tide* 34/26 (27 June 1953): 851–2.

Hussey, Dyneley. 'Music – A Royal Occasion.' *Listener* 49/1268 (18 June 1953): 1027, 1029.

Irvine, J. Thorburn. '*Gloriana*' [Letter]. *The Times*. 22 June 1953.

Keller, Hans. 'The Half-year's New Music.' *Music Review* 83/948 (August 1953): 209–21.

Kinross [pseud.]. 'Gala Performance.' *Punch* 224/5880 (17 June 1953): 706–707.

Klein, John W. '*Gloriana*' [Letter]. *Musical Opinion* 76/910 (August 1953): 652.

—— '*Gloriana*' [Letter]. *Musical Opinion* 77/913 (October 1953): 11–13.

—— 'Some Reflections on *Gloriana*.' *Tempo* 29 (Autumn 1953): 16–21.

Knaggs, Philip. 'Uproar' [Letter]. *Sunday Express*. 14 June 1953.

Knyvett, Grenville. '*Gloriana*.' *Royal College of Music Magazine* 49/3 (November 1953): 67–9.

[Lawrence, John.] [Untitled]. *News of the World*. 14 June 1953.

Lewis, Anthony. '*Gloriana*' [Letter]. *The Times*. 16 June 1953.

Littlefield, Joan. 'Britten's Coronation Opera.' *Canon* 7/1 (August 1953): 19–21.

D.M. [Donald Mitchell.]. 'A Pocket Guide to *Gloriana*.' *Musical Opinion* 76/910 (July 1953): 603–5.

M.M.M. 'Letters to Australia.' *Canon* 7/8 (March 1953): 333–6.

Mann, William. 'London Repetitions of Britten's *Gloriana* Bring Revised Verdict on Opera.' *Musical America* 74/5 (March 1954): 50.

Mayer, Tony. 'L'Affaire *Gloriana*.' *Opera* 4/8 (August 1953): 456–60.

Mitchell, Donald. 'Some Observations on *Gloriana*.' *Monthly Musical Record* 83/952 (December 1953): 225–60.

—— '*Gloriana*' [Letter]. *Musical Opinion* 76/912 (September 1953): 711.

—— '*Gloriana*' [Letter]. *Musical Opinion* 77/914 (November 1953): 79.

Montagu, George. '*Gloriana* at Covent Garden.' *London Musical Events* 8/8 (August 1953): 10, 11, 39.

—— 'Musical Survey.' *London Musical Events* 8/8 (August 1953): 17–21.

Montagu-Nathan, M. 'Radio in Retrospect.' *Musical Opinion* 76/910 (July 1953): 587–8.

Mortlock, C.B. '*Gloriana* Falls Short of Glory.' *Church Times* 136/4714 (12 June 1953): 436.

E.N. [Ernest Newman.]. '*Gloriana*.' *The Sunday Times*. 14 June 1953.

Newman, Joseph. 'Music Fit for a Queen.' *New York Herald Tribune*. 14 June 1953.

Notcutt, Arthur. 'London Events Range from *Gloriana* to Glyndebourne.' *Musical Courier* 148/1 (August 1953): 6–7.

Pollen, Arthur J. 'Britten Can Take It' [Letter]. *Daily Express*. 22 June 1953.

Porter, Andrew. 'Music of Today: *Gloriana*.' *London Musical Events* 8/8 (August 1953): 12–14.

—— 'Opera Diary: *Gloriana.' Opera* 4/9 (September 1953): 566.

—— 'Britten's *Gloriana.' ML* 34/4 (October 1953): 277–87.

H.S.R. 'Opera and Ballet in London: *Gloriana.' Musical Opinion* 76/910 (July 1953): 585.

Redlich, H. F. 'Urauffuhrung von Brittens Kronungsoper *Gloriana.' Musikleben* 6 (July–August 1953).

Rhodes, Harold W. '*Gloriana*' [Letter]. *The Times*. 19 June 1953.

Roberts, E. M. '*Gloriana*' [Letter]. *The Times*. 22 June 1953.

Rotter, J. [pseud.]. 'Not So Glorious Now' [Letter]. *News Chronicle*. 11 June 1953.

C. S. 'Gala Performance at the ROH.' *Birmingham Post*. 9 June 1953.

E. S. '*Gloriana.' Music and Musicians* 1/11 (July 1953): 3.

E. S. 'London Concerts and Opera.' *Music and Musicians* 1/12 (August 1953): 16.

Sear, H. G. 'Needle in a Haystack.' *Daily Worker*. 9 June 1953.

Sellers, Elizabeth. '*Gloriana*' [Letter]. *The Times*. 19 June 1953.

Shawe-Taylor, Desmond. 'Royal Operas.' *New Statesman* 45/1162 (13 June 1953): 701.

—— '*Gloriana*, Cheltenham, Glyndebourne.' *New Statesman* 45/1163 (20 June 1953): 729.

Sherwood, Roy. '*Gloriana*: Pathos and Pageantry.' *Belfast Newsletter*. 10 June 1953.

—— 'Gala Night for *Gloriana.' Birmingham Mail*. 9 June 1953.

Siderfin, Rev. John K. 'Nerve-fraying Art: Has It Forgotten Its Mission?' [Letter]. *Daily Telegraph*. 11 June 1953.

Smith, Andrew. 'Tale of the First Elizabeth.' *Daily Herald*. 9 June 1953.

Smith, C. 'Elizabeth II Attends Premiere of Benjamin Britten's Latest Opera.' *Musical America* 73/9 (July 1953): 7.

Smith, Cecil. 'The Performance.' *Opera* 4/8 (August 1953): 467–9.

Spens, M. '*Gloriana*' [Letter]. *Music and Musicians* 1/12 (August 1953): 23.

Stopes, Marie. '*Gloriana*' [Letter]. *The Times*. 20 June 1953.

J. T. 'An Improved *Gloriana.' Star*. 12 June 1953.

Vaughan Williams, Ralph. '*Gloriana*' [Letter]. *The Times*. 18 June 1953.

Watkins, D. '*Gloriana*' [Letter]. *Music and Musicians* 1/12 (August 1953): 23.

Williams, Stephen. '*Gloriana* – An Ideal Tribute.' *Edinburgh Evening News*. 9 June 1953.

—— 'Elizabeth II Sees Bow of *Gloriana.' New York Times*. 9 June 1953.

—— 'Coronation Opera.' *New York Times*. 14 June 1953.

Wolfe, Peter. 'Facing the Music: Almost Glory.' *What's On*. (19 June 1953)

Wood, Sinjon. [pseud.]. '*Gloriana*' [Letter]. *Musical Opinion* 76/911 (August 1953): 652.

—— '*Gloriana*' [Letter]. *Musical Opinion* 77/913 (October 1953): 13.

—— '*Gloriana*' [Letter]. *Musical Opinion* 77/ 916 (January 1954): 205.

—— '*Gloriana*' [Letter]. *Musical Opinion* 77/917 (February 1954): 269.

Wyatt, Woodrow. '*Gloriana*' [Letter]. *The Times*. 20 June 1953.

4. SUBSEQUENT PERFORMANCES

(a) Concert Performances

(i) Extracts in Concert Performance: 28 June 1953, Aldeburgh

Diapason [Hendrik Sprutyenburg, pseud.]. 'Fine Climax at Aldeburgh: Highlights from *Gloriana.' East Anglian Daily Times*. 29 June 1953. (Also appeared in *Ipswich Suffolk Chronicle and Mercury*. 3 July.)

(ii) **Extracts in Concert Performance:** 12 July 1953, Queen's Hall, Barnstaple

'Lord Harewood Introduces Fifteen Operas.' *North Devon Journal Herald*. 16 July 1953.

'Earl of Harewood Introduces Operatic Concert.' *Bideford and North Devon Weekly Gazette*. 17 July 1953.

(iii) **Extracts in Concert Performance:** 26 July 1953, Guildhall of St. George, King's Lynn

'For artistry This Recital Stood Out.' *Lynn News and Advertiser*. 28 July 1953.

(iv) **Concert Performance,** 22 November 1963, Royal Festival Hall, London

'Triumphant Return of *Gloriana*.' *The Times*. 23 November 1963.

Cooper, Martin. 'England: Slack Season.' *Musical America* 84/1 (January 1964): 68.

Fairfax, Bryan. 'The Neglected Britten.' *Music and Musicians* 12/3 (November 1963): 42, 61.

Goodwin, Noel. '*Gloriana* Reawakened.' *Music and Musicians* 12/5 (January 1964): 30.

Hamburger, Paul. 'Glory Be to Britten.' *New Statesman* 66/1707 (29 November 1963): 802–804.

Henderson, Robert L. '*Budd* and *Gloriana* Reconsidered.' *Tempo* 68 (Spring 1964): 31–33.

Mason, Colin. '*Gloriana* at the Royal Festival Hall.' *Guardian*. 23 November 1963.

Mitchell, Donald. 'A Neglected Masterpiece: Britten's *Gloriana*.' *Listener* 73/1087 (14 November 1963): 809.

A. P. [Andrew Porter.]. '*Gloriana*.' *Opera* 15/1 (January 1964): 66–67.

Tracey, Edmund. 'London Music.' *MT* 107/1451 (January 1964): 36–37.

(b) **Revised Version, New Production, Sadler's Wells, 1966**

'Characters of Britten Opera Captured.' *The Times*. 22 October 1966.

A. B. [Alan Blyth.]. 'London Opera Diary – *Gloriana*.' *Opera* 18/4 (April 1967): 339.

Baker, George. 'The Musical Scene.' *Music Teacher and Piano Student* 45/12 (December 1966): 475, 497.

Chapman, Ernest. 'Britten's *Gloriana* Revived.' *London Musical Events* 21/12 (December 1966): 8–9.

Dean, Winton. '*Gloriana*.' *MT* 107/1486 (December 1966): 1072–1073.

Evans, Peter. 'Britten in Merrie England.' *Listener* 76/1962 (3 November 1966): 663.

Goodwin, Noel. 'The Triumph of *Gloriana*.' *Music and Musicians* 15/4 (December 1966): 16–17.

Greenfield, Edward. 'London Report.' *Hi-fi / Musical America* 17/2 (February 1967): [*Musical America*] 27.

Keller, Hans. 'Two Interpretations of *Gloriana* As Music Drama: 1: A Re-affirmation.' *Tempo* 79 (Autumn–Winter 1966–7): 2–5.

Klein, John W. 'Britten's Major Setback.' *Musical Opinion* 90/1069 (October 1966): 13, 15.

—— 'Elizabeth and Essex' *Music and Musicians* 15/3 (November 1966): 16, 17, 49.

Mason, Eric. 'The Change Does Britten Good.' *Daily Mail*. 22 October 1966.

Mitchell, Donald. 'Public and Private Life in Britten's *Gloriana*.' *Opera* 17/10 (October 1966): 767–774.

Natan, A. 'Gotter und Konige: Premieren in Covent Garden und Sadler's Wells.' *Opern Welt* 1 (January 1967): 20–22.

Payne, Anthony. 'New Essex for *Gloriana*.' *Music and Musicians* 15/8 (April 1967): 42.

Porter, Andrew. 'Gloriana.' *MT* 107/1484 (October 1966): 854–858.

H. D. R. [Harold Rosenthal.]. 'Gloriana.' *Opera* 17/12 (December 1966): 987–990.

H. R. S. 'Opera and Ballet in London – Sadler's Wells Opera.' *Musical Opinion* 90/1071 (December 1966): 129.

Walsh, Stephen. 'Two Interpretations of Gloriana as Music Drama: 2: A New Impression.' *Tempo* 79 (Autumn–Winter 1966–7): 5–9.

(c) Other Performances

(Cincinnati, 1956; London, 1967; Lisbon, 1967; Brussels, 1967; Munster, 1968; London, 1968–9; Aberdeen, 1971; London, 1972; Munich, 1972; London (Concert Performance), 1973; London, 1975; Vienna, 1975; Radio Broadcast (1973 Concert Performance Recording), 1977; London (Camden Festival), 1983; Manchester (RNCM), 1984; London, 1984; New York, 1984; Video Recording, 1988; Aberdeen, 1989.)[1]

'First Recordings of Unfamiliar Britten.' *American Record Guide* 28 (May 1962): 720–725.

'Belgium: Wells at the Monnaie.' *Opera* 18/11 (November 1967): 917.

'Munster.' *NZM* 129/ 7&8 (July–August 1968): 298.

'Gastspiel der Sadler's Wells Opera London: Gloriana.' *Oper und Konzert* 10/10 (1972): 10.

Blyth, Alan. 'Elizabeth II.' *Music and Musicians* 16/3 (November 1967): 38.

—— 'ENO in Vienna.' *Opera* 26/Festival Issue (Autumn 1975): 46–47.

—— 'On Video: Gloriana.' *Opera* 39/10 (October 1988): 1258–1259.

Cairns, David. 'Gloriana.' In *Responses*, 78–87. London: Martin Secker and Warburg, 1973.

Chapman, Ernest. 'Gloriana at the Coliseum.' *London Musical Events* 24/4 (April 1969): 30.

Crowther, Richard. 'Lisbon: May 15 – June 6.' *Opera* 18/11 (November 1967): 885.

Fairman, Richard. 'Gloriana (Chelsea Opera Group at the Logan Hall (Camden Festival), March 22).' *Opera* 34/6 (June 1983): 684–685.

Goodwin, Noel. 'Festival from Philanthropy.' *Music and Musicians* 15/11 (July 1967): 30–31.

—— 'Gloriana.' *Music and Musicians* 22/3 (November 1973): 59.

Grier, Sydney. 'Less Immediate Gloriana.' *Music and Musicians* 17/8 (April 1969): 54.

A. J. [Arthur Jacobs.]. 'Gloriana.' *Opera* 18/10 (October 1967): 848–849.

—— 'Gloriana.' *Opera* 20/4 (April 1969): 355.

Jonen, Louis John. 'Cincinnati.' *Musical Courier* 153/8 (June 1956): 33–34.

Joseph, Jeffrey. 'Radio and Television.' *Music and Musicians* 25/12 (August 1977): 44–47.

Kemp, Ian. 'Aberdeen.' *MT* 112/1540 (June 1971): 581.

Kennedy, Michael. 'Gloriana (RNCM Opera Theatre, Manchester).' *Opera* 35/2 (February 1984): 213–214.

Kerner, L. 'Music: Sic Transit Gloriana (ENO at the Met).' *Village Voice* 29/30 (July 1984): 79.

Koegler, Horst. 'Modl's Mesmeric Gloriana, Munster.' *Opera* 19/8 (August 1968): 633.

Milnes, Rodney. 'Video Reviewed.' *Gramophone* 64/760 (September 1988): 363.

Monelle, R. 'Gloriana: Haddo House Choral and Operatic Society at Haddo House.' *Opera* 40/6 (June 1989): 744–745.

Northcott, Bayan. 'Gloriana.' *Music and Musicians* 21/2 (October 1972): 59.

---

[1] All unsigned articles are arranged in chronological order.

Oppens, K. 'Von Gangstern, Koeniginnen, Krieg und Frieden: der Gastspiel der English National Opera in New York.' *Opern Welt* 25/8–9 (August–September 1984): 76–77.

Porter, Andrew. 'Musical Events: Triumph of Oriana.' *New Yorker*. 30 July 1984.

Rosenthal, Harold. 'London Opera Diary: *Gloriana*.' *Opera* 23/10 (October 1972): 938–940.

—— '*Gloriana*.' *Opera* 26/5 (May 1975): 489.

Rothon, Grenville. 'Munich: *Gloriana*.' *Opera* 23/Festival Issue (Autumn 1972): 97–98.

Sabin, Robert. 'New Music: Britten's *Gloriana* in Vocal Score.' *Musical America* 75/13 (November 1955): 26.

—— 'Benjamin Britten: *Gloriana*.' *Notes* 13/2 (March 1956): 331.

Sadie, Stanley. '*Gloriana*.' *MT* 125/1695 (May 1984): 282.

Schmidt-Gare, H. 'Sadler's Wells Opera spielt *Gloriana* in Adele-Sandrock-Look.' *NZM* 133/10 (October 1972): 587.

Sutcliffe, James Helme. 'Munster.' *Opera News* 33/1 (7 September 1968): 38.

Szmolyan, W. 'Brittens *Gloriana* in der Volksoper.' *ÖMz* 30/7 (July 1975): 380.

Taubman, H. 'May Festival.' *New York Times*. 20 May 1956.

Tuggle, Robert A. 'London.' *Opera News* 33/1 (7 July 1968): 37.

Wendland, J. 'Ereignis und Rettung des Abends: Martha Moedl.' *Opern Welt* 1/8 (August 1968): 30–31.

Zachariasen, B. 'New York: The English National Opera's Long-awaited Visit.' *Ovation* 5 (September 1984): 36.

5. RELATED WORKS and REVIEWS OF PUBLICATIONS[2]

(a) Original version (A)

Mann, William. 'The Vocal Score.' *Opera* 4/8 (August 1953): 460–464.

(b) Second Lute Song (B)

'New Music: Britten: The Second Lute Song of the Earl of Essex, from *Gloriana*.' *London Musical Events* 9/8 (August 1954): 29.

Keys, Ivor. 'The Second Lute Song (from *Gloriana*).' *ML* 36/1 (January 1955): 104.

(c) Choral Dances (C) and (G)

'Priaulx Rainier Requiem.' *The Times*. 17 April 1956.

'Mainly Vocal.' *New Statesman and Nation*. 21 April 1956.

Keller, Hans. 'The Half-year's New Music.' *Music Review* 16/1 (February 1955): 53–64.

Keys, Ivor. 'Choral Dances from *Gloriana*.' *ML* 35/3 (July 1954): 270.

Main, Basil. 'Music apt for voices: Rainthorpe Hall Concert.' *Eastern Daily Press*. 12 September 1955.

Mitchell, Donald. 'London Music: Some First Performances: Choral.' *MT* 96/1344 (February 1955): 92.

---

2 Reviews of versions and related works appear here in the order in which the works appear in the List of Sources.

Sabin, Robert. 'New Music: Choral Episodes from *Gloriana.' Musical America* 75/13 (November 1955): 26.

Siebert, F. Mark. 'Benjamin Britten's Choral Dances from *Gloriana.' Notes* 13/3 (June 1956): 530.

(d) **Symphonic Suite (D)**

Keller, Hans. 'The Half-year's New Music.' *Music Review* 16/3 (August 1955): 228–233.
—— 'Major and Minor Britten.' *Music Review* 17/3 (August 1956): 269–270.

Mason, Colin. 'Symphonic Suite *Gloriana* by Benjamin Britten. Full Score.' *ML* 36/3 (July 1955): 303–304.

Mitchell, Donald. 'London Music: Some First Performances: Orchestral.' *MT* 96/1349 (July 1955): 378.

(e) **March from the Courtly Dances, arranged for orchestra (E)**

'Suffolk'. *Making Music* 25 (summer 1954): 16.

(f) **Courtly Dances arranged for small orchestra (H)**

Simmons, David. 'Concert Notes.' *Strad* 78/934 (February 1968): 395–396.

(g) *Gloriana* (revised version) (M)

Evans, Peter. '*Gloriana*: an opera in Three Acts, Opus 53. Full Score.' *ML* 72/3 (August 1991): 488–489.

Mark, Christopher. 'Rescue from neglect.' *MT* 132/1777 (March 1991): 133–134.

(h) **Symphonic Suite (version with chorus) (P)**

B. B. [Benjamin Britten.]. 'Three Scenes from *Gloriana.' Aldeburgh Festival Programme Book* 1970: 14–15.

Index

Compiled by Judith Henderson

References in chapters 1–5 to individual sources are indexed, but not those which appear in the List of Sources (chapter 6). Publications referred to in the text, but not listed in the Bibliography (chapter 7), are indexed here under author.

Contributors

PAUL BANKS is a musicologist specializing in music of the nineteenth and twentieth centuries. After ten years on the staff of the Music Department at Goldsmiths' College, London, he took up his present position, as Librarian of the Britten–Pears Library, in 1989. He was appointed Special Professor in Nineteenth-Century Studies at the Department of Music, the University of Nottingham, in 1992.

PETER EVANS was, for many years until his retirement, Professor of Music at Southampton University. After early research in seventeenth-century music he has worked mainly on twentieth-century topics, and his *The Music of Benjamin Britten* is the most extensive study of the composer's output in print.

ROBERT HEWISON is a cultural historian, broadcaster and critic. He is an authority on John Ruskin, and has published a three-volume history of the arts in Britain since 1939. He is a regular broadcaster on BBC Radio 3, and has written on the arts for *The Sunday Times* since 1981.

ANTONIA MALLOY is a music graduate of Worcester College, Oxford and the University of Surrey. As Halstead Scholar, Worcester College, she is currently preparing a doctoral thesis on *Gloriana*. Her other research interests include *Owen Wingrave*, orchestration, music-theatre and Harrison Birtwistle.

DONALD MITCHELL is a leading scholar of the music of Gustav Mahler and Benjamin Britten, and has published widely on both composers. *Letters from a Life: Selected Letters and Diaries of Benjamin Britten*, edited jointly with Philip Reed, was published in 1991. Dr Mitchell is a Trustee of the Britten-Pears Foundation, and recently retired as Chairman of the Performing Right Society.

PHILIP REED is the Staff Musicologist at the Britten-Pears Library. *Letters from a Life: Selected Letters and Diaries of Benjamin Britten*, edited jointly with Donald Mitchell, was published in 1991 and was followed by the Cambridge Opera Handbook on *Billy Budd*, edited jointly with Mervyn Cooke, in Spring 1993. Philip Reed and Mervyn Cooke are now working on a Handbook on the *War Requiem*.

ROSAMUND STRODE worked as Benjamin Britten's music assistant for many years, and was subsequently Keeper of Manuscripts and Archivist at the Britten–Pears Library. She is currently preparing a biography of Imogen Holst.